Employment Trends in the United States, Japan, and the European Community

Employment Trends in the United States, Japan, and the European Community:

A Comparative Economic Study

Eckhardt Wohlers

Günter Weinert

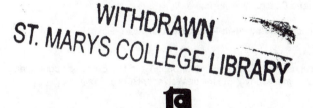

Transaction Books
New Brunswick (USA) and Oxford (UK)

Library of Congress Catalog Number: 87–34232
ISBN: 0-88738-230-4
Printed in the United States of America

Library of Congress Cataloging-in-Publication Data

Wohlers, Eckhardt.
   Employment trends in the United States, Japan and the European community:
a comparative economic study / Eckhardt Wohlers, Günter Weinert.
      p.   cm.
   Bibliography: p.
ISBN 0-88738-230-4
   1. Labor supply—United States.   2. Labor supply—Japan. 3. Labor supply—
European Economic Community countries.   I. Weinert, Günter.   II. Title.
HD5724.W565   1988   87-34232
331.12—dc19

P R E F A C E

Since the first oil crisis in 1973, unemployment has increased markedly in nearly all Western industrialized countries. However, this alone is an insufficient description of labour market trends, as there have been substantial differences in employment performance among countries and regions. For example, after 1973 the number of persons employed continued to rise distinctly in the USA but decreased on average in the European Community. Certain countries have apparently been less successful than others at overcoming employment problems.

The present study was completed in 1985, having been commissioned by the West German Ministry for Economic Affairs. Its purpose is to present and attempt to explain differences in employment trends between the USA, Japan and EC member countries during the period from 1973 to 1983. The empirical analysis focuses on differences between countries concerning growth rate and structure, real wage level and wage structure, labour market flexibility and the socio-economic framework; these differences are evaluated as possible causes of differing employment performance.

The authors are staff members of the HWWA-Institute of Economic Research, Hamburg, in the departments "Money, Business Cycles and Public Finance" and "World Business Cycles", respectively.

Hans-Jürgen Schmahl

C O N T E N T S

T A B L E S

DIAGRAMS

INTRODUCTION

The unemployment figures in all western industrialized countries have shown a marked upward trend in the last ten years. As far as employment is concerned, however, there have been much wider differences in the performance of individual countries or economic areas. For example, the number of persons employed in the European Community contracted slightly on average between 1973 and 1983; there were differences from one country to another, with the Federal Republic of Germany experiencing an appreciable reduction. In Japan, by contrast, employment increased by an average of 0.9 % per year and in the USA it expanded by as much as 1.7 % per year, leading some observers to speak of an "American employment miracle". This term is misleading, however, since the "employment miracle" in the USA in the seventies was not a new phenomenon; new jobs were being created there on an even larger scale in the sixties. It is only since the labour market problems have become more acute that increased attention is being paid to the continuing growth in employment in the USA, particularly by observers in Europe.

This study seeks to establish why the net supply of jobs continued to increase in some countries while in others job losses outweighed the creation of new jobs, despite the fact that all the countries were exposed to similar pressures from exogenous shocks such as the oil price crises and the changeover to floating exchange rates. The examination covers the USA, Japan and the European Community's (EC) economically most important member states, namely France, the Federal Republic of Germany, Italy and the United Kingdom. All references to the EC mean the Community of Nine; Greece, which did not join the EC until the eighties, is left out of account, as are the new member states of Spain and Portugal. In several cases, the lack of adequate statistical material has caused more detailed analysis requiring greater disaggregation to be limited to a comparison of developments in the USA and Germany.

The period under examination extends from 1973 to 1983. The merits of choosing 1973 as the base year lie primarily in the fact that it contained two strong exogenous shocks in the shape of the final abandonment of fixed exchange rates and the first oil shock, both of which necessitated considerable adjustment. In all of the countries examined in the study, 1973 marked a more or less sharp break in employment trends. The period was terminated at 1983 mainly for statistical reasons, since data on important variables were available only up to that year during the drafting of the study.

Differences in employment trends in individual countries can have a variety of causes, such as

- differences in the pace and structure of growth,

- differences in real wage trends and in the wage structure,

- differences in the labour market's flexibility, adaptability and willingness to adjust, and

- differences in fundamental concepts of economic policy.

The issues under examination in this report therefore involve an extremely wide spectrum of facts and interrelationships. The resources available for carrying out the study were small by comparison with the scale of the task, so that it was not possible to deal with all aspects exhaustively.

The difficulty of identifying universally valid causes increases considerably as the number of countries in the comparison rises. The more countries involved, the greater the number of special factors obscuring and distorting the theoretically correct relationships. The problems are compounded by statistical deficiencies. In some areas there are considerable gaps, particularly in the case of Italy, and only too often the comparability of data is seriously impaired by differences in definition, collection and processing. The lower the level of aggregation, the more serious the divergences. Hence in many cases comparisons can only be made at a relatively high level of

Employment Trends

aggregation or at extremely great expense. Many seemingly plausible hypotheses are impossible to verify empirically for lack of adequate statistical material or can only be tested indirectly. This applies especially to such factors as labour market flexibility or the effect of the socio-economic framework and economic policy measures. These constraints should be borne in mind when assessing the results of the study.

Chapter 1

EMPLOYMENT TRENDS IN THE USA, JAPAN AND THE EC
- SIMILARITIES AND DIFFERENCES

1.1 Introduction

Empirical studies such as the present one require a broad and thorough statistical basis. As so often, however, there is a wide divergence between what is needed and what is available. The disparity is present in the employment statistics themselves, the comparability of which is sometimes severely limited by differences in the methodology and in the principles of collection and definition. Employment is generally equated with gainful activity, and this is the sense used here; employed persons comprise all employees, self-employed persons and unpaid family workers. Employees include also apprentices, part-time workers, temporary workers, occasional and seasonal workers employed during the survey period.[1]

Although all the countries considered in this study basically follow this definition, in practice there are differences that in some cases seriously limit the comparability of the employment statistics.[2] For example, some countries calculate their employment figures using the national concept, whereas others base them on the resident concept.

---

1 Cf. for example STATISTICAL OFFICE OF THE EUROPEAN COMMUNITIES (Eurostat), Employment and Unemployment, 1985, p. 45; Erwin WARTENBERG, Entwicklung der Produktion, Beschäftigung und Abeitsproduktivität in der Bundesrepublik Deutschland im internationalen Vergleich, in: WiSta 10/1984, p. 854.

2 Cf. EUROSTAT, op.cit.; INTERNATIONAL LABOUR OFFICE (ILO), Yearbook of Labour Statistics 1984, introduction to the chapter "Employment", p. 239; STATISTISCHES BUNDESAMT, Statistisches Jahrbuch 1983, introduction to "Internationale Übersichten, Erwerbstätigkeit". With regard to the problem of the international comparison of statistical data, see also Elmar HÖNEKOPP, Hans ULLMANN, Auf dem Weg zur Dienstleistungsökonomie? in: MittAB No. 2/1980, p. 256.

Some obtain employment statistics from sample surveys of the labour market or of households, while others use social security statistics or payroll data and company surveys, so-called "establishment surveys". The definitions of the categories of employed persons also differ; for example, unpaid family workers may be allocated to different categories. Senior managers are also frequently treated differently in the classification according to employment status; in some countries they are counted as self-employed, while elsewhere they are classed as employees.

Further differences occur in the treatment of temporary and occasional workers, primarily concerning the period for which a person must work to count as employed. In Japan, for example, this "work threshold" is set at a very low level, with every person in paid work for a minimum of one hour during the survey period counting as employed, or more accurately not unemployed.[1] This very broad interpretation of employment undoubtedly goes a long way towards explaining why Japan's unemployment rate is low by international standards.[2]

Serious reservations must be made about the comparability of sectoral employment data for the various countries; comparability decreases progressively as the level of disaggregation increases, owing primarily to the different ways in which data are defined and collected. Almost every country has its own method, deviating more or less widely

---

1 Cf. Angelika ERNST, Beschäftigungsprobleme und Beschäftigungspolitik in Japan, in: MittAB, No. 2/1981, p. 88.

2 Cf. Angelika ERNST, Arbeitslosigkeit und Unterbeschäftigung in Japan, in: MittAB, No. 1/1978, p. 46; Roland SCHLUMPF, Der Anschein von Vollbeschäftigung in Japan, in: Arbeitslosigkeit - Schicksal der achtziger Jahre?, published by the Economics Staff of Neue Zürcher Zeitung, Zurich 1983, pp. 89 ff.; Koji TAIRA, Japan's low unemployment: economic miracle or statistical artifact? in: Monthly Labor Review, No. 7/1983, pp. 3 ff.; Constance SORRENTINO, Japan's low unemployment: an in-depth analysis, in: Monthly Labor Review, No. 3/1984, pp. 18 ff.

from those used in other countries. International classification systems such as ISIC (the International Standard Industrial Classification) or NACE (the General Industrial Classification of economic activities within the EC) are used chiefly by international organizations and have not yet had much impact on national statistics.

The differences between concepts used for classifying the services sector and its branches in various countries are particularly marked, largely owing to the complexity of the sector; this also explains the lack of a uniform, universally accepted definition.[1] Given the diversity of the sector, the concept of services is often very broad, being used to encompass all products that do not represent material goods. On the basis of this definition, services are generated in every branch of activity; hence, all institutional classifications underlying most statistics are only a more or less fitting approximation, oriented toward the main aspect of economic activity. The recorded size of the services sector therefore depends partly on the level of company specialization and on the extent to which service activities have split off from the agricultural and industrial sectors.

In addition to this broad classification, there are other narrower ones. For example, the wholesale and retail trade, transport, storage and communication, finance, insurance and real estate are treated as separate branches of economic activity and only the remaining activities are classed as services; this is the approach adopted by the Federal Republic of Germany and the USA. Many countries also exclude government services. Generally this is done for practical reasons rather than being the result of a particular definition of services.

---

1 On the problem of classifying services, see also Manfred WEGNER, Die Schaffung von Arbeitsplätzen im Dienstleistungsbereich, in: IFO-Schnelldienst No. 7/1985, pp. 3 f., Michael URQUHART, The employment shift to services: where did it come from? in: Monthly Labor Review, No. 4/1984, p. 16 and Ludwig BEREKOVEN, Der Dienstleistungsmarkt in der Bundesrepublik Deutschland, Vol. I, Göttingen 1983, pp. 5 ff.

This study is based on the broad institutional "negative classifi-cation", whereby the services sector comprises all branches of economic activity not predominantly involved in the production of physical goods. Branches such as wholesale and retail trade, trans-port, financing etc. are simply components of the services sector. This does not solve the problem of the comparability of data, but only mitigates it or shifts it to a lower level, for even a broad definition of the services sector such as this leaves conceptual differences between countries. For example, in the USA the services provided by public utilities and the entire branch of repair services are classed under services, whereas in the Federal Republic of Germany they fall within the industrial sector. There also remain differences in the classification of individual sub-groups of services.

This study is based largely on statistical data from international organizations such as the OECD, the ILO and the EC, since they use a uniform classification system for all countries and attempt as far as possible to adjust national data to that system and to make them comparable. Even so, complete comparability cannot always be achieved, for sometimes standardization clearly boils down to a mere standardization of branch terminology, especially when using highly disaggregated data.

The data supplied by these organizations is far less comprehensive than the material available from national sources; the statistics on the services sector, in particular, are at a relatively high level of aggre-gation. Hence, when dealing with certain issues it is necessary to fall back on national statistics as well, despite the problems involved. In these cases, every effort has been made to make them as comparable as possible.

1.2 Main Characteristics of Employment Trends in the USA, Japan and the EC

Unemployment has been on a rising trend in the industrialized countries since 1973; unemployment rates have risen appreciably everywhere. There are similarities between the performances of the USA, Japan and the EC countries, to the extent that none has been spared an increase in unemployment (cf. Table 1 and Diagram 1). However, the universal rise in unemployment rates does not adequately reflect labour market tendencies in individual countries, since employment trends[1] exhibit substantial macroeconomic and sectoral differences.

1.2.1 Macroeconomic Employment Trends

In the USA the unemployment rate rose, despite an appreciable growth in employment. In the ten years from 1973 to 1983 alone, the number of persons in employment - wage earners and salaried employees, self-employed persons and unpaid family workers - increased by 15.77 million, an annual average rise of 1.7 % (see Table 1). It is true that the rate of increase was lower than in the preceding ten years, but the slowdown was far less pronounced than in other countries. The growth in employment in the USA is therefore no new phenomenon, though this is the impression many publications on the "American employment miracle" tend to convey. Clearly, it simply stands in more marked contrast with the falling employment levels in many other countries. In Japan, too, the employment trend was still increasing between 1973 and 1983, rising at an average of 0.9 % a year. Here the slowdown in relation to the Sixties was sharper than in the USA.

---

1 Unless indicated otherwise, references to employment mean civilian employment.

Table 1   EMPLOYMENT AND UNEMPLOYMENT

		USA	Japan	EC (Nine)	Germany	France	Italy	UK
TOTAL EMPLOYMENT[1]								
Thousands	1962	66702	45560	100475	26289	18737	20270	24185
	1973	85064	52590	103018	26411	20865	19057	24694
	1983	100834	57330	101827	24649	21154	20350	23470
Annual change								
(%)	1962-73	2.2	1.3	0.2	0.0	1.0	-0.6	0.2
	1973-83	1.7	0.9	-0.1	-0.7	0.1	0.7	-0.5
AGRICULTURE								
Thousands	1962	5034	12670	15689	3307	3998	5923	1066
	1973	3572	7050	9400	1924	2348	3489	724
	1983	3541	5310	6951	1371	1697	2526	628
Annual change								
(%)	1962-73	-3.1	-5.2	-4.5	-4.8	-4.9	-4.7	-3.4
	1973-83	-0.1	-2.8	-3.0	-3.3	-3.0	-3.1	-1.5
INDUSTRY[2]								
Thousands	1962	23219	14210	43007	12574	7327	7341	11356
	1973	28225	19570	43159	12554	8238	7470	10482
	1983	28253	19930	36275	10352	7145	7352	7882
Annual change								
(%)	1962-73	1.8	3.0	0.0	-0.0	1.1	0.2	-0.7
	1973-83	0.0	0.2	-1.7	-1.9	-1.4	-0.2	-2.8
SERVICES[3]								
Thousands	1962	38448	18680	41779	10410	7412	7006	11763
	1973	53265	25970	50459	11933	10279	8098	13488
	1983	69037	32090	58602	12926	12312	10472	14961
Annual change								
(%)	1962-73	3.0	3.0	1.7	1.3	3.0	1.3	1.3
	1973-83	2.6	2.1	1.5	0.8	1.8	2.6	1.0
UNEMPLOYMENT RATE[4]								
as percentage	1973	4.8	1.3	3.0	0.8	2.6	6.2	3.0
of labour	1980	7.0	2.0	5.9	3.0	6.3	7.5	6.6
force	1981	7.5	2.2	7.6	4.4	7.3	8.3	9.9
	1982	9.5	2.4	8.9	6.1	8.1	9.0	11.4
	1983	9.5	2.6	10.1	8.0	8.3	9.8	12.6
	1973-83	7.1	2.0	6.0	3.8	5.4	7.3	7.1

1 Civilian employment (excluding armed forces). -- 2 Mining and quarrying, manufacturing, electricity, gas and water, construction (ISIC divisions 2-5). -- 3 ISIC divisions 6-9, including government. 4 Standardized unemployment rates (OECD), EC excluding Denmark, Ireland and Luxembourg.

Source: OECD: Labour Force Statistics; EUROSTAT: Employment and Unemployment; authors' calculations.

Diagram 1   EMPLOYMENT AND UNEMPLOYMENT

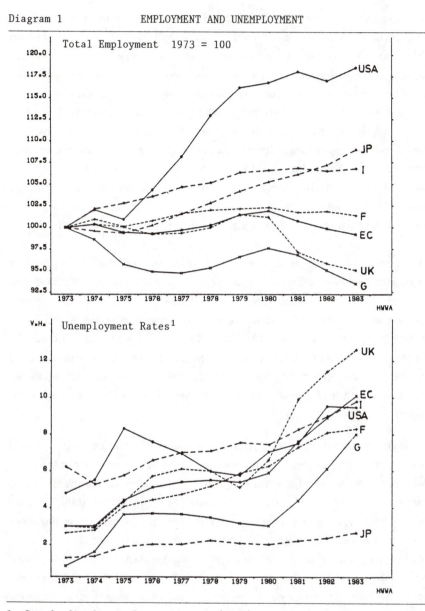

1 Standardized unemployment rates (OECD), in percentages.

Key: USA = United States of America; JP = Japan; EC = European
      Community; G = Federal Republic of Germany; F = France;
      I = Italy: UK = United Kingdom.

Source: See Table 1.

Similarities and Differences   25

The employment trend in the EC was far less favourable. Here the number of persons employed contracted marginally on average between 1973 and 1983, whereas in the previous ten years it had increased slightly. Nevertheless, there were marked differences between the major EC countries. In Italy employment increased considerably over the period, although it should be borne in mind that Italy, unlike other countries, had suffered a sharp contraction in employment in the previous ten years. In France the number of persons employed also rose slightly during the period under examination, while it declined in the United Kingdom and the Federal Republic of Germany, especially the latter. Of all the countries under consideration, Germany had the worst employment performance between 1973 and 1983.

There were also differences in the development of the "structure" of employment, measured in terms of professional status (cf. Table 2 and Diagram 2). These were most pronounced among non-agricultural self-employed persons, where there was a sharp rise averaging 3.3 % a year in the USA between 1973 and 1983. There were also substantial increases in Japan and, especially since the beginning of the eighties, in the United Kingdom. By contrast, the number of self-employed stagnated in the Federal Republic of Germany and actually declined slightly in France.

Employment in all countries showed a clear correlation with cyclical developments. However, the range of fluctuation, measured by deviations from trend, differed from one country to another; it was particularly high in the USA and lowest in France and Italy.[1] Hence in the USA cyclical fluctuations had a stronger impact on employment than in the major EC countries; more employees were dismissed during downturns, and probably at an earlier stage, but on the other hand more job-seekers were hired more quickly as economic activity recovered. An international comparison of employment developments

1 See also Bernd HOF, Sektorale Beschäftigungsentwicklung in den Vereinigten Staaten und in der Bundesrepublik Deutschland, in: iw-trends, No. 2/1984, pp. 12 f.

Employment Trends

Table 2   EMPLOYMENT ACCORDING TO PROFESSIONAL STATUS
            - non-agricultural activities -

		USA	Japan	Germany	France	Italy[1]	UK
EMPLOYMENT							
All activities							
Thousands	1962	61667	33580	22982	14739	14347	23119
	1973	81492	45430	24487	18517	15568	23970
	1983	97293	52020	23278	19457	17824	22842
Annual change							
(%)	1962-73	2.6	2.8	0.6	2.1	0.8	0.3
	1973-83	1.8	1.4	-0.5	0.5	1.4	-0.5
EMPLOYEES							
Thousands	1962	54901	25220	20210	12449	10621	21760
	1973	75501	35630	22145	16407	11978	22232
	1983[a]	88376	41590	21179	17429	13386	20861
Annual change							
(%)	1962-73	2.9	3.2	0.8	2.5	1.1	0.2
	1973-83	1.7	1.6	-0.4	0.6	1.9	-0.6
SELF-EMPLOYED[2]							
Thousands	1962	6165	5220	2111	2290	3726	1359
	1973	5451	6400	1863	2110	3590	1738
	1983[a]	7540	6910	1858	2028	3868	1982
Annual change							
(%)	1962-73	-1.1	1.9	-1.1	-0.6	-0.3	2.3
	1973-83[b]	3.3	0.8	-0.0	-0.4	2.0	1.3
UNPAID FAMILY							
WORKERS							
Thousands	1962	601	3150	661	-	-	-
	1973	539	3380	479	-	-	-
	1983	376	3520	241	-	-	-
Annual change							
(%)	1962-73	-1.0	0.6	-2.9	-	-	-
	1973-83	-3.5	0.4	-6.6	-	-	-

1 In the case of Italy, data on employees and self-employed persons
are available only up to 1979. -- 2 Including unpaid family workers
in the case of France, Italy and the United Kingdom. -- a 1979 in
the case of Italy. -- b 1973-79 in the case of Italy.

Source: OECD: Labour Force Statistics; authors' calculations.

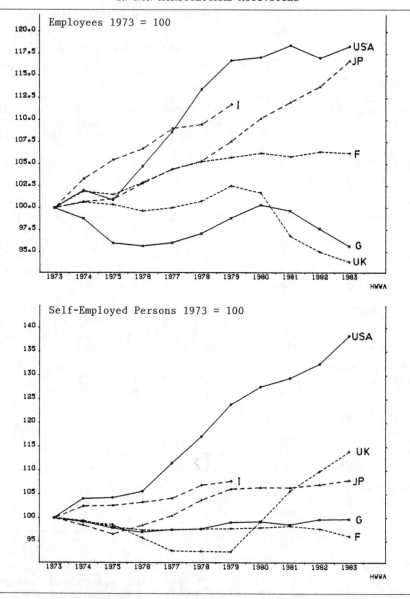

Diagram 2   EMPLOYEES AND SELF-EMPLOYED PERSONS
IN NON-AGRICULTURAL ACTIVITIES

Key: USA = United States of America; JP = Japan; G = Federal Republic of Germany; F = France; I = Italy: UK = United Kingdom.
Source: See Table 2.

during a particular cyclical phase - such as the present recovery - has little meaning unless differences in responsiveness and possible differences in lags are taken into consideration; indeed, it could lead to the wrong conclusions being drawn.

1.2.2 Employment by Sector

The differences in the employment performance of the USA, Japan and the EC at the macroeconomic level are also reflected in sectoral employment trends. The disparities were smallest in agriculture and forestry (including fishing), where the decline in employment continued in most countries between 1973 and 1983, although generally at a slightly slower rate than in the sixties. Only in the USA was the decrease in agricultural employment barely perceptible. The sector's share of total employment continued to contract everywhere (see Table 3).

The contrasts were more marked in the industrial sector,[1] although here too the share of total employment fell in all countries. Table 1 shows that industrial employment more or less stagnated in the USA over the decade to 1983 and actually increased slightly in Japan. In almost all the major EC countries, by contrast, the underlying trend was distinctly downwards, in Italy only slightly so. There were sharp fluctuations in industrial employment everywhere, a reflection of the sector's heavy dependence on economic cycles.

The main factor determining employment in industry was the trend in manufacturing, where more than 70 % of all industrial jobs were concentrated in the countries in question between 1973 and 1983 (see Table 4).[2]

1 Mining, manufacturing, electricity, gas and water and construction, using the ISIC classification (categories 2-5).

2 Gaps in the statistical material make it difficult to compare employment trends in different branches of industry. For example, comparable employment figures are available only from 1977 onwards in the case of Italy and only up to 1982 for all countries.

Table 3   EMPLOYMENT BY SECTOR
                    - percentages of total employment -

		USA	Japan	EC (Nine)	Germany	France	Italy	UK
EMPLOYMENT Total[1]		100	100	100	100	100	100	100
AGRICULTURE	1962	7.5	27.8	15.6	12.6	21.3	29.2	4.4
	1973	4.2	13.4	9.1	7.3	11.3	18.3	2.9
	1981	3.5	10.0	7.1	5.5	8.4	13.4	2.6
	1982	3.6	9.7	6.8	5.5	8.2	12.4	2.7
	1983	3.5	9.3	6.8	5.6	8.0	12.4	2.7
INDUSTRY	1962	34.8	31.2	42.8	47.8	39.1	36.2	47.0
	1973	33.2	37.2	41.9	47.5	39.5	39.2	42.4
	1981	30.1	35.3	37.4	43.5	35.2	37.6	35.8
	1982	28.4	34.9	36.5	42.7	34.5	37.1	34.7
	1983	28.0	34.8	35.6	42.0	33.8	36.1	33.6
SERVICES	1962	57.6	41.0	41.6	39.6	39.6	34.6	48.6
	1973	62.6	49.4	49.0	45.2	49.3	42.5	54.6
	1981	66.4	54.7	55.5	51.0	56.4	49.0	61.5
	1982	68.0	55.4	56.7	51.8	57.3	50.5	62.6
	1983	68.5	56.0	57.6	52.5	58.2	51.5	63.8

1 Civilian employment.

Source: OECD: Labour Force Statistics; authors' calculations.

Diagram 3   EMPLOYMENT IN INDUSTRY AND SERVICES

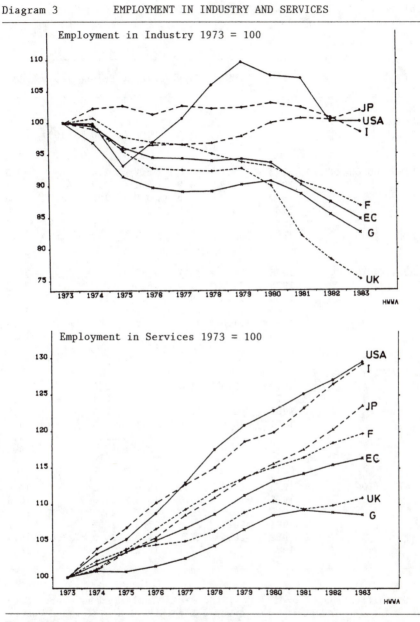

Key: USA = United States of America;   JP = Japan;   EC = European
      Community;   G = Federal Republic of Germany;   F = France;
      I = Italy;   UK = United Kingdom.
Source: See Table 1.

Similarities and Differences   31

Table 4   EMPLOYMENT IN INDUSTRY[1]

                         - percentage shares -

		USA	Japan	Germany	France	Italy[2]	UK
INDUSTRY Total		100	100	100	100	100	100
MINING AND QUARRYING	1973	2.3	0.7	3.2	2.4	-	3.5
	1975	2.9	0.9	3.1	2.2	-	3.5
	1980	3.2	0.6	3.0	1.9	2.9	3.8
	1981	3.7	0.5	3.2	1.9	2.9	4.0
	1982	3.6	0.5	3.1	1.9	2.9	4.1
	1983	3.3	0.5	3.1	-	-	4.1
MANUFACTURING	1973	74.6	73.7	77.2	71.3	-	75.8
	1975	74.0	71.9	78.5	72.0	-	76.2
	1980	72.4	69.9	77.7	71.7	70.6	74.8
	1981	72.3	70.3	77.3	71.3	69.7	73.7
	1982	71.8	70.2	77.6	71.4	69.5	73.4
	1983	70.6	70.6	77.3	-	-	73.4
ELECTRICITY, GAS, WATER	1973	3.4	1.7	1.6	2.0	-	3.3
	1975	3.8	1.7	2.1	2.1	-	3.5
	1980	3.9	1.5	2.1	2.4	-	3.8
	1981	4.0	1.6	2.1	2.5	-	4.1
	1982	4.2	1.7	2.3	2.7	-	4.2
	1983	4.4	1.8	2.4	-	-	4.2
CONSTRUCTION	1973	19.7	23.9	18.0	24.3	-	17.4
	1975	19.4	25.6	16.4	23.6	-	16.8
	1980	20.5	28.0	17.2	24.0	26.5	17.7
	1981	20.1	27.6	17.3	24.3	27.4	18.2
	1982	20.4	27.5	17.0	24.0	27.6	18.4
	1983	21.8	27.1	17.2	-	-	18.2

1 Classification according to ISIC. -- 2 In Italy the electricity, gas and water industries are grouped together with mining and quarrying.

Source: OECD: Labour Force Statistics; EUROSTAT: Employment and Unemployment; authors' calculations.

However, manufacturing's share of total industrial employment decreased in most countries; the decline was fairly marked in the USA, Japan and the United Kingdom but only slight in the Federal Republic of Germany and France. By contrast, the employment shares of energy and water[1] increased in all countries, as did that of construction everywhere except in France and the Federal Republic of Germany. Overall, the shifts in the sectoral structure of industrial employment were more pronounced in the USA and Japan than in the EC countries.

In all of the countries under examination, the proportion of employment in the services sector (including government)[2] increased between 1973 and 1983 and there was a substantial increase in the number of persons employed in this sector (cf. Table 1 and Diagram 3). The growth was largest in the USA and Italy; in these countries and in Japan more new jobs were created in services than were lost in other sectors. Here too, the Federal Republic of Germany brought up the rear, with the creation of jobs in services lagging far behind the loss of jobs in other areas.

The rise in employment in the services sector showed a conspicuous levelling-off in some of the major EC countries since the end of the seventies; in the Federal Republic of Germany the trend has even turned downwards. In trade, transport and communications, which are particularly sensitive to changes in economic activity, the cyclical contraction in employment was particularly sharp owing to the length of the downturn and in many cases was not offset to the extent seen in previous cycles by increases in employment in other branches of services, notably in the public sector.

1   In Italy the electricity, gas and water industries are grouped together with mining.

2   Wholesale and retail trade and restaurants and hotels, transport, storage and communications, financing, insurance real estate and business services, community, social and personal services (divisions 6-9 of the ISIC).

Similarities and Differences   33

No link could be detected between the strength of the rise in employment in the services sector and the size of the sector's share of total employment between 1973 and 1983. There is no evidence that "catching-up" phenomena, for example, caused employment in the sector generally to increase more strongly in countries where services account for a small share of total employment than in those where their share was high. The average increase was approximately the same in the two countries with the highest and lowest proportions of employment in services - the USA and Italy. In the Federal Republic of Germany, where services accounted for a smaller share of employment than in most other countries, the number of persons employed in the sector showed a below-average increase (see Table 3 and Diagram 3).

Analysis of the development of individual branches' shares of total employment in services reveals similarities in employment trends within the sector in many countries (cf. Table 5). The number of persons employed in wholesale and retail trade and restaurants and hotels and in transport and communications tended to increase at below-average rates almost everywhere, and their shares consequently fell. By contrast, finance, insurance and other business services showed above-average increases in employment numbers and gains in percentage shares in all countries, though there were differences in the size of changes in share.

There were large differences in the division comprising community, social and personal services, which accounted for more than 40 % of all jobs in the services sector in all countries except Japan (see Table 5). From 1973 to 1983 the employment share of this division virtually stagnated in the USA and probably also in Japan,[1] but in all

---

1 In the case of Japan the trend can only be estimated approximately, owing to changes in branch definitions; since 1979 business services have been grouped with financing and insurance, whereas previously they had formed part of the branch community, social and personal services.

Table 5   EMPLOYMENT IN THE SERVICES SECTOR[1]

- percentage shares -

		USA	Japan[2]	Germany	France	Italy	UK
SERVICES SECTOR Total		100	100	100	100	100	100
WHOLESALE & RETAIL TRADE, RESTAURANTS & HOTELS	1973	33.7	42.0	32.7	31.7	-	33.1
	1975	33.4	42.1	31.4	30.4	-	32.2
	1980	32.6	41.8	30.1	29.0	38.9	32.3
	1981	32.6	41.9	29.7	28.9	39.0	31.8
	1982	32.5	41.7	29.1	28.7	38.7	31.8
	1983	32.5	40.9	28.6	-	-	31.8
TRANSPORT AND COMMUNICATION	1973	9.3	13.0	13.5	12.0	-	11.8
	1975	9.0	12.4	13.1	11.9	-	11.4
	1980	8.6	11.7	12.0	11.4	11.6	10.7
	1981	8.5	11.3	11.8	11.3	11.5	10.4
	1982	8.3	11.2	11.8	11.4	11.0	9.9
	1983	7.7	10.9	11.8	-	-	9.5
FINANCING & INSURANCE, REAL ESTATE & BUSINESS SERVICES	1973	11.6	6.1	10.9	12.0	-	11.5
	1975	11.5	6.3	11.1	12.3	-	11.5
	1980	12.8	10.6	11.6	13.1	5.3	12.4
	1981	13.0	10.9	11.9	13.2	5.6	12.8
	1982	13.4	11.2	12.0	12.9	5.8	13.3
	1983	14.1	11.4	12.2	-	-	13.6
COMMUNITY, SOCIAL AND PERSONAL SERVICES	1973	45.5	38.9	43.0	44.3	-	43.6
	1975	46.2	39.2	44.4	45.5	-	45.0
	1980	46.1	35.9	46.3	46.5	44.2	44.7
	1981	46.0	35.9	46.6	46.6	44.0	45.0
	1982	45.8	35.9	47.1	46.9	44.5	45.0
	1983	45.7	36.8	47.4	-	-	45.1

1 Classification according to ISIC. -- 2 New classification of the Branches "financing and insurance" and "community, social and personal services" from 1979 onwards; figures on either side of that date are not comparable.

Source: OECD: Labour Force Statistics; EUROSTAT: Employment and Unemployment; authors' calculations.

Similarities and Differences   35

the major EC countries it was still rising in the early eighties, in some countries strongly. The increase in the division's share was above-average in the Federal Republic of Germany.

1.2.3 The Services Sector as a Reservoir of Jobs - a Comparison of Developments in the USA and the Federal Republic of Germany

A more detailed analysis of employment trends in the various branches of the services sector and of the nature of newly created jobs would clearly help determine the reasons for differences in the performance of individual countries. However, such an undertaking is severely limited by the statistical material available, so that it must be confined primarily to a comparison of developments in the Federal Republic of Germany and the USA. National statistics must therefore be used, but this raises the problem of the comparability of data, since the employment statistics of the two countries are based on different branch classification systems and job characteristics. Approximate comparability can nevertheless be achieved, at least for the development by branches.[1] The results are presented in Table 6.

The figures show that between 1974[2] and 1983 the underlying trends in many branches of the services sector were similar in the two countries. There were differences primarily in the extent of job-creation:

1 The comparison is based on data on wage earners and salaried employees only, since corresponding figures are not available for self-employed persons and unpaid family workers. The data relate to employees liable to social insurance and civil servants in the case of Germany, to employees on nonagricultural payrolls in that of the USA. The relatively detailed breakdown of data for the USA was rearranged according to the German classification system (the Federal Institute of Labour's classification by economic activity). In this way approximate comparability could be achieved for at least a certain number of services.

2 The choice of 1974 as the initial year is based solely on statistical grounds; data broken down to the same disaggregated level are not available for the Federal Republic of Germany before that date.

- Business services[1] generated strong employment stimuli in both countries. The number of employees in this branch increased by a much higher percentage than in the sector as a whole. Nevertheless, in the USA the rise was significantly larger and the proportion of the sector's total workforce engaged in business services was appreciably higher than in the Federal Republic of Germany. This reflects the fact that specialization and the separation of service activities from the industrial sector are more advanced in the USA than in the Federal Republic of Germany,[2] where the proportion of business services performed by firms in manufacturing industry is still higher than in the USA,[3] so that the employment effects appear not in the services sector but in industry.

- Health services in both countries provided a further strong boost to employment; here again, the number of persons employed rose faster than in the sector as a whole. In the USA it was principally the private part of the health sector that showed above-average employment gains. In the public part, which is much smaller and comprises mainly municipal and state hospitals, the increase was below the average.[4]

- There were also above-average increases in employment in restaurants and hotels in both countries, while in finance and insurance the number of employees increased at more or less the same rate as in the services sector as a whole.

---

1 Services provided chiefly for enterprises. The number of persons employed in business services in the USA is broken down for the various branches, but in the German statistics only business consultancy and legal services are shown separately; all other business services are grouped under "Other services".

2 See also Manfred WEGNER, op.cit., p. 5; Michael URQUHART, op.cit., p. 18.

3 Cf. Franz-Josef BADE, Produktionsorientierte Dienste - Gewinner im wirtschaftlichen Strukturwandel, in: DIW-Wochenbericht No. 16/1985, p. 203.

4 Cfl. Michael URQUHART, op.cit., p. 19.

Table 6   EMPLOYEES IN THE SERVICES SECTOR[1]

Branches of activity	Federal Republic of Germany[2]					United States of America[3]				
	Employment in thousands[4]		Increase or decrease		Percentage share of employment 1983	Employment in thousands[5]		Increase or decrease		Percentage share of employment 1983
	1974	1983	absolute ('000s)	% p.a.		1974	1983	absolute ('000s)	% p.a.	
Transport	1034.5	933.7	-100.8	-1.1	4.3	2575.5	2543.4	-32.1	-0.1	2.8
Communication	499.3	518.8	+19.5	+0.4	2.4	1202.5	1326.5	+124.0	+1.1	1.5
Wholesale & retail trade	2840.8	2770.8	-70.0	-0.3	12.6	13755.8	15624.6	+1868.8	+1.4	17.4
Finance, insurance	727.8	787.2	+59.4	+0.9	3.6	3524.5	4434.1	+909.6	+2.6	4.9
Restaurants & hotels	344.2	427.5	+83.3	+2.4	2.0	4108.9	6008.8	+1899.9	+4.3	6.7
Cleaning & personal care	290.7	307.6	+16.9	+0.6	1.4	888.3	937.2	+48.9	+0.6	1.0
Education, the arts, advertising	1137.1	1407.6	+270.5	+2.4	6.4	7709.8	8763.1	+1053.3	+1.4	9.7
of which: education	-	-	-	-	-	6948.8	7711.2	+762.4	+1.2	8.6
private	-	-	-	-	-	990.1	1207.3	+217.2	+2.2	1.3
public	-	-	-	-	-	5958.7	6503.9	+545.2	+1.0	7.2

(Continued)

Employment Trends

Table 6 (continued)

Branches of activity	Federal Republic of Germany[2]					United States of America[3]				
	Employment in thousands[4]		Increase or decrease		Percentage share of employment 1983	Employment in thousands[5]		Increase or decrease		Percentage share of employment 1983
	1974	1983	absolute ('000s)	% p.a.		1974	1983	absolute ('000s)	% p.a.	
Health & veterinary services	791.5	1083.7	+292.2	+3.6	4.9	4853.0	7067.6	+2214.6	+4.3	7.9
private	-	-	-	-	-	3886.7	5948.4	+2061.7	+4.8	6.6
public	-	-	-	-	-	966.3	1119.2	+152.9	+1.7	1.2
Services, primarily for enterprises[6]	170.3	239.8	+69.5	+3.9	1.1	3075.3	5262.3	+2187.0	+6.2	5.9
business services	-	-	-	-	-	2027.4	3595.0	+1567.6	+6.6	4.0
legal services	-	-	-	-	-	324.9	602.4	+277.6	+7.1	0.7
miscellaneous services[7]	-	-	-	-	-	723.0	1064.9	+341.9	+4.4	1.2
Other services[8]	647.5	836.6	+189.1	+2.9	3.8	2320.9	3650.8	+1329.9	+5.2	4.1
Government	1897.8	2085.5	+187.7	+1.1	9.5	7245.0	8120.9	+875.9	+1.3	9.0
Private non-profit organizations	311.0	384.4	+73.4	+2.4	1.8	1437.9	1521.9	+84.0	+0.6	1.7

(Continued)

Similarities and Differences

Table 6 (continued)

| | Federal Republic of Germany[2] | | | | | United States of America[3] | | | | |
| Branches of activity | Employment in thousands[4] | | Increase or decrease | | Percentage share of employment 1983 | Employment in thousands[5] | | Increase or decrease | | Percentage share of employment 1983 |
	1974	1983	absolute ('000s)	% p.a.		1974	1983	absolute ('000s)	% p.a.	
Services sector overall	10692.5	11783.2	+1090.7	+1.1	53.6	52697.4	65261.2	+12563.8	+2.4	72.5
excl. government & private non-profit organizations	7503.8	8214.2	+710.4	+1.0	37.4	44014.4	55618.4	+11603.9	+2.6	61.8
ALL BRANCHES	22402.1	21974.9	-427.2	-0.2	100.0	78265.0	89978.0	+11713.0	+1.6	100.0

1 In accordance with the classification system of the Federal Institut of Labour; the figures for the USA were obtained by rearranging the original data based on ISIC 1972. -- 2 Wage earners and salaried employees liable to social insurance and civil servants. -- 3 Employees on nonagricultural payrolls. -- 4 On 30th June in both years. -- 5 Annual averages. -- 6 For Germany, only legal services and business consultancy; for the USA, "business services", legal services, accounting and auditing, engineering and architectural services. -- 7 Accounting and auditing, engineering and architectural services. -- 8 Real estate agents and managers, investment management; for Germany, includes a number of activities carried out for enterprises and which are included among "business services" in the USA; for the USA, includes social services and repair services.

Sources: Amtliche Nachrichten der Bundesanstalt für Arbeit, No. 8/1984; STATISTISCHES BUNDESAMT: Finanzen und Steuern: Personal des öffentlichen Dienstes, 1974 und 1983; US DEPARTMENT OF LABOR: Employment and Earnings; authors' calculations.

- Finally, there were broadly similar trends in some services in which the number of employees rose by less than the average, particularly personal services such as cleaning and personal care.

The similarities in employment trends were less distinct in distributive services, that is to say the wholesale and retail trades, transport and communications. Nonetheless, the two countries had one point in common in that employment in these activities performed less well than in the services sector as a whole. In the USA the number of persons employed in the wholesale and retail trades and in communications did rise, and there was a small contraction in transport. In the Federal Republic of Germany, on the other hand, employment declined in both transport and the wholesale and retail trades.

Marked contrasts emerged in education, the arts and advertising, and especially in education within this field. Employment growth here was still well above average in Germany, but in the USA it fell short to an equal degree. The restrained performance in the USA was determined by the public sector. In the private education sector employment increased more or less in line with the expansion in the services sector as a whole.

All in all, there were substantial similarities between the USA and the Federal Republic of Germany as regards the trend of wage and salary workers in various services between 1973 and 1983. Fundamental differences were to be found primarily in education; in most other branches the underlying trend was broadly similar in both countries. Disparities in these other branches were due chiefly to the extent of new job creation, and were frequently substantial.

In contrast to developments in the number of persons in dependent employment, the figures on self-employed persons and unpaid family workers appear to exhibit greater differences even in the basic trend. At any event, the number of such persons in the services sector of the USA increased considerably between 1973 and 1983; the rise of 3.3 % a year was even larger than the increase in employees.

This category accounts for around 10 % of employment in the sector in both the USA and Germany, but in Germany there was a fall of almost 1 % a year over the same period, while the number of employees increased by the same percentage.[1]

In the USA the rapidly growing ranks of the self-employed generated considerable employment stimuli via the establishment of new firms. The importance of this factor can be gauged from the fact that the majority of all new jobs were created by small, relatively "young" and rapidly expanding firms.[2] According to studies conducted by Birch, two-thirds of the net increase in jobs between 1969 and 1976 were attributable to firms with twenty workers or less, and a further 15 % to firms with between 21 and 100 employees. Around four-fifths of all new jobs created during that period were in enterprises that were four years old or less.[3] Other studies arrive at similar conclusions.[4] They also show that the bulk of new company establishment and job creation occurred in the services sector. In the Federal Republic of Germany, by contrast, the propensity to establish firms and create jobs was far less pronounced than in the USA. This is reflected indirectly in the figures in Table 6, which show that in Germany around 70 % of all new jobs in the services sector were in the education and health services and in central and local government; in the USA the proportion was less than one-third.

1 In France too, the number of self-employed and unpaid family workers in the services sector declined between 1973 and 1983. In the United Kingdom, on the other hand, it rose, especially after the end of the seventies.

2 Cf. David L. BIRCH, Dynamik der Kleinen, in: Wirtschaftswoche 19/1984, pp. 138 ff.; Anon., How the U.S. is able to create so many jobs, in: Business Week, 16.7.1984, pp. 34 ff.; Richard GREENE, Tracking job growth in private industry, in: Monthly Labor Review, No. 9/1982, pp. 3 ff.

3 Cf. David L. BIRCH, op.cit., p. 146 and the table on page 142.

4 Cf. for example the overview in Richard GREENE, op.cit., pp. 3 ff.

It would appear that in the USA the desire to increase incomes was often not the decisive motive for striking out into self-employment. In many cases the reason was probably as much the lack of job opportunities; a similar trend has also been evident in the United Kingdom in recent years. An indication of this can be found in income trends. Studies by the US Department of Labor have concluded that in 1982 the income of a self-employed person averaged only about 70 % of the income of a salaried employee in the same occupation, despite longer working hours; in the case of women the ratio was even worse. In 1978, by contrast, self-employed persons had still ranked ahead of paid employees in the income charts.[1]

These data should be treated with circumspection, however. First, in 1982 the effects of the preceding recession were still being felt; recessions usually have a stronger impact on the incomes of the self-employed than on those of wage earners and salaried employees. Secondly, the average incomes of self-employed persons and salaried employees are not fully comparable owing to structural differences. For example, the average income of employees include the incomes of government employees in 1982, but not in 1978. And thirdly, it is not clear from the statistics how unpaid family workers and the second jobs that some employees held were treated.

1.2.4 The Quality of the Newly Created Jobs - the "Bad Jobs" Issue

The question of the quality of the newly created jobs frequently plays a part in the debate about the "American employment miracle". It is often claimed that most of the new jobs are "bad jobs".[2] By this are

---

1 Cf. Eugene H. BECKER, Self-employed workers: an update to 1983, in: Monthly Labor Review No. 7/1984, p. 18.

2 See for example Werner SENGENBERGER, Das amerikanische Beschäftigungssystem - dem deutschen überlegen? in: Wirtschaftsdienst No. 8/1984, p. 401; Werner SENGENBERGER, Zur Flexibilität im Beschäftigungssystem. Ein Vergleich zwischen den USA und der Bundesrepublik Deutschland, Munich 1984, p. 17. The UN Economic Commission for Europe (ECE) has evidently also expressed a similar view - see Handelsblatt, 12.3.1985, "Die neuen Arbeitsplätze in den USA sind meist nicht besonders hochwertig".

meant mainly jobs that are of short duration, vulnerable to cyclical fluctuations and often associated with long working hours and poor working conditions; a further characteristic is that the pay is close to the relatively low legal minimum wage.[1] The term "bad job" introduces a strong value judgement into the debate, often intentionally, since it suggest that such jobs are barely worth taking. The definition given also leaves considerable scope for interpretation.

There are undoubtedly many jobs that display these features in the USA, as in other countries, and probably a large proportion of them are to be found in the services sector. However, opinions are sharply divided on the proportion of bad jobs among existing and newly created jobs, and of course on the way in which they should be assessed. Taking Ginzberg as his authority, Sengenberger claims that the majority of the newly created jobs in the USA should be classed as bad jobs.[2] This is denied by other authors, however.[3] According to Birch, lowly occupations - he cites doormen, guards, auxiliary hospital staff or staff in fast food restaurants by way of example - account for only about 11 or 12 % of all services, a proportion that has remained largely unchanged for the last 30 years.[4]

Indeed, even if a very broad interpretation of the term "bad jobs" is used, empirical evidence suggests that bad jobs make up a rather small percentage of the expansion in employment in the USA. As

1 Cf. Werner SENGENBERGER, Das amerikanische Beschäftigungssystem, op.cit., p. 401.

2 Cf. Werner SENGENBERGER, Das amerikanische Beschäftigungssystem, op.cit., p. 401.

3 Cf. Diana WINKLER-BÜTTNER, Die Beschäftigungsentwicklung in den USA und in der Bundesrepublik, in: Wirtschaftsdienst No. 7/1984, p. 345, and the discussion paper by Janet L. NORWOOD in: BUNDES-ANSTALT FÜR ARBEIT (ed.): Wirtschafts- und Arbeitsmarktentwicklung in den USA und in der Bundesrepublik Deutschland, BeitrAB No. 96, pp. 85 ff.

4 Cf. David L. BIRCH, op.cit., p. 142.

Employment Trends

Table 7 shows, more than four-fifths of the net new jobs created between 1973 and 1982[1] were in white collar occupations. In service activities in the narrower sense, where common opinion has it that the bulk of the jobs classed as "bad" are to be found,[2] the number of jobs also increased considerably, but they accounted for less than one-fifth of newly created jobs.

Of course, the white collar jobs include some with low qualification requirements and correspondingly low pay. If this were adopted as the sole criterion for defining a "bad job", as is clearly sometimes the case, the number of such jobs would obviously be greater; for example, it would include cashiers in chain stores and certain sales personnel. However, with the exception of cashiers, these were not occupations that were expanding particularly rapidly. The largest increases occurred in activities at a higher level of qualification;[3] computer specialists and EDP staff, nurses and medical assistants, engineers and technicians, activities in accounting and law, non-agricultural managerial activities and bank staff accounted for more than 40 % of all new jobs created between 1973 and 1982 in the USA and for one-fifth of employment at the end of the period. These activities will continue to be seen as a considerable "jobs reservoir" in the future.[4]

1 Changes in the occupational statistics prevented data for 1983 being taken into consideration.

2 The jobs of service and food preparation staff in fast food restaurants, auxiliary staff in hospitals and nursing homes, private security staff and doormen are generally classed as "bad jobs".

3 See also Carol Boyd LEON, Occupational winners and losers: Who they were during 1972-80, in: Monthly Labor Review, No. 6/1982, pp. 18 ff.

4 See George T. SILVESTRI, John M. LUKASIEWICZ, Marcus E. EINSTEIN, Occupational employment projections through 1995, in: Monthly Labor Review, No. 11/1983, pp. 44 ff.

Table 7 USA: EMPLOYED CIVILIANS BY OCCUPATION

Occupation	Number of persons employed, thousands		Increase or decrease		Percentage share of employment in 1982
	1973	1982	absolute, thousands	% p.a.	
TOTAL EMPLOYED	84 409	99 526	15 117	1.8	100.0
White collar workers	40 384	53 470	13 086	3.2	53.7
Professional and technical	11 777	16 951	5 174	4.1	17.0
Accountants	750	1 193	443	5.3	1.2
Computer specialists	287	751	464	11.3	0.8
Engineers	1 094	1 574	480	4.1	1.6
Lawyers, judges, etc.	344	630	286	7.0	0.6
Nurses, dietitians and therapists	970	1 736	766	6.7	1.7
Health technologists and technicians	330	657	327	8.0	0.7
Managers and administrators (excl. agriculture)	8 644	11 493	2 849	3.2	11.5
Sales workers	5 415	6 580	1 165	2.2	6.6
Clerical workers	14 548	18 446	3 898	2.7	18.5
Bank tellers	326	561	235	6.2	0.6
Bookkeepers	1 661	1 968	307	1.9	2.0
Cashiers	1 048	1 683	635	5.4	1.7
Computer and peripheral equipment operators	216	588	372	11.8	0.6
Secretaries	3 066	3 847	781	2.6	3.9
Blue Collar workers	29 869	29 597	-272	-0.1	29.7
Craft and kindred workers	11 288	12 272	984	0.9	12.3
Operatives (except transport)	10 972	9 429	-1 543	-1.7	9.5
Transport equipment operatives	3 297	3 377	80	0.3	3.4
Non-farm labourers	4 312	4 518	206	0.5	4.5
Service workers in the narrow sense[1]	11 128	13 736	2 608	2.4	13.8
Private households	1 353	1 042	-311	-2.9	1.0
Other services	9 775	12 694	2 919	2.9	12.8
Farm workers	3 027	2 723	-304	-1.2	2.7

1 Domestic staff, cleaning and food service workers, health service workers, personal service workers, security workers.
Source: US DEPARTMENT OF LABOR: Handbook of Labor Statistics.

Employment Trends

In contrast to white collar activities and service occupations in the narrower sense, the number of blue collar jobs in the USA declined slightly overall between 1973 and 1982. Here too, there was a trend towards activities requiring higher qualifications. The number of unskilled or semi-skilled workers decreased markedly, while that of skilled workers and craftsmen continued to rise swiftly. Among blue collar occupations also, an increasing shift in activities from the industrial to the services sector can be detected. For instance, maintenance and repair work were increasingly undertaken by specialized service companies; the growing demand for such services was one of the reasons for the rise in the number of skilled workers and craftsmen.[1]

Overall, jobs requiring higher qualifications accounted for the majority of the jobs created in the USA after 1973. The claim that "bad jobs" had accounted for most of the new employment is not confirmed by the evidence, unless the main criterion were salary below the average labour income for all employees. If that were the case, many service occupations would be classed as "bad jobs", including some that would not count as such on grounds of working conditions, for pay in these fields was indeed often lower than in other branches of economic activity.[2] However, wage differentials are not a suitable classification criterion; they are a characteristic of a market economy and reflect differences in relative scarcity and different performance and qualification requirements. They thus also fulfil an important function in directing workers to particular occupations.

The debate about "bad jobs" has little relevance to the solution of employment problems, for "bad jobs" are better than "no jobs", if that is the only alternative. They can even be viewed in a positive

---

1 Cf. Carol Boyd LEON, op.cit., pp. 24 f.

2 According to Sengenberger, some wages are close to the legal minimum, which is only one-third or less of the wage of a worker in the steel or automobile industries. Cf. Werner SENGENBERGER, Das amerikanische Beschäftigungssystem, op.cit., p. 401.

light; unlike the German economy, the US economy has succeeded until recently in creating not only jobs requiring high qualifications but also jobs with a lower level of skill - though at lower pay - and has thus provided employment opportunities for problem groups as well. In the Federal Republic of Germany, by contrast, the prospects for such groups have become worse, if anything; only too often the alternative is long-term unemployment. Sometimes, however, even that is clearly regarded as more desirable than "inferior" jobs. The difference in outlook is also evident in the debate on ways of overcoming the employment problem. Whereas the quality of jobs is not an issue in the USA except in a very few instances, in Germany it assumes considerable importance.

1.2.5 Trends in the Supply of Labour

The problems that employment trends have caused in the labour markets of many countries have been exacerbated by developments on the supply side. The supply of labour, measured in terms of the labour force,[1] increased in all countries to a greater or lesser extent between 1973 and 1983. The relative increase in the USA was the largest by far; despite the creation of many additional jobs, unemployment also increased. In the Federal Republic of Germany, by contrast, the labour force grew much more slowly than in the other countries and the increase began later (see Diagram 4). In the case of the USA and Japan, the expansion in the supply of labour was merely a continuation of a trend that had already been present in the sixties. In many EC countries, however, it was a new phenomenon; France was an exception in this regard. In these countries the underlying trend had been flat from the midsixties to the early seventies and in some it had actually been downwards.

---

1 Employed persons and unemployed persons seeking work.

Employment Trends

Diagram 4   WORKING-AGE POPULATION AND LABOUR FORCE

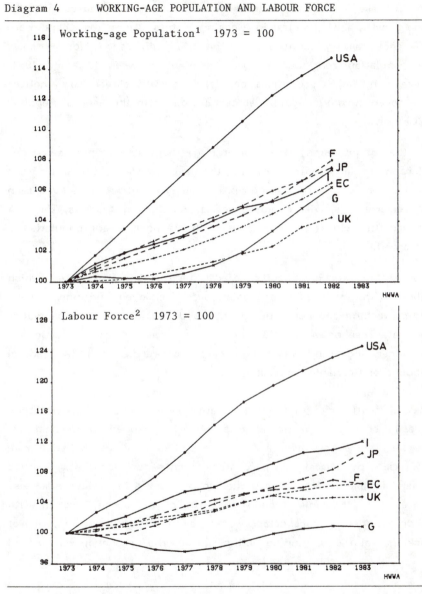

Key: USA = United States of America;   JP = Japan;   EC = European
      Community;   G = Federal Republic of Germany;   F = France;
      I = Italy;   UK = United Kingdom.
1   Population from 15 to 64 years. -- 2   Persons employed and unemployed.

Source: See Table 1.

Similarities and Differences   49

The increase in the labour force had essentially two causes: population growth and changes in working habits. Here too there were differences among countries; in the USA and Japan, for example, the population continued to grow strongly between 1973 and 1983, whereas in the EC countries population growth slowed down noticeably, even turning negative at certain stages in the Federal Republic of Germany.

On the other hand, the working-age population[1] increased considerably in all countries during the last decade as a result of the "baby boom" of the fifties and sixties; many countries have even seen an acceleration since the mid-seventies. As Diagram 4 shows, the USA also led the field as far as expansion in the working-age population is concerned.

Changes in working habits affect the participation rate, which indicates the ratio of the labour force (employed and unemployed) to the working-age population.[2] In the USA and Japan the participation rate rose between 1973 and 1983, whereas in most EC countries the underlying trend was flat or even downwards, as in the Federal Republic of Germany (see Table 8).

The substantial rise in the participation rate in the USA is primarily a result of higher participation by American women in the last two decades; since the beginning of the sixties their participation rate has risen by almost 20 percentage points to over 60 %. Married women, in particular, entered the labour market in greater numbers. Whereas in 1960 only around one-fifth of all married women with children under 6 years of age worked or at least had the intention of working, at the beginning of the eighties the proportion was around

---

1 Population from 15 to 64 years.

2 In some cases the participation rate is also defined as the labour force as a proportion of the total population. This definition will not be used in this study.

Employment Trends

Table 8   PARTICIPATION RATES[1]

                                  - percentages -

		USA	Japan	Germany	France	Italy	UK
PARTICIPATION RATE Total	1962	66.1	74.6	70.7	68.3	64.9	71.9
	1965	66.6	71.9	70.5	67.2	61.8	72.8
	1970	67.7	72.0	69.5	67.7	59.5	72.4
	1975	69.1	70.4	67.9	67.9	58.9	73.5
	1980	72.3	71.8	66.6	68.1	60.3	74.3
	1981	72.7	72.1	66.1	67.6	60.5	73.6
	1982	72.9	72.3	65.4	67.3	60.0	73.3
	1983	73.1	73.0	64.7	66.4	60.0	72.8
PARTICIPATION RATE Female	1962	42.7	58.7	49.2	-	38.5	47.3
	1965	44.3	55.8	49.0	-	34.6	49.0
	1970	48.9	55.4	48.1	48.3	33.5	50.7
	1975	53.2	51.7	49.6	51.2	34.6	55.1
	1980	59.7	54.9	50.0	54.4	39.4	58.3
	1981	60.6	55.2	50.1	54.4	40.1	57.1
	1982	61.4	55.9	49.8	54.6	39.9	57.4
	1983	61.9	57.2	49.5	54.3	40.5	57.8

1 Labour force as a proportion of the working-age population.

Source: OECD: Labour Force Statistics.

one-half.[1] Female participation rates have also increased in many EC
countries, though by far less than in the USA. The increase in the
labour supply remained small, however, since there was a simultaneous decline in the participation rate among men; in the Federal
Republic of Germany, for example, this was the result of longer
schooling and the possibility of early retirement.

1 Cf. Janet L. NORWOOD, Labor market contrasts: United States and
   Europe, in: Monthly Labor Review, No. 8/1983, p. 4.

In the USA the large number of women entering the labour market for the first time was absorbed surprisingly smoothly. Between 1973 and 1983 the number women available for work increased by 13,7 million; more than 80 % of them found a job. The number of women in work rose by almost $11^1/_2$ million, more than twice the figure for men; more than 70 % of all newly created jobs were taken by women. The successful integration of women into the job market is also evident from the female unemployment rate, which rose by less than the average between 1973 and 1983 and in recent years was even below the male rate.[1] The proportion of women increased to a greater or lesser extent in all branches of economic activity, including blue collar occupations.[2]

Overall, demographic factors and changes in working habits had a far stronger effect on the labour supply in the USA than in the other countries. In addition, the demographic developments in the USA showed a substantial "lead" over Europe; the "baby boom" began far earlier in the USA and the birth rate also began to fall sooner than in Western Europe, namely in the first half of the sixties. The US Department of Labor therefore estimates that the labour market pressures stemming from population growth will begin to slacken in the second half of this decade.[3] In the European countries, a corresponding easing of labour market conditions is not generally expected until the nineties.

1.2.6 Similarities and Differences - a Resumé

A number of similarities and differences can be detected in the employment trends in the USA, Japan and the EC between 1973 and 1983. There were similarities in that in all countries

1 Cf. Diana WINKLER-BÜTTNER, op. cit., p. 343.
2 Cf. Carol Boyd LEON, op. cit., pp. 19 ff.
3 Cf. also Janet L. NORWOOD, Labor market contrasts, op. cit., p. 5.

- the underlying employment trend was less favourable than it had been in the sixties and early seventies;

- the services sector increased its share of total employment, while those of agriculture and industry declined; the shift in the pattern of employment coincided broadly with the "three sector" hypothesis;

- the labour force increased to a greater or lesser extent, mainly owing to demographic factors; and

- the unemployment trend was upwards.

Differences emerged mainly in that employment increased in some countries but declined in others. There were also fairly large differences in the pace and in some cases the timing of developments affecting the labour market.

Of all the countries examined here, the USA made the greatest progress between 1973 and 1983 in mastering the employment problem, even though the growth in the labour force was largest there. The number of new jobs far outweighed the number lost, so that even a substantial proportion of the persons entering the labour market were able to find a job. For that reason, the number of unemployed increased less markedly in percentage terms than in most other countries.

The Federal Republic of Germany, by contrast, recorded the worst performance in tackling the employment problem. During the period under examination many more jobs were eliminated than created, so that the number of unemployed rose for that reason alone. The growth in the labour force, which began later than elsewhere, compounded the problem, causing unemployment to rise far more quickly than in any of the other countries in question, which fell somewhere between these two extremes as far as labour market developments are concerned.

The creation of new jobs was concentrated in the services sector in all of the countries. However, it would be a mistake to deduce from this that the differences in employment performance are essentially a structural problem, caused by differences in the rate of progress towards the service-oriented society. The example of the USA illustrates this point clearly; the employment performance of the United States was better than that of most other countries in the services sector, but it was also better than that of at least the EC countries in the industrial sector as well. This was all the more significant, since the separation of service activities from industry is far more advanced in the USA than in the EC. Hence the creation of jobs in business services shows up in the industrial sector to a far greater extent in the EC than in the USA; but for that, the EC's industrial employment record would have been even worse.

Finally, attention should be drawn to a circumstance of significance to this study. In most of the countries the statistics on the services sector are inadequate, the only exception being the USA. Comprehensive statistics are available on the industrial sector and especially manufacturing, but data on services are very sparse, making empirical analysis extremely difficult.

1.3 Reasons for Differences in Employment Trends - an Overview

The examination of employment trends in the USA, Japan und the EC revealed clear differences. Since all the countries in question are essentially market-directed economies, it seems logical to assume that the same fundamental employment determinants apply. The reasons for differences in employment performance are therefore to be sought first in differences in developments in and/or significance of these determinants in individual countries.

As mentioned above, the factors that primarily suggest themselves as the causes of the differences in employment performance between the USA, Japan and the EC are the following:

54   **Employment Trends**

- differences in growth rates and in the structure of growth;

- differences in the development of real wages and wage structures;

- differences in the labour markets' flexibility, adaptability and willingness to adjust;

- differences in fundamental conceptions of economic policy.

There is a link between economic growth and employment trends; differences in growth rates between countries might therefore be a cause of divergences in employment performance. However, lasting disparities such as those seen in the period under consideration presuppose differences in underlying growth trends. A lack of international cyclical synchronization, for example, would have caused only temporary discrepancies, not more enduring differences in growth rates and employment. Diverging growth trends themselves would have needed explaining, for economic growth is also the result of a multiple process and hence ultimately only an indirect determinant of employment.

The structure of growth can also have a significant influence on employment. The increase in overall output may be more labour-intensive in one country but more capital-intensive in another, even though the actual rate of growth may be the same. The growing importance of the services sector is often cited as an example of this; since productivity in services is generally lower than in industry, growth in a country with a services sector that is larger or growing faster than elsewhere is expected to be more labour-intensive than in countries where services account for a smaller proportion of the economy.

Arguments that a substantial part of the expansion in employment in the USA is due to demographic factors - primarily the steep increase in the resident and working populations - and to the sharp rise in female participation rates[1] also ultimately rest upon differences in the structure of growth. It is claimed that these factors generated increased demand for more labour-intensive services that was met by expanding production. However, this would presuppose a fairly close relationship between private consumption or demand for services on the one hand and population growth and participation rates on the other.

Differences in wage costs might be a further cause of divergences in employment, although their effect on employment is a controversial issue. The proponents of the neo-classical school see wages, or rather real wages, as the essential determinant of employment. In their view, the employment problem can be solved primarily by reducing real wages or holding the rise in real wages below the rate of productivity growth. Post-Keynesians also do not deny that real wages have an effect on employment in principle, but they do not consider the link to be as clearcut as the neo-classical economists assume. They believe there may even be market situations in which unemployment may be increased by real wage cuts and reduced by real wage rises.[2]

The post-Keynesians cite another reason why they consider wage policy a poor tool for solving the employment problem - the authorities' lack of "control" over real wages. Wage policy can influence only nominal wages, whereas it is real wages that determine employment. It is in no way certain that a reduction in nominal wages, for example, will lead to a corresponding reduction in real wages. It is also conceivable that firms might try to improve their market position by passing on their cost advantages. The end result would merely be

1 See for example Werner SENGENBERGER, Das amerikanische Beschäftigungssystem, op. cit., p. 400.

2 Cf. Gerhard SCHMITT-RINK, Reallohnniveau und unfreiwillige Arbeitslosigkeit. Neo-klassische und neokeynesianische Erklärungsansätze, in: WISU, No. 1/1985, p. 35.

a process of deflation, at the end of which real wages would be just as high as before the reduction in nominal wages, if not higher.

This is not an inevitable mechanism, however, since it can be counteracted via the monetary policy. Even if the money supply remains unchanged, falling prices will sooner or later generate expansive impulses and hence provide a counterweight to the deflationary spiral. Keynes also realized this possibility. The neo-classical argumentation is generally based on the assumption that monetary policy is guided by capacity growth, implying a rising money supply.

Macroeconomic real wage levels alone do not adequately reflect the full employment effects of wages, however. The underlying microeconomic wage relationships are equally important; indeed, in a market economy they may be the more important influence, with the macroeconomic real wage level being merely a derived aggregate. The wage structure can only fulfil its guidance function in unregulated labour markets. Only in such markets does it have the necessary flexibility to react quickly to new market conditions and in turn to generate an adjustment in employment. In "cartelized" markets this function is seriously limited. If wage structures are no longer determined by the market and if they are adjusted only tardily or not at all to changed market conditions, it is inevitable that they will have repercussions on employment. Hence differences in the employment performances of individual countries may stem partly from differences in the flexibility and adaptibility of wage structures.

An efficient labour market presumes a high degree of flexibility. Flexibility will be affected by many factors, for example, by the institutional and legal framework, the degree of organization of market participants, and the mobility and adaptability of the supply of and demand for labour. The labour market is here defined in fairly wide terms to include work opportunities for self-employed persons. Differences in labour market flexibility are thus a further possible source of divergences in the employment performance of various countries.

Finally, economic policy can also contribute towards differences in employment performance. The socio-economic framework and macro-economic policy influence employment via their effects on growth and also have an impact on labour market conditions. Finally, the labour market policy enables economic policymakers to have a direct impact on employment.

Differences in employment performances in different countries can therefore be due to a variety of causes. The chapters that follow will examine which factors can explain employment differences between the USA, Japan and the EC between 1973 and 1983 and how strong their effect was. It should be noted, however, that interdependence between the various factors makes empirical analysis significantly more difficult.

Chapter 2

GROWTH AND PRODUCTIVITY IN THE USA, JAPAN AND THE EC - THEIR IMPACT ON THE EMPLOYMENT TRENDS

2.1 Macroeconomic Growth and the Structure of Growth Processes

2.1.1 Growth and Hours of Work

Since there is a link between development employment and economic growth, differences in the pace of growth may help explain differences in employment trends. Lasting divergences in employment performance such as those observed between the USA and the Federal Republic of Germany presuppose differences in growth trends; temporary disparities in growth rates due to a lack of cyclical synchronization would not be a sufficient explanation.

Measured in terms of real gross domestic product, there were many similiarities in the growth of real GDP in the USA, Japan and the EC between 1973 and 1983. Growth in all countries slowed down considerably from the rates recorded in the sixties and early seventies (see Table 9) and growth differentials narrowed in many cases. The average rate of increase in real GDP in the USA was 1.9 % a year between 1973 and 1983, barely higher than the 1.7 % rate recorded in the EC. The disparity was larger only vis-à-vis the United Kingdom, where the rate of growth was significantly below the EC average (see Table 9 and Diagram 5). Hence the divergences in employment performance between the USA and the EC, at any rate, cannot be explained by differences in growth rates.

As in earlier years, Japan was an exception. Economic growth in Japan slowed down considerably between 1973 and 1983, but it was still approximately twice as fast as in the USA or the EC. If the comparison of employment performance were confined to Japan and the EC, one might be tempted to attach greater importance to this

Table 9   EMPLOYMENT, REAL GROSS DOMESTIC PRODUCT

AND PRODUCTIVITY

- average percentage rates of change -

	Employment[1]		Real GDP[2]		Productivity[3]	
	1962-73	1973-83	1962-73	1973-83	1962-73	1973-83
USA	2.2	1.5	4.1	1.9	1.8	0.4
Japan	1.3	0.9	9.7	3.7	8.3	2.8
EC	0.2	-0.1	4.6	1.7	4.3	1.8
Germany	0.1	-0.6	4.4	1.6	4.3	2.2
France	0.9	0.2	5.5	2.3	4.5	2.1
United Kingdom	0.2	-0.5	3.3	1.1	3.1	1.6
Italy	-0.6	0.6	5.0	1.8	5.5	1.2

1 Total employment, as defined in the national accounts. -- 2 Gross domestic product at constant prices. -- 3 Real gross domestic product per person employed.

Source: OECD: National Accounts; authors' calculations.

difference, but it loses significance if the USA is included, for the expansion in employment was much greater in the USA than in Japan, despite slower growth.

Nor do changes in working hours provide an explanation for the employment differentials between the USA, Japan and the EC. Working hours per worker fell between 1973 and 1983 in all of the countries in question. The average reduction in the length of the working week was actually greater in the EC than in the USA or Japan; it can be assumed that the same applied to other components of working hours, such as holiday entitlements or part-time working.[1]

1 See also Gernot MÜLLER, Das "Beschäftigungswunder" in den USA, in: WSI-Mitteilungen, No. 9/1984, pp. 503 f.; Donato ALVAREZ, Brian COOPER, Productivity trends in manufacturing in the U.S. and 11 other countries, in: Monthly Labor Review, No. 1/1984, pp. 53 f., especially Table 3.

Diagram 5   GROWTH AND PRODUCTIVITY

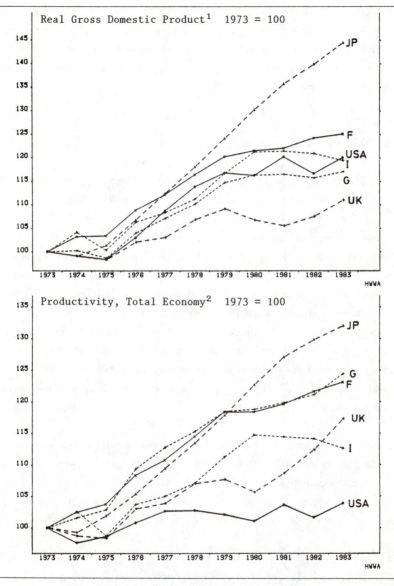

Real Gross Domestic Product[1]   1973 = 100

Productivity, Total Economy[2]   1973 = 100

Key: USA = United States of America;   JP = Japan;   EC = European
       Community;   G = Federal Republic of Germany;   F = France;
       I = Italy;   UK = United Kingdom.
1 At 1980 prices. -- 2 Gross domestic product per person employed.

Source: See Table 9.

Growth and Productivity   61

If one assumes an inverse relationship between working hours and employment, as the advocates of a reduction in working hours do, the larger reduction in working hours in the EC should have produced a relative improvement in the labour market. In reality, however, employment in the EC virtually stagnated, whereas it rose significantly in the USA.

2.1.2 The Structure of Growth Processes

An explanation for the different employment trends in the USA, Japan and the EC is sometimes sought in the "structure" of the growth process. The American "employment miracle" between 1973 and 1983 is thus attributed partly to the relatively large services sector in the USA and its rapid growth.[1] It is claimed that since both the productivity level and productivity gains in the services sector are generally lower than in industry, growth in countries with a larger and/or more rapidly expanding services sector is more "labour-intensive" than in countries where services account for a smaller share of the economy and/or are expanding more slowly. The increasing prominence of the labour-intensive services sector is also seen as one of the causes of the general slowdown in the overall rate of productivity growth.[2]

Measured in relation to total employment, the services sector is indeed much larger in the USA than in the other countries (see Table 10). In the USA more than 70 % of all persons in employment worked in the services sector in 1983, compared with between 50 and 60 % in Japan and most of the EC countries. However, it is not the service

---

1 Cf. Bundesanstalt für Arbeit (ed.), Wirtschafts- und Arbeitsmarkt-entwicklung in den USA und in der Bundesrepublik Deutschland, op. cit., p. 216.

2 Cf. Ronald E. KUTSCHER, Jerome A. MARK, The service-producing sector: some common perceptions reviewed, in: Monthly Labor Review, No. 4/1983, p. 21.

Table 10 EMPLOYMENT AND OUTPUT SHARES OF
THE MAJOR SECTORS OF THE ECONOMY IN 1973 AND 1983
- percentages -

	Agriculture		Industry[1]		Services[2]	
	1973	1983	1973	1983	1973	1983
Share of gross domestic product - at current prices -						
USA	3.8	2.0	33.4	31.0	62.8	67.0
Japan	5.6	3.2	44.1	40.3	50.3	56.5
Germany	3.0	2.0	48.8	42.1	48.2	55.9
France	7.1	4.2	40.4	36.2	52.5	59.6
Italy	7.7	5.7	41.9	39.2	50.4	55.1
United Kingdom	2.9	2.0	42.1	39.4	55.0	58.6
- at constant prices -						
USA	3.0	2.6	35.7	31.4	61.3	66.0
Japan	5.5	3.3	42.4	45.8	52.1	50.9
Germany	2.4	2.3	47.8	42.4	49.8	55.3
France	6.4	5.4	41.7	38.8	51.9	55.8
Italy	7.2	7.0	42.9	40.3	49.9	52.7
United Kingdom	1.9	2.1	43.3	39.6	54.8	58.3
Share of total employment[3]						
USA	4.4	3.6	28.7	24.1	66.9	72.3
Japan	15.8	11.5	37.4	34.7	46.8	53.8
Germany	7.2	5.5	47.4	41.7	45.4	52.8
France	10.9	7.9	37.8	32.2	51.3	59.9
Italy	16.4	12.0	37.9	34.5	45.7	53.5
United Kingdom[4]	2.9	2.7	42.4	33.6	54.7	63.7

1 Mining and quarrying, manufacturing, electricity, gas and water,
construction. -- 2 Wholesale and retail trade, restaurants and
hotels, transport and communication, financing, insurance, business
services, community, social and personal services. -- 3 Employment as
defined in the national accounts. -- 4 Employment as defined in the
labour force statistics.

Source: OECD: National Accounts and Labour Force Statistics; national
statistics; authors' calculations.

sector's share of employment but its share of gross product that is the appropriate measure for investigating the employment effect of structural factors such as the size of the sector in the various countries. The "labour intensity" of growth depends on the proportion of output and growth attributable to labour-intensive activities.

The service sector's share of real gross product was also higher in the USA than in the other countries between 1973 and 1983, although the differences were smaller than in employment shares (see Table 10). On the other hand, the growth in the services sector was no faster in the USA than in EC countries and in fact was slower than in Japan (see Table 11 and Diagram 6); the same holds true for most branches of the sector.

A comparison of employment and output shares shows that on average for the years from 1973 to 1983 the services sector's share of employment was appreciably higher than its share of real gross product in the USA and slightly higher in France and the United Kingdom. In the Federal Republic of Germany and Italy the opposite was the case; here the sector's output share exceeded its employment share. In Japan the two measures were more or less equal.

This leads to a remarkable finding on the level of productivity (real gross product per person employed): in some countries productivity in the services sector over the period from 1973 to 1983 was above rather than below the average for the economy as a whole. The opposite applied only in the USA, where the difference was fairly marked, and in France and the United Kingdom, where it was far less pronounced. In the private sector productivity was lower than in the economy as a whole only in the USA and Japan, although the differences were not very large. In most EC countries, on the other hand, productivity in the services sector excluding government was above the overall average.

Hence, the frequent claim that there is a clear productivity differential between industry and the services sector cannot be substantiated for most of the countries examined here. Even in the USA, where the disparity was largest, average productivity in the services sector as a whole over the period from 1973 to 1983 was only just over one-quarter below that of industry, and in the private branches of the sector it was even less marked. It is true that productivity gains in services were small, but they were only slightly greater in industry. In most other countries, however, productivity growth in the services sector was faster than in industry and the differential between the two more pronounced (see Table 11 and Diagram 7); in the Federal Republic of Germany productivity gains were approximately the same in both sectors.

This all suggests that little weight should be attached to structural factors such as the different relative size of the services sectors to explain differences in employment performance, particularly between the USA and the EC countries. According to simulation estimates, the absolute increase in employment in the USA between 1973 and 1983 would have been reduced by less than one-tenth if the services sector had been proportionately as small as in the EC countries and the productivity differential between the industry and services sectors had been of a similar order.[1]

It should be borne in mind, however, that the measurement of productivity is extremely problematic in the services sector.[2] Calculating output is fraught with difficulty, especially where government is concerned, and deflating the results poses still more problems. Inter-

---

1 For the sake of simplicity, no account was taken of productivity increases in these calculations.

2 On the problems of measuring productivity in services, see Jonathan GERSHUNY, Ian D. MILES, The New Service Economy, London 1983, pp. 33 ff.; John W. KENDRICK, Beatrice N. VACCARA (eds.), New Developments in Productivity Measurement and Analysis, Chicago and London 1980, especially the contributions by Mayer/Gomez-Ibanez and Searle/Waite, pp. 293 ff.

Diagram 6   GROSS DOMESTIC PRODUCT IN INDUSTRY AND
IN THE SERVICES SECTOR

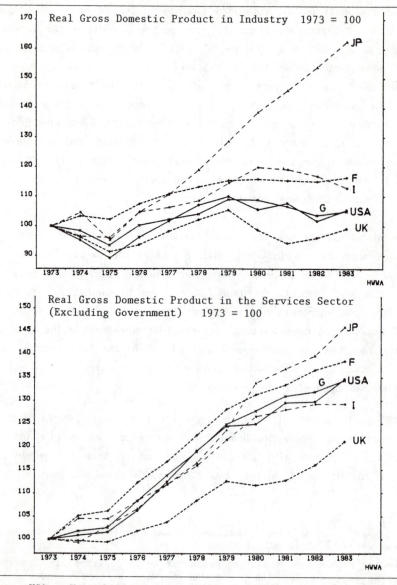

Key: USA = United States of America; JP = Japan; G = Federal Re-
      public of Germany; F = France; I = Italy; UK = United King-
      dom.
Source: See Table 11.

Employment Trends

Diagram 7   PRODUCTIVITY IN INDUSTRY AND IN THE
SERVICES SECTOR

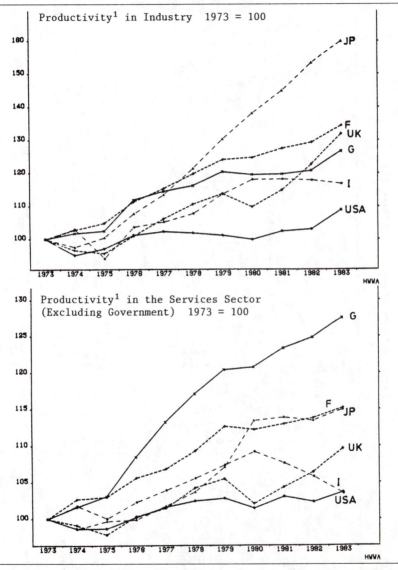

Key: USA = United States of America;   JP = Japan;   G = Federal Re-
        public of Germany;   F = France;   I = Italy; UK = United Kingdom.
1   Real gross domestic product per person employed. -- 2   Including
government.
Source: See Table 11.

Growth and Productivity   67

Table 11   GROSS DOMESTIC PRODUCT AND PRODUCTIVITY, BY KIND OF ACTIVITY, 1973-83

– annual average percentage changes –

| | Agriculture | Total | Industry | | | |
			Mining & quarrying	Manu-facturing	Electricity, gas, water	Construc-tion
Real gross domestic product						
USA	0.3	0.5	1.1	0.8	1.8	-1.7
Japan	-1.1	5.0	0.9	6.2	4.2	-0.1
Germany	1.0	0.5	-2.8	0.7	3.0	-1.0
France	0.6	1.5	-2.9	1.8	5.7	-0.8
Italy	1.5	1.2	–a	1.8	-0.4a	-0.2
United Kingdom	2.0	-0.1	13.5	-1.7	1.6	-2.1
Productivity[3]						
USA	1.0	0.9	-3.0	1.6	0.1	-2.2
Japan	1.2	4.8	3.2	6.5	3.1	-1.2
Germany	4.3	2.4	-1.7	2.7	2.3	1.2
France	3.7	3.0	0.8	3.2	3.1a	1.0
Italy	4.2	1.6	–a	2.2	-1.6a	0.1
United Kingdom	3.5	2.8	14.9	1.5	1.9	-0.1

(Continued)

Employment Trends

Table 11 (continued)

| | Services sector[1] | | | | | For comparison: Services sector including government[2] |
	Total	Wholesale and retail trade, restaurants & hotels	Transport, communications	Financing, insurance, business services	Social & personal services	
	Real gross domestic product					
USA	3.0	2.3	2.7	3.9	2.8	2.6
Japan	3.8	3.5	3.2	5.4	2.6	3.8
Germany	3.0	1.3	3.4	3.8	3.8	2.8
France	3.3	2.2	3.3	3,7[b]	4,7[b]	3.1
Italy	2.6	2.3	3.0	2,8[b]	-[b]	2.4
United Kingdom	1.9	-0.2	0.9	3.8	3.2	1.7
	Productivity[3]					
USA	0.4	0.1	1.9	-0,8	0.2	0.4
Japan	1.4	1.6	2.4	2.6	-0.7	1.5
Germany[4]	2.5	1.6	4.0	2.6	1.6	1.9
France	1.4	1.5	2.8	0,5[b]	0,8[b]	1.4
Italy	0.3	0.2	1.6	-1,0[b]	-[b]	0.2
United Kingdom	0.9	-0.9	2.0	1.0	0.5	0.7

1 Services sector excluding government and private non-profit organizations. -- 2 Services sector including government and private non-profit organizations. -- 3 Real gross domestic product per person employed. -- 4 Branches of the services sector defined in accordance with the German classification system. -- a In Italy mining and quarrying and electricity, gas and water are grouped as a single branch. -- b Social and personal services are included with financing, insurance and other services.

Source: OECD: National Accounts and Labour Force Statistics; national statistics; authors' calculations.

Growth and Productivity

national comparisons are further complicated by differences of definition. Furthermore, it is questionable whether the level of productivity
can be adequately expressed by the usual measure, that is to say
real gross domestic output per person employed; for example,
measurement on this basis would show the renting of dwellings to be
highly productive, owing to the relatively high gross value-added and
the small number of employees. At any event, a comparison of productivity levels is more uncertain than a comparison of changes in
productivity over time.

2.1.3 The Impact of Changes in Population and Employment Behaviour

Differences in population changes and in employment behaviour are
sometimes used to help explain differences in employment performance
between the USA, Japan and the EC. For example, Sengenberger
considers that a substantial part of the large increase in employment
in the USA is attributable to the comparatively sharp increase in the
resident and working-age populations and in labour force participation of women.[1] This argument rests ultimately on differences in the
structure of the growth process, that is to say a disproportionately
large increase in the private demand for services in the USA. It
assumes a relatively close relationship between population changes
or employment behaviour on the one hand and private consumption
or demand for services on the other.[2] Two factors above all make
such a close relationship less plausible: the income dependency of
consumption and the effect of price relationships on consumption
structure.

---

1 Cf. Werner SENGENBERGER, Das amerikanische Beschäftigungssystem,
   op. cit., p. 400.

2 Sengenberger assumes "a fairly constant ratio between the resident
   population and the demand for particular services over the short
   run"; Werner SENGENBERGER, Das amerikanische Beschäftigungssystem,
   op. cit., P. 400.

Employment Trends

A growing population signifies no more than rising demand, including the demand for services. The extent to which this materializes depends crucially on the development of real incomes. A decline in real per capital income - as a result of population pressure on the supply side of the labour market and a consequent fall in wages, for example - could partly or wholly neutralize the demand-side effects of population growth on private consumption. This alone greatly weakens the link between population growth and a growth in consumption.

Furthermore, the demand for services is not only income-elastic but also price-elastic, an aspect that is often neglected. A disproportionately large increase in the demand for services should cause the prices of services to rise more rapidly than those of industrial goods. This creates an incentive to replace services either by goods that perform the same function more cheaply - the washing machine in place of the laundry, the television set in place of the cinema - or by do-it-yourself or by services from the underground economy.[1] A relatively close relationship between population changes and the consumption of services is to be expected only where services are provided free of charge, or all consumers are obliged to receive them or to share in meeting their cost. This applies to the education and health services and to a range of services provided by public authorities. However, population growth is not the sole determinant, even in the fields of education and health care; other factors such as education and health policies are also important.

All things considered, a close or even rigid relationship between population growth and employment behaviour on the one hand and private consumption or the demand for services on the other appears to be rather implausible; it is the exception rather than the rule. On closer inspection, therefore, the theory that the relatively good employment performance in the USA is attributable largely to the

1 Cf. Manfred WEGNER, op. cit., p. 9.

Table 12   TOTAL PRIVATE CONSUMPTION AND THE CONSUMPTION OF SERVICES, 1973-83[1]

- average annual percentage changes -

| | Private consumption total | Consumption of services[2] | | | | | | |
		Total	Health and medical care	Transport & communication[3]	Education & entertainment	Personal services	Restaurants, cafes and hotels	gross rent, fuel and power
USA	2.7	3.4	3.7	2.0	4.2	1.2	2.4	3.3
Japan	3.1	4.3	5.6	2.9	3.9	3.4	-[a]	5.5
Germany	2.0	2.8	2.8	1.9	1.9	1.7	0.7	3.1
France	3.0	4.4	6.6	3.5	5.3	1.8	2.0	4.2
Italy	1.9	2.3	4.4	2.7	3.5	3.3	2.2	2.3
United Kingdom	1.2	1.1	2.4	1.7	2.7	-0.3	-0.5	1.2

1 At constant prices. -- 2 The definition of the total consumption of services differs from those of the components listed. -- 3 Expenditure on private automobiles included for Japan, excluded for the other countries. -- a Included among "Personal services".

Source: OECD: National Accounts; national statistics; authors' calculations.

Employment Trends

Diagram 8   TOTAL PRIVATE CONSUMPTION AND THE CONSUMPTION
OF SERVICES[1]

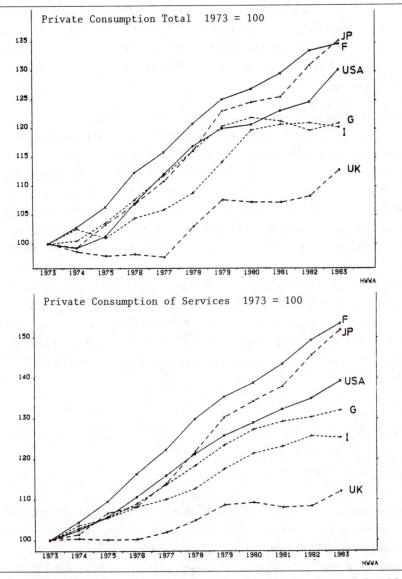

Key: US = United States of America; JP = Japan;   G = Federal Republic
       of Germany; F = France; I = Italy; UK = United Kingdom.
1 At constant prices.

Source: See Table 12.

Growth and Productivity   73

comparatively rapid population growth and the rise in female participation rates does not seem very convincing. It would require the
growth in private consumption and especially the demand for services
to be considerably stronger in the USA than in the other countries;
in fact, assuming similar patterns of growth on the expenditure
side, overall growth would have had to be faster than in the other
countries.

Empirical evidence gives a different picture, however (see Table 12
and Diagram 8). Although the population and the participation rate
increased much more rapidly in the USA than in the other countries
between 1973 and 1983, the increase in overall private consumption
in the USA was not much higher than in the Federal Republic of
Germany and Italy and was actually lower than in France and Japan;
there was a pronounced "growth differential" only with respect to
the United Kingdom. The same applies to the consumption of services.
This suggests that no great significance should be attached to the
differences in demographic trends and participation rates between
the USA, Japan und the EC countries in seeking to explain the
differences in employment trends. Nevertheless, here too it should
be borne in mind that analysis is made more difficult by problems of
definition, particularly regarding the consumption of services.

2.2 Productivity and Employment

2.2.1 Productivity - the Evidence

By definition, there is a close ex post correlation between growth,
productivity and employment. Since growth rates were broadly
similar, the differences in the employment performance of the USA,
Japan and the EC countries between 1973 and 1983 were therefore
reflected in productivity (see Table 9 and Diagram 5). Employment
rose substantially in the USA, while productivity showed only a
moderate increase. In the EC countries, on the other hand, average

74   **Employment Trends**

productivity gains were much larger. They were greatest in Japan, however, where economic growth was also appreciably faster than in the other countries. There were differences in the scale of productivity growth in all the major branches of economic activity (see Table 11 and Diagram 7); even in the services sector there were pronounced disparities between the various countries, despite the comparatively small differences in rates of growth.

In all the countries, both prodictivity growth and economic growth were much slower between 1973 and 1983 than they had been in the sixties and early seventies, although the extent of the slowdown differed from country to country. In the USA, the rise in productivity slowed down much more than economic growth. In most EC countries the reverse was the case; growth showed a more marked weakening, whereas productivity gains declined less. Italy was an exception; here a sharp decline in the rate of growth was accompanied by an even steeper fall in productivity gains. The picture in Japan was similar. Put another way, the trend towards more labour-intensive production intensified further between 1973 and 1983 in the USA, whereas in most EC countries growth became even more capital-intensive, despite a pronounced increase in the supply of labour.

The slowdown in productivity growth has attacted particular notice in the USA, but it has not yet been explained satisfactorily.[1] A number of econometric studies have examined possible causes such as the structure and quality of the capital stock, the quality of labour, expenditure on research and development, the increase in energy costs, structural change, the weakness of investment and

---

1 Cf. Manfred WEGNER, The Employment Miracle in the United States and Stagnating Employment in the European Community. Commission of the European Communities, Economic Papers, No. 17, July 1983; Janet L. NORWOOD, Arbeitsplatzbeschaffung als Herausforderung im wirtschaftlichen Wandel, in: Bundesanstalt für Arbeit (ed.), Wirtschafts- und Arbeitsmarktentwicklung in den USA und in der Bundesrepublik Deutschland, op. cit., pp. 18 ff.

growth, the decline in capital intensity, conflicts over income distribution, inflation and even the degree of regulation of the economy, but in many cases there remaines a substantial "unexplained remainder" [1] All that is certain is that there is no single explanation for the general slowdown in productivity growth; a whole series of factors have clearly contributed to it. The underlying slowdown in productivity gains in the "mature" industrialized countries and the general weakening of economic growth are worthy subjects of research, but they are not the concern of this study. However, it will be necessary to consider some of those causes of these phenomena which are expected to show a particularly close link with the performance of employment.

2.2.2   Determinants of Productivity

The link between economic growth, productivity and employment is expressed by the identity

$$GDP_r = P_E \cdot E \qquad (1)$$

where GDP_r represents real gross domestic product,

E employment and

P_E productivity per worker

---

1   Cf. for example Martin Neil BAILY, The Productivity Growth Slowdown, in: Martin Neil BAILY, Arthur M. OKUN (eds.), The Battle against Unemployment and Inflation, 3rd edition, New York and London 1982, pp. 198 ff.; J.R. NORSWORTHY, Michael J. HARPER, Kent KUNZE: The Slowdown in Productivity Growth: Analysis of some Contributing Factors, in: Brookings Papers on Economic Activity, No. 2/1979, pp. 387 ff.; John W. KENDRICK, Productivity Trends and the Recent Slowdown: Historical Perspective, Causal Factors, and Policy Options, in: American Enterprise Institute: Essays in Contemporary Economic Problems, Washington 1979, pp. 17 ff.; John W. KENDRICK, International Comparisons of Recent Productivity Trends, in: American Enterprise Institute: Essays in Contemporary Economic Problems, Washington 1981, pp. 125 ff.; OECD, Productivity Trends in the OECD Area, Working Party No. 2 of the Economic Policy Committee, Paris 1980; The Decline in Productivity Growth, Proceedings of a Conference held in June 1980, Federal Reserve Bank of Boston, Conference Series No. 22.

so that

$$p_E = \frac{GDP_r}{E} \qquad (2)$$

The following relationship[1] exists between the rates of change (d):

$$dGDP_r = dp_E + dE \qquad (3).$$

Identities shed no light on the nature of the relationship between employment and productivity; they only depict the result of economic processes and say nothing the nature or course of these processes or about the factors involved. They do not reveal how the observed configuration of growth, productivity and employment came about.

The determinants of productivity must therefore be examined first in the search for a connection between employment and productivity. Productivity growth is determined mainly endogenously, as are economic growth and increases in employment. Only productivity potential is really "exogenous", being determined by the state of technology and technological progress. Decisions on the manner, scale and intensity with which potential is exploited are made in the course of the economic process; a whole range of factors come into play in this regard, so that the actual development of productivity in the economy as a whole remains open, even if productivity potential is high. What is measured ex post as a productivity gain can differ considerably from what could have been expected purely on the basis of the given technical parameters.[2]

---

1 To be mathematically correct, equation (3) should read
$$dGDP_r = dp_E + dE + dGDP_r \cdot dp_E$$
However, at low rates of growth the multiplication term is insignificant, so that the above approximation is generally used for economic analyses.

2 Cf. Eckhardt WOHLERS, Beschäftigungsfeindlicher Produktivitäts-fortschritt? in: Wirtschaftsdienst, No. 1/1985, p. 45.

The main possible influences on productivity are:[1]

a) Technological progress

- Technological knowhow
- Research and development
- Technology transfer

b) Quantitative factors

- Availability of labour and capital
- Availability of natural resources

c) Qualitative factors

- Composition and quality of labour
- Composition and quality of capital

d) Resource allocation

e) Returns to scale

f) Structural change

- Structure of demand
- Structure of production

g) Process-related factors

- Growth and capacity utilization
- Factor costs
- Factor price relationship, substitution effects
- Inflation

---

1 The list of factors influencing productivity is based on John W. KENDRICK, Productivity Trends and the Recent Slowdown, op. cit., pp. 19 ff.; Douglas TODD, Some aspects of industrial productivity performance in the European Community: an appraisal, in: COMMISSION OF THE EUROPEAN COMMUNITIES, European Economy, No. 20/1984, pp. 12 ff.; Martin Neil BAILY, op. cit.; Bernd ROHWER, Wachstum, Produktivität und Beschäftigung, in: Jahrbuch für Sozialwissenschaft, Vol. 34/1983, No. 1, pp. 142 ff.; Klaus ROSE, Produktivität, in: Handwörterbuch der Sozialwissenschaften, Vol. 8, Göttingen 1964, pp. 616 ff.; Niklaus BLATTNER, Bruno MORDASINI, Die Arbeitsproduktivität in der Schweiz 1960-1980: Entwicklung und Versuche der Erklärung, in: Die Volkswirtschaft, Vol. 55, 1982, pp. 53 ff.; Anon., Der Produktivitätsfortschritt in der Bundesrepublik und seine Bestimmungsfaktoren, in: Monatsberichte der Deutschen Bundesbank, No. 1/1980, pp. 12 ff.

h)   Exogenous "shocks"

i)   Economic policy

j)   Socio-economic factors
      - Political and social conditions
      - Managerial expertise and entrepreneurship.

In turn, more or less close relationships may exist between the groups of determinants. Take technical progress, for example. For labour productivity, advances in production processes, i.e. the introduction of more efficient production techniques, primarily are of great relevance. Advances in products, i.e. product innovation, have only an indirect effect on productivity, by coupling new products and procedures, for example.[1] Process-related technical progress causes substitution effects and thus influences capital intensity. It can raise the quality of production procedures and natural resources, improve the efficiency of resource allocation and affect the level of returns to scale.[2] Technical progress is an exogenous factor over the short term, but it can be influenced over the longer term, via research and development, for example.

The main quantitative factors are the availability of labour, capital and natural resources. Substitution effects, such as shifts in the volume of factor inputs, are often also included under this heading.[3] However, substitution effects are only a "derived" determinant; the extent of substitution depends in turn on other factors, not least the change in factor price ratio. If the analysis relates to labour productivity, as in this case, the capital goods provided for each workplace - in other words, the capital intensity - are also extremely important.

---

1 Cf. Bernd ROHWER, op. cit., pp. 143 f.
2 Cf. Bernd ROHWER, op. cit., pp. 144; Klaus ROSE, op. cit., p. 617.
3 As in Niklaus BLATTNER, Bruno MORDASINI, op. cit., p. 53; Klaus ROSE, op. cit., p. 617.

The efficiency of the production plant and the available "human capital" are qualitative factors. Plant efficiency is determined by the modernity of the capital stock and the volume and pattern of investment; investment is the medium by which technical progress is "embodied" in the economic process. The "human capital" available depends primarily on the level of qualification of the workforce and the efficiency of training. Other factors also come into play, however, such as the structure of the labour supply or the state of workers' health.[1] There are links between qualitative and process-related factors. The latter affect the quality of capital via investment activity, but they also influence the quality of labour by modifying workers' inclination to seek higher qualifications, for example. Resource allocation influences production efficiency and hence productivity; the intensity of competition plays an important role in this. The returns to scale deriving from the advantages of mass production can also become important for productivity growth.

The pace of productivity growth can also depend on changes in the structure of demand and output. The "current" theory is that the disproportionately large expansion in services, which are deemed to be labour-intensive, tends to depress the productivity rate for the economy as a whole. The general slowdown in productivity growth in the industrial countries is partly ascribed to structural factors such as this;[2] however, the findings of the analysis of the effects of growth on employment performance suggest that no great importance should be attached to them.

In the course of the economic process, productivity is also affected by growth and the capacity utilization rate, as well as factor costs or factor price relationships; the latter play a crucial part in determining

---

1 Cf. John W. KENDRICK, Productivity Trends and the Recent Slowdown, op. cit., pp. 48 f.

2 Cf. Henning KLODT, Vor der Trendwende? in: Wirtschaftswoche, No. 16/1984, p. 94.

Employment Trends

whether technical progress is labour-saving or capital-saving. The other production costs also play a role, however, for the main motive behind process innovation is to improve the overall ratio of costs to earnings; the ratio of wage costs to capital costs is only one of several determinants, albeit a particularly weighty one.[1] Economic policy and exogenous "shocks", such as those triggered by dramatic increases in the prices of energy products or other raw materials, often also exert an influence on productivity via the economic process.[2]

Socio-economic factors such as social conditions and the fundamental conceptions of economic policy or the power of associations and institutions can also have an impact on productivity, for example via acceptance or rejection of technical innovations or restriction of leeway in economic activity. Factors such as managerial expertise and entrepreneurship help determine the efficiency of production, the volume and pattern of investment and the application of technical progress. They are therefore also important from the point of view of productivity.

Some of these factors determine productivity growth mainly over the long term. This is true of technical progress, the availability and composition of factors of production, resource allocation, returns to scale and some socio-economic factors. They are largely exogenous in the sense that over the shorter run their effect on factor productivity can be influenced only gradually, if at all, and is thus predetermined. Short and medium-term productivity growth depend to a considerable degree on process-related determinants.

Every change in productivity actually has some effect on employment. However, in countries at a similar stage of development, like those

---

1 Cf. Bernd ROHWER, op. cit., p. 145.
2 Cf. for instance Martin Neil BAILY, op. cit., pp. 198 ff.; OECD, Productivity Trends in the OECD Area, op. cit., pp. 69 ff.

under consideration here, exogenous productivity increases in the sense stated above should actually occur on a similar scale everywhere; they therefore seem to have little relevance as a cause of differences in productivity and employment trends. It must be conceded that differences do occur when new technologies are introduced. For example, the USA and Japan undoubtedly have a lead over the European countries in microelectronics;[1] however, the employment performance between 1973 and 1983 probably did not yet reflect this to any significant degree.

The main reasons for differences in employment and productivity trends in the USA, Japan and the EC between 1973 and 1983 are therefore to be sought primarily among those factors that have a significant effect on developments over the short and medium term. Since investigations so far have virtually eliminated differences in the rate and pattern of growth as possible causes, the factors that remain to be considered are disparities in factor costs or factor price relationship in economic policy and in the social and legal framework.

1 See also Dietmar KELLER, The International Competitiveness of Europe, the USA and Japan, in: Intereconomics, No. 2/1985, pp. 59 ff.; HWWA-Institut für Wirtschaftsforschung-Hamburg, Internationale Wettbewerbsfähigkeit und strukturelle Anpassungserfordernisse, supplementary volume 3 to HWWA-Strukturbericht 1983, Hamburg 1984, pp. 66 ff. and 103 ff.

Chapter 3

THE EMPLOYMENT EFFECTS OF WAGE BEHAVIOUR AND LABOUR MARKET FLEXIBILITY IN THE USA, JAPAN AND THE EC

3.1 Wages and Employment - a Brief Theoretical Sketch

There are few who would deny the close link between the behaviour of wages and employment, but the nature of the link and of the transmission mechanism are the subject of controversy. Neo-classical theory holds that the demand for labour is determined primarily by price in the shape of wages - or more precisely real wages; there is an inverse relationship between employment and real wages. This approach is based essentially on a microeconomic outlook. It is the behaviour of labour costs that is crucial to employment; the macro-economic demand effects of wages are of secondary importance.

Real wage increases can thus affect employment in many ways:[1]

- by impairing the viability of existing jobs; if a job becomes un-profitable, it is only a matter of time before it will be eliminated;

- by reducing the return on capital; over the medium term, a fall in capital profitability will depress investment and cause unemployment due to "capital deficiency".

- by changing relative factor prices; if labour becomes more expensive in relation to capital, there will be an incentive to substitute capital for labour.

---

1 See for example Peter KALMBACH, Lohnhöhe und Beschäftigung: Ein Evergreen der wirtschaftspolitischen Debatte, in: Wirtschafts-dienst, No. 7/1985, pp. 370 ff.; Herbert GIERSCH, Arbeit, Lohn und Beschäftigung, in: Weltwirtschaftliches Archiv, No. 119 (1983), p. 10; OECD, Real Wages and Employment, Working Party No. 1, Paris 1982, p. 3.

These links are not denied by Keynesians; nor are they questioned by the advocates of a simplifying "purchasing power theory of wages", although they hold that the negative employment effects of higher labour costs at the microeconomic level will be offset in the economy as a whole by the demand effects of higher wages and that in times of underemployment and spare capacity they will actually be outweighed. At least during those periods, they claim, there is no inverse relationship between real wages and employment at the macro-economic level, but probably the opposite.

In general, Keynesian economists differentiate more than the pro-ponents of the "purchasing power theory of wages" in assessing the links between real wages and employment. They concede that there may be circumstances in which unemployment is exacerbated by real wage reductions and eased by real wage increases,[1] but this is not the general rule. The Neo-Keynesians also admit that the long-term effects may differ from the short-term effects. For example, Malinvaud considers that the employment impact of real wage increases will probably be positive over the short term owing to the immediate stimulus to demand but negative over the medium to long term owing to the reduction in profitability. Overall, he judges the long-term effects to be stronger than the short-term ones.[2] Keynesians thus also acknowledge the existence of an inverse relationship between real wages and employment, at least over the long term.

They nevertheless criticize the conclusions for economic policy that the neo-classicists draw from the relationship between real wages and employment. According to the neo-classical view, the key to solving the employment problem lies solely in wage policy. Wage restraint on

1 Cf. Gerhard SCHMITT-RINK, op. cit., p. 35.

2 Cf. Edmund MALINVAUD, Wages and Unemployment, in: The Economic Journal, No. 92 (1982), pp. 1 ff.

Employment Trends

the part of the trade unions would lead to a relative or absolute fall in real wages and hence stimulate employment. It is this that many Keynesians question, however; they consider it far from certain that restraint in nominal wage behaviour will lead to a fall in real wages. They argue that in the context of strong competition that usually characterizes periods of weak economic activity, a policy of nominal wage restraint would be more likely to depress prices. This would trigger a deflationary spiral that would in turn lead to increased uncertainty and hence have a destabilizing effect, and the intended relative or absolute fall in real wages would not materialize.

The danger of a deflationary spiral was stressed by Keynes himself.[1] This was one of the main reasons why he proposed an expansion of demand or of the money supply instead of a reduction in nominal wages (nominal wage restraint under today's conditions) as a remedy for unemployment. The transmission mechanism between nominal and real wages indeed is the Achilles' heel of neo-classical employment policy. Wage policy exercises direct control only over nominal wages, whereas it is real wages that are crucial to employment. Whether nominal wage restraint produces similar behaviour in real wages depends on several factors, most of all monetary policy. A deflationary spiral is not inevitable, however. It will only occur if monetary policy restricts the money supply when prices are falling. The danger of a deflationary spiral will not arise if wage restraint is coupled with a policy of expanding the money supply in line with capacity.

Various wage structures are possible for any given real wage level. Even a relatively high level of real wages can be consistent with employment needs if the underlying wage structure accords with

---

1 Cf. John Maynard KEYNES, The General Theory of Employment, Interest and Money, London, Melbourne and Toronto 1967, chapter 19, pp. 257 ff. However, Keynes considered that unemployment was due to the trade cycle, whereas the neo-classicists assume that the causes of unemployment are essentially non-cyclical.

market forces. If it does not, even low real wages cannot guarantee a high level of employment. In order to achieve equilibrium in the labour market, either the level of real wages would have to be adjusted to suit the "wrong" structure or vice versa.

Hence the macroeconomic level of real wages alone does not adequately express the employment effects of wages; the wage structure must also be taken into consideration. If the wage structure were taken as given, it would mean seeking a solution to the employment problem solely by adjusting the level of real wages, and thus forfeiting the use of an important and efficient instrument. However, the wage structure can perform its guidance function properly only if it is sufficiently flexible; it is trammelled in "cartelized" markets.

A number of other factors must also be considered in connection with the links between wages and employment. Some affect the level and structure of wages, some determine the processes of co-ordination and adjustment occurring in the labour market. "Labour market conditions" of this kind include the nature of wage determination, the degree of market cartelization, the regional and occupational mobility of labour, firms' labour market behaviour and all institutional and legal arrangements that influence events in the labour market. In this context, the labour market should be defined fairly widely to include also work opportunities for self-employed persons.

Given the many and complex relationships between wages and employment, it is not surprising that the numerous empirical studies on this problem, mostly econometric analyses, sometimes arrive at very different results.[1] The main aspect investigated has been the rela-

1 See the extensive documentation on this matter in OECD, Real Wages and Employment, op. cit., pp. 31 ff.

tionship between the macroeconomic wage level and unemployment.[1] Some studies have proved - or rather not falsified - an inverse relationship between the two variables, while others have not confirmed it.

The differences in the results are undoubtedly due partly to the differences of approach. However, it is also pertinent to ask whether the econometric models used hitherto are not too simple, given the complex relationships and many interdependences between the variables involved:[2]

- Econometric models look at only a limited number of variables, so that they do not paint a rounded picture of reality. The effects of explanatory factors that are omitted are attributed to those that are considered.

- There are also positive relationships between real wages and employment via the supply side; most econometric models pay little heed to supplyside effects.

- In interdependent models the direction of dependence is not clearly identified, but left open to interpretation.

This study cannot discuss the links between wages and employment in depth; it must be assumed that the reader is largely familiar with the theoretical background. The above considerations have served primarily to clarify the ground that must be covered in analyzing the

---

1 The German economic research institutes have also examined the links between the wage structure and employment in their latest reports on the structure of the Germany economy. Cf. Kurt VOGLER-LUDWIG, Auswirkungen des Strukturwandels auf den Arbeitsmarkt, Ergänzungsband zur Ifo-Strukturberichterstattung 1983, Munich 1983, pp. 53 ff.; DEUTSCHES INSTITUT FÜR WIRTSCHAFTSFORSCHUNG, Auswirkungen des Strukturwandels auf den Arbeitsmarkt, Anforderungen des Strukturwandels an das Beschäftigungssystem, Schwerpunktthema im Rahmen der Strukturberichterstattung 1983, Berlin 1983, pp. 91 ff.

2 See also OECD, Real Wages and Employment, op. cit., p. 31.

differences in the employment performance of the USA, Japan and the EC. The brief theoretical sketch has shown that wages can be assumed to affect employment. Differences between countries' employment performances can therefore have the following causes:

- Differences in the behaviour of the macroeconomic real wage level;
- differences in the behaviour or flexibility of wage structures;
- differences in other labour market conditions.

If differences in real wage behaviour can be detected, it is necessary to enquire into the causes. They may stem from differences in nominal wage developments from one country to another or in adjustment mechanisms between nominal and real wages; for that reason nominal wage develpoments must also be investigated. This aspect is also of considerable importance with regard to the interpretation of economic policy. At the same time, the differences in productivity trends must not be ignored; the way in which they fit into the picture must be examined.

3.2 Macroeconomic Wage Level, Productivity and Employment - Empirical Findings

3.2.1 Real Wages - Definition and Empirical Calculation

Real wages are generally taken to be money wages adjusted for variations in the value of money:

$$wr = \frac{wn}{P_G} \tag{1}$$

where wr stands for real wages

wn   nominal or money wages

P_G the general price level.

Real wages are determined from money wages and movements in the value of money; the result of this process cannot be clearly predicted in advance. Two problems arise in determining real wages empirically:

- the choice of suitable money wage variables and
- the question of an appropriate deflator.

Cost aspects are in the forefront when examining the employment impact of wages, so that the money wage variable must include all costs attributable to labour. These comprise not only direct labour costs, i.e. wages in the strict sense, but also non-wage labour costs such as employers' social security contributions or firms' voluntary social benefits. A recently published study by the Austrian Institute for Economic Research covering the period from 1960 to 1981 clearly that non-wage labour costs have become an increasingly heavy item of expenditure in all the countries under examination here (see Table 13).[1] For long periods they rose noticeably faster than direct labour costs; it was not until the end of the seventies that the rate of increase slowed down.

In most EC countries non-wage labour costs increased faster than in the USA and Japan between 1973 and 1981. Moreover, in all EC countries except the United Kingdom the level of such costs was far higher than in the USA and Japan, mainly owing to differences in the financing of social security. Private provision predominates in the USA and Japan, with trade union pension funds making a substantial contribution in the USA. In the United Kingdom social security is financed primarily by central government, while France, Italy and the Federal Republic of Germany have special social security systems in

---

1 For a detailed definition of ancillary labour costs, see Alois
   GUGER, Internationaler Arbeitskostenvergleich nach Industrie-
   branchen, in: Österreichisches Institut für Wirtschaftsforschung
   (Wifo), Monatsberichte, No. 6/1985, pp. 359 ff.; SWEDISH EMPLOYERS'
   CONFEDERATION, Wages and total labour costs for workers, Inter-
   national Survey 1971-1981, 1984, p. 7.

Table 13   INTERNATIONAL COMPARISON OF NON-WAGE LABOUR COSTS
FOR INDUSTRIAL WORKERS
- as a percentage of hourly wages -

	1960	1972	1978	1981
USA	17.7	26.7	34.5	37.4
Japan	13.5	16.2	19.2	18.6
Federal Republic of Germany	42.4	51.7	67.4	76.9
France	60.7	67.5	85.5	79.9
Italy	77.3	91.3	95.1	86.2
United Kingdom	16.1	21.8[a]	36.0	43.0

a   1973.

Source: Alois GUGER: Internationaler Arbeitskostenvergleich nach Industriebranchen, Österreichisches Institut für Wirtschaftsforschung, Monatsberichte, No. 6/1985, Table 5.

which part of the contributions are paid by employers.[1] If social
security is financed out of tax revenues, firms obviously also contribute indirectly, but this does show up in non-wage labour costs.

In order to record the largest possible proportion of non-wage labour
costs, the money wage variables are calculated on the basis of compensation of employees paid by resident producers. The nominal wage
is then the compensation of employees per worker or per man/hour.
From the costs standpoint the hourly calculation would no doubt be
sufficient, since it also reflects the cost effects of a reduction in
working hours, but in many countries the figures for hours worked
relate only to manufacturing. International comparisons that also
encompass other sectors are therefore generally based on wages per
worker. That approach has also been adopted for this study. In
addition, a "hourly wage" has been estimated, on the assumption that

1 Cf. Alois GUGER, op. cit., p. 360.

annual working hours per employee are the same outside manufacturing as they are within the sector.[1] The assumptions concerning
working hours outside manufacturing are somewhat problematic, so
that the calculated variable is only an approximation. The "productivity per man-hour", which is also an estimate, is based on the
same data. Here an additional assumption was required with regard
to the ratio of the working hours of the self-employed to those of
wage and salary earners.

The choice of the price deflator for calculating real wages is a
further problem. The objective is to adjust nominal wages for fluctuations in the value of money; this calls for a macroeconomic price
indicator. Two deflators are commonly used in empirical analysis - the
GNP price index and the consumer price index. The real wages
calculated on these two bases differ markedly in some countries, but
little in others (see Table 14). The differences stem primarily from
differences in the treatment of external influences on the price
series. Changes in import prices are reflected directly in consumer
prices, but not in the GDP deflator. As in most works, the expression used in this study for real wages will be the quotient of
compensation of employees per worker or per man-hour and the GDP
deflator.

3.2.2 The Behaviour of Real Wages in the USA, Japan and the EC

In all of the countries under examination, real wages - or rather
real wages per worker - rose less sharply on average between 1973
and 1983 than in the sixties and early seventies. Whereas the rates
of growth of real GDP converged in most countries, there remained
considerable differences in the rate of real wage increase (see Table
15). In the USA real wages increased by no more than 0.5 % a year

1 Figures on average annual working hours per worker in manufacturing from 1970 onwards are published by the Institut der deutschen Wirtschaft. See INSTITUT DER DEUTSCHEN WIRTSCHAFT, Internationale Wirtschaftszahlen, various years.

Table 14   REAL WAGES CALCULATED USING VARIOUS DEFLATORS[1]
            - average annual percentage change, 1973-83 -

	All activities[2]	Industry	Services sector (excl. government)
USA			
Real wages (1)	0.5	1.1	0.5
real wages (2)	-0.4	0.0	-0.5
Japan			
Real wages (1)	3.8	4.0	3.5
Real wages (2)	1.7	1.8	1.4
Germany			
Real wages (1)	1.9	2.5	1.7
Real wages (2)	1.5	2.1	1.4
France[3]			
Real wages (1)	2.9	-	-
Real wages (2)	2.7	-	-
Italy			
Real wages (1)	1.9	1.6	1.3
Real wages (2)	2.6	2.3	2.0
United Kingdom			
Real wages (1)	1.3	1.7	0.8
Real wages (2)	1.3	1.8	1.0

1 Real wages (1) = Compensation of employees per worker, deflated
                     using the GDP price index.
   Real wages (2) = Compensation of employees per worker, deflated
                     using the consumer price index.

2 Total economy.

3 No figures are available on compensation of employees by kind of
   activity.

Source: Authors' calculations based on OECD, EC and national data.

Table 15   REAL WAGES, PRODUCTIVITY AND EMPLOYMENT

- total economy, average annual percentage changes -

	Real wages[1]		Productivity		Wage and salary earners[2]
	per worker	per man-hour	per person employed	per man-hour	
USA					
1962-73	1.9	-	2.0	-	2.8
1973-83	0.5	0.7	0.4	0.6	1.4
Japan					
1962-73	7.9	-	8.3	-	3.1
1973-83	3.8	4.1	2.8	3.1	1.5
Germany					
1962-73	4.6	-	4.3	-	0.7
1973-83	1.9	2.7	2.3	3.1	-0.0
France					
1962-73	4.4	-	4.5	-	2.1
1973-83	2.9	4.8	2.1	3.9	0.4
Italy					
1962-73	6.0	-	5.5	-	0.6
1973-83	1.9	3.4	1.2	2.7	0.6
United Kingdom					
1962-73	3.2	-	3.1	-	0.1
1973-83	1.3	1.7	1.6	2.0	-0.7

1 Deflated using the GDP price index.

2 As defined in the national accounts.

Source: Authors' calculations based on OECD, EC and national data.

Wage Behaviour and Labor Market Flexibility   93

on average, but in the EC countries the rise was between three and four times as high, and even more rapid in France. The largest real wages rises, however, occured in Japan, as in earlier years. Real wages per man-hour presented a similar picture.

There were also considerable differences over time (see Diagram 9). In the USA, though not in the other countries, real wages per worker declined in 1974 and 1975 following the first oil crisis; they rose again for a period after 1975 as economic activity recovered, but little subsequently. In most other countries, however, they increased more or less continuously throughout the seventies. It was not until the beginning of the eighties that the rate of increase slowed down slightly in Japan and markedly in France and actually came to a standstill in Italy and Germany. Only the United Kingdom deviated from this pattern; here there was a slight decline in real wages in the second half of the seventies, but then they began to rise again sharply.

Real wages per man-hour behaved rather differently over time in some countries. In some, the rate of increase had already slowed down appreciably by the mid-seventies; the slowdown was permanent in the case of Italy and sporadic in that of Japan. In France the pace slackened for a while in the late seventies but then accelerated sharply again, especially during the period when working hours were being shortened by the Mitterand government. In the United Kingdom, on the other hand, real wages per man-hour rose far less rapidly than real wages per worker in the early years of this decade. In the USA and Germany the two measures moved roughly parallel.

In most countries, real wages in the services sector (excluding government) rose less rapidly than in industry between 1973 and 1982 (see Diagram 10).[1] Japan was an exception; here the increase was

1 Only real wages per worker could be calculated, owing to a lack of data on working hours in individual branches of activity. However, for France even that was impossible, since comparable figures on compensation of employees by kind of activity are not available.

Diagram 9   REAL WAGES[1]

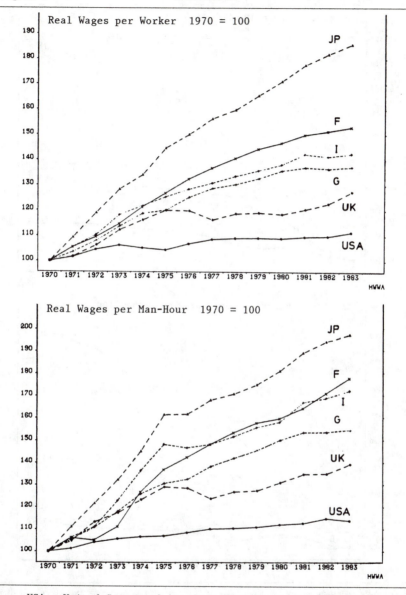

Real Wages per Worker   1970 = 100

Real Wages per Man-Hour   1970 = 100

Key: USA = United States of America; JP = Japan; G = Federal Republic
      of Germany; F = France; I = Italy; UK = United Kingdom.

1 Deflated using the GDP price index.

Source: See Table 15.

Wage Behaviour and Labor Market Flexibility

Diagram 10   REAL WAGES, BY SECTOR[1]

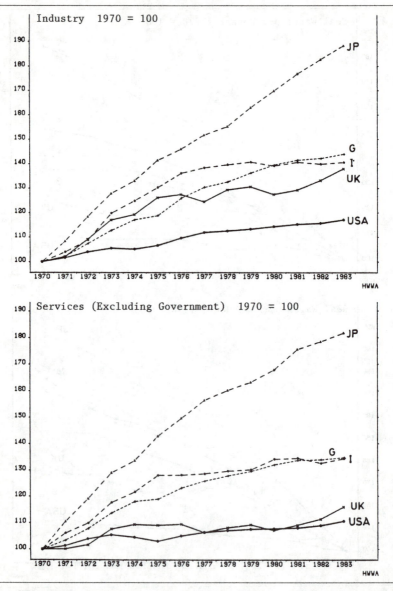

Industry   1970 = 100

Services (Excluding Government)   1970 = 100

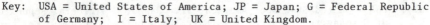

Key: USA = United States of America; JP = Japan; G = Federal Republic
       of Germany;   I = Italy;   UK = United Kingdom.

1   Deflated using the GDP price index.

Source: See Table 14.

broadly similar in both sectors. The differences in the USA were substantial, with real wages in industry rising continuously from 1974 to 1982 - albeit far less sharply than in most other countries - and almost stagnating in the services sector. There was a similar development in the United Kingdom, although with wider fluctuations. Here real wages in the services sector fell slightly overall from the mid-seventies onwards. In the Federal Republic of Germany, on the other hand, the rise in the services sector only slowed down at first, though it too came to a standstill at the beginning of the eighties.

In Italy real wages rose strongly in the first half of the seventies, but since 1976 they roughly stagnated in the industry and increased only little in the private part of the services sector. On the contrary, in the government sector there obviously remained a substantial real wage increase, hence in the services sector as whole real wages rose distinctly up to the eighties.

To summarize, it will be seen that the differences in overall real wage developments in individual countries were not due to differences in the main branches of economic activity but occurred equally in both industry and services. The country "ranking" is the same in both sectors. In both cases the highest real wage increases occured in Japan, whereas the USA brought up the rear. The EC countries were positioned between these two extremes, with the Federal Republic of Germany - and probably also France - towards the upper part of the range.

3.2.3 Employment Effects of Real Wage Developments - the Concept of the Real Wage Gap

The preceding overview has shown that substantial differences emerged in the behaviour of real wages in the USA, Japan and the EC between 1973 and 1983. In an expanding economy, real wage developments alone say nothing about the employment effects of wages; productivity must also be taken into account. In principle, an increase in real wages can be expected to have an adverse impact on employment only if it exceeds the rise in productivity, or more precisely the "employment-neutral" rise in productivity, that is the increase of productivity which would take place if the factor input ratio remained unchanged. The difference between the rise in real wages and productivity gains has come to be called the "real wage gap". It is regarded as a measure of whether the level of real wages in an economy is consistent with full employment or not.[1]

3.2.3.1   The Concept of the Real Wage Gap

Several methods have been devised for measuring the real wage gap. Some attempt to quantify it directly,[2] while others estimate its effects on the basis of the so-called adjusted wage ratio;[3] both approaches deal essentially with the same relationship. The real wage gap can be expressed as the discrepancy between the actual real wage and the "full-employment" real wage, that is the wage consistent with full employment of labour:[4]

$$wg = \frac{wr}{wrn} \tag{2}$$

where wg stands for the real wage gap,

> wr   real wages per worker and
>
> wrn   "full-employment" real wages per worker.

---

1   Cf. Manfred WEGNER, The Employment Miracle in the United States, op. cit., p. 36.

2   See for instance Jeffrey D. SACHS, Real Wages and Unemployment in the OECD Countries, Brookings Papers on Economic Activity, No. 1/1983, pp. 255 ff.

3   Cf. Henning KLODT, Lohnquote und Beschäftigung - die Lohnlücke, Kieler Arbeitspapiere, No. 230, Kiel 1985.

4   It is not necessary to differentiate real wages and productivity per worker from real wages and productivity per man-hour in order to illustrate the concept of the real wage gap. It is usually based on data per worker, the approach that has been adopted here. The real wage gap on the basis of man-hours can be deduced in a similar way.

Expressed in rates of change, equation (2) becomes:

$$dwg = dwr - dwrn \qquad (3).$$

If it is also assumed that the "full-employment" real wage rise matches the "employment-neutral" productivity increase, the change in the real wage gap can also be expressed as:

$$dwg = dwr - dpn \qquad (4)$$

where dpn stands for the "employment-neutral" productivity increase.

The same relationship can also be portrayed using the adjusted wage ratio. The wage ratio, which is the ratio of wages to national income, can also be expressed as follow:

$$WS = \frac{wr}{p} \cdot \frac{WE}{E} \cdot \frac{GDP_M}{GDP_{FC}} \qquad (5)$$

where WS stands for the wage ratio,

        p   productivity,

        WE   wage and salary earners,

        E   employment,

        GDP_M gross domestic product at market prices and

        GDP_{FC} gross domestic product at factor cost (national income)

In terms of rates of changes, we then have:

$$dWS = dwr - dp + d\left(\frac{WE}{E}\right) + d\left(\frac{GDP_M}{GDP_{FC}}\right) \qquad (6).$$

Substituting the "employment-neutral" productivity increase for the actual increase we get the adjusted wage ratio

$$dWS_a = dwr - dpn + d\left(\frac{WE}{E}\right) + d\left(\frac{GDP_M}{GDP_{FC}}\right) \qquad (7)$$

or

$$dWS_a = dWS + (dp - dpn) \qquad (8).$$

The first two terms on the right-hand side of the equation (7) represent the change in the real wage gap. This can therefore also be measured as

$$dwg = dWS + (dp-dpn) - d\left(\frac{WE}{E}\right) - d\left(\frac{GDP_M}{GDP_{FC}}\right) \qquad (9).$$

Changes in the wage ratio can therefore also provide information on development in the real wage gap. To do so, however, it must be adjusted for the wage-induced productivity rise; any changes in the ratio of wage and salary earners to total employment and in the quotient of GDP at market prices divided by national income must also be taken into account.

Empirical measurement of the level of the real wage gap raises a serious problem, that of determining the "full-employment" real wage or the "full-employment" wage ratio. It finally requires the marginal productivity of labour to be quantified. Even using a production function, this hardly is possible or necessitates making severely restrictive assumptions. For that reason it is usual to adopt a different approach. One or several base years are chosen in which there was full employment and it is postulated that real wages in that year were consistent with full employment.[1] The full-employment real wage path is then extrapolated using the "employment-neutral" productivity increase. Since our main concern here is to explain differences in the

---

1 This is the course adopted by Sachs and others. Cf. Jeffrey D. SACHS, op. cit., p. 259. However, the assumption that wages were consistent with full employment in a year of full employment is in no way conclusive owing to lags.

Employment Trends

employment performance of various countries, arguments based on developments in the real wage gap will suffice.

However, this simply shifts the problem elsewhere, since for this we need to know the "employment-neutral" productivity increase, which also entails serious problems of calculation. The "employment-neutral" productivity rise can differ quite markedly from the actual measured increase. As explained in the preceding chapter, the productivity gain is the result of a process involving a large number of factors, including wage behaviour. For example, if wage costs rise faster than capital costs, labour becomes relatively more expensive, creating an incentive to accentuate the substitution of capital for jobs. This leads to an increase in capital intensity and an additional wage-induced productivity increase; the actual productivity increase is greater than it would have been if factor price relationships had remained unchanged. Giersch points out another "structural" effect.[1] If large real wage increases make labour-intensive jobs unviable, sooner or later such jobs will be eliminated, labour-intensive production processes will be abandoned and firms with below-average productivity will be squeezed out of the market. This too leads to an acceleration in the increase in labour productivity.

3.2.3.2 "Employment-neutral" Productivity Increase

"Employment-neutral" productivity increase can be interpreted as that rise in productivity that would occur if factor input ratio remained unchanged. To calculate it, the actual productivity increase would have to be split into a quasi-exogenous "technical progress element" and a "factor substitution element". The "technical progress element"

---

1   Cf. Herbert GIERSCH, Produktivität und Beschäftigung, in: Produktivität, Eigenverantwortung, Beschäftigung, published by the Verband Deutscher Maschinen- und Anlagenbau (VDMA) and the Institut der deutschen Wirtschaft (IW), 1983, pp. 37 f.

would then represent the "employment-neutral" productivity increase and the "factor substitution element" that part of the rise in productivity resulting from a change in the ratio of factor inputs.

In principle, such a subdivision is possible if one adopts a production theory approach and a number of associated assumptions, which would undoubtedly give rise to fierce debate. The starting point is to attribute the growth in the real output of an economy to two effects - an increase in inputs of labour and capital and a rise in total factor productivity. In other words, after accounting for the contribution to the growth in output stemming from increased factor inputs, there remains a residual attributable to other factors; this is generally identified as technical progress.[1]

The rise in total factor productivity can be equated with the "technical progress element" of productivity rise. For total factor productivity at time t, the following equation applies:

$$TP_t = \frac{Pr_t}{w_o L_t + r_o C_t} \qquad (10)$$

where Pr stands for real output,

L	labour,
C	capital,
w	the price of labour and
r	the price of capital.

w_o and r_o, which are the constant prices of the production factors at time t = o, are used for weighting. For this purpose, the assumption that

$$Pr_o = w_o \cdot L_o + r_o \cdot C_o \qquad (11)$$

1 Cf. also COMMISSION OF THE EUROPEAN COMMUNITIES, Annual Economic Review 1984-85, in: European Economy, No. 22/1984, pp. 97 f.; Douglas TODD, op. cit., pp. 15 ff.

appears to be appropriate. An equation for the change in total factor productivity can be deduced from (10); it is

$$dTP = dp - k \cdot d(\frac{C}{L}) \qquad (12)$$

where p stands for labour productivity and

$$\frac{C}{L} \qquad \text{capital intensity}$$

and

$$k = \frac{r_o \cdot C_o}{w_o \cdot L_o + r_o \cdot C_o} \qquad (13).$$

In view of (11),

$$k = \frac{r_o \cdot C_o}{Pr_o} = 1 - \frac{w_o \cdot L_o}{Pr_o} \qquad (13a)$$

also applies for (13).

The second term on the right-hand side of equation (12) can be interpreted as the "factor substitution element" of the statistically measured productivity increase. For simplicity, it is assumed that the contribution of substitution to the increase in average labour productivity is proportional to the change on the ratio of factor inputs. The coefficient k is identical with the profit share at time t = o. In the calculations that follow, 1973 was used as the base year where t = o. The price of labour is represented by compensation of employees per worker or per man-hour; it is assumed that self-employed persons draw a labour income in the same amount. Changes in capital intensity are measured by the quotient of gross fixed capital formation at constant prices (excluding residential buildings)[1]

1 The figures on gross fixed capital formation are drawn from OECD sources (OECD, Flows and Stocks of Fixed Capital 1955-1980) and from national statistics. In some cases, the latest figures hat to be estimated.

divided by total employment or hours worked. No figures on gross fixed capital formation are available for Italy, however, so that neither capital intensity nor "employment-neutral" productivity increase could be calculated for that country.

The approach adopted here was developed by the HWWA for its reports on the structure of the economy.[1] It is more comprehensive than the approaches commonly used, since it requires no a priori assumptions about a particular kind of production function.[2] This allows greater scope for interpreting the "factor substitution element".

Dividing the observed productivity increase into a "technical progress element" - total factor productivity - and a "factor substitution element" is based on certain assumptions that are not unproblematic.[3] For example, it involves the notion that a movement along the production function - in other words a change in factor input ratio - should be distinguished from a shift in the production function. However, this presupposes a particular kind of technical progress that has a "neutral" effect on labour and capital. A further problem lies in recording overall productivity as a residual, since any errors in recording and measurement will affect it. For that reason the figures that follow should be treated with caution and considered only as approximations.

1 Cf. HWWA-INSTITUT FÜR WIRTSCHAFTSFORSCHUNG-HAMBURG, Analyse der strukturellen Entwicklung der deutschen Wirtschaft, Strukturbericht 1980, Materialband 1, Hamburg 1980, p. 19 f.

2 Authors generally postulate either a Cobb-Douglas production function (e.g. Todd) or a production function of the CES type (e.g. Klodt, Krugman). Cf. Douglas TODD, op. cit.; Henning KLODT, Lohnquote und Beschäftigung, op. cit.; Paul KRUGMAN, The real wage gap and employment, in: Annales de l'INSEE, Nos. 47-48(1982.

3 See for instance Douglas TODD, op. cit., pp. 15 f.; COMMISSION OF THE EUROPEAN COMMUNITIES, Annual Economic Review 1984-84, p. 98.

3.2.3.3 Productivity Growth and Substitution Effects - Empirical Findings

Table 16 shows developments in labour productivity and its components in the USA, Japan and the EC countries between 1973 and 1983.[1] The following conclusions can be drawn:

-   In all countries the general slowdown in productivity growth in the seventies and early eighties was due mainly to a pronounced weakening of the rise in total factor productivity; in the USA there was actually a slight fall on average over the period 1973-83. The latitude for "employment-neutral" real wage increases was therefore greatly reduced everywhere.

-   In all the countries the "factor substitution element" was larger on average than the "technical progress element" during the period under examination. In the sixties and early seventies, on the other hand, the reverse had been true.

-   In most countries, the "factor substitution element", that is to say the productivity increase dependent on substitution, was about as high between 1973 and 1983 as in earlier years; in France it was actually a little higher, and only in Japan was it slightly lower.

-   The scale of substitution-related productivity increase differed from one country to another. It was comparatively small in the USA, much larger in the EC countries and largest in Japan. This corresponds to the trend in capital intensity (see Diagram 11). The rise was smallest in the USA and largest in Japan.

-   substitution-related productivity increase fluctuated much less over time than the growth of total factor productivity. This was mainly a consequence of the method of calculation; since the "technical progress element" is recorded as a residual, fluctuations

---

1   See also Diagrams 2a to 2c in the Appendix.

Table 16

COMPONENTS OF LABOUR PRODUCTIVITY

- average annual percentage changes -

| | Labour productivity | | "Technical progress element"[1] | | "Factor substitution element"[2] | | for comparison: Capital intensity[3] | |
	per worker	per man-hour	per worker	per man-hour	per worker	per man-hour	Capital input per worker	Capital input per man-hour
USA								
1962-73	2.0	-	1.5	-	0.6	-	2.3	-
1973-83	0.4	0.6	-0.3	-0.1	0.7	0.7	2.3	2.6
Japan								
1962-73	7.8	-	5.5	-	2.2	-	10.4	-
1973-83	2.8	3.1	0.9	1.1	1.9	2.0	5.7	6.0
Germany								
1962-73	4.3	-	2.9	-	1.4	-	5.6	-
1973-83	2.3	3.1	0.9	1.4	1.4	1.8	4.2	5.0
France								
1962-73	4.5	-	3.2	-	1.3	-	4.4	-
1973-83	2.1	3.9	0.5	1.4	1.6	2.5	4.3	6.2
United Kingdom								
1962-73	3.1	-	2.2	-	1.0	-	3.9	-
1973-83	1.6	2.0	0.5	0.7	1.1	1.3	3.5	4.0

1 Total factor productivity. -- 2 The part of productivity growth due to changes in the ratio of factor inputs. -- 3 Capital input per worker or per man-hour; capital = gross fixed capital formation (excluding residential construction) at constant prices.

Source: Authors' calculations using OECD and national statistical data.

Employment Trends

Diagram 11   CHANGES IN CAPITAL INTENSITY[1]

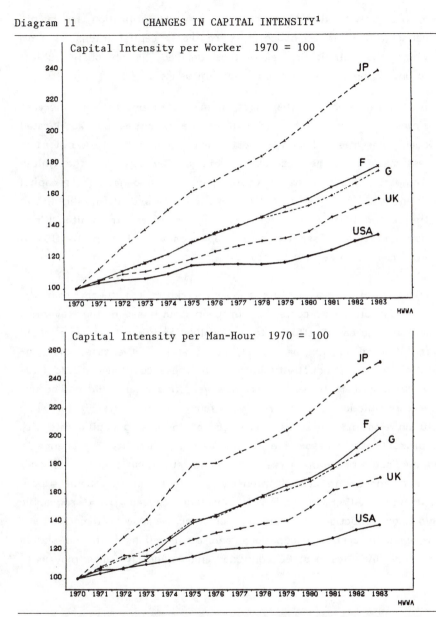

Key: USA = United States of America; JP = Japan; G = Federal Republic
       of Germany;   F = France;   UK = United Kingdom.

1 Capital input per worker or per man-hour.

Source: See Table 16.

in productivity due to changes in capacity utilization are mainly reflected in this component. By contrast, capital intensity, from which the substitution element is derived, is obviously subject to only comparatively weak cyclical influences.

- In several countries the substitution-related productivity increase slowed down in the second half of the seventies but accelerated again thereafter. This was most pronounced in the USA but much less marked in the Federal Republic of Germany and the United Kingdom. This too has its counterpart in the behaviour of capital intensity. The rise in capital intensity slowed down slightly in the second half of the seventies in Germany and the United King- dom and to a lesser extent in Japan as well, but in the USA it even came to a temporary standstill.

At first sight, these results appear to refute the theory that the strong rise in wage costs in European countries in the seventies stimulated increased efforts to rationalize and led to a more rapid substitution of labour for capital; had that been the case, the sub- stitution-related productivity increase in these countries should have been greater than in the sixties; however, this clearly did not occur. This contradiction can be resolved fairly easily. The "factor sub- stitution element" measures the effect of increasing capital intensity on productivity, irrespective of the reasons behind it. The change in relative factor prices as a result of rising labour costs is not the only cause of increasing capital intensity. Another lies in labour supply constraints, either reflecting a shortage caused by demographic factors or reductions in working hours or because bottlenecks have developed in certain occupations and qualifications.[1] In the sixties and early seventies most EC countries enjoyed nearly full employment;

---

1 The dividing line between the two types of causes is blurred, since a labour shortage induces wage increases and hence also has repercussions on the factor price ratio. Wage increases of this kind, which are a response to market forces, are to be viewed differently from wage increases in times of rising unemployment.

Employment Trends

Italy was an exception to some extent. The supply of labour was fairly limited and was further tightened by reductions in working hours. During this period the reason for rising capital intensity therefore lay primarily in labour supply constraints.

In the seventies and early eighties, by constrast, all the EC countries moved from a labour shortage to a surplus. The labour supply increased everywhere owing to demographic factors, while at the same time employment contracted in some countries. If wages had been sufficiently flexible, this should have curbed the trend towards increasing capital intensity and led to decreasing substitution-related productivity increase. The fact that the rise in capital intensity continued almost unabated can be explained by the strong increase in the pressure to substitute capital for labour owing to the trend in labour costs. In the Federal Republic of Germany the increase in the pressure of competition as a result of the continued real appreciation of the Deutsche Mark was another factor. The thesis of rising wage-induced pressure to rationalize does not therefore conflict at all with the trend of substitution-related productivity increase described above.

In the USA, by contrast with the EC countries, the change in the labour supply had already occured in the sixties. The relatively low capital intensity and comparatively small substitution-related pro-ductivity increase during that period indicate that wage policy took greater account of the change than was the case in the European countries, so that the wage-induced pressure to rationalize remained within bounds

Japan is in a special position among the countries considered. In the sixties and early seventies considerable efforts were made to reduce the lead of the "old" industrial countries and to build up an industry with modern standards of technology. This was necessarily accom-panied by an "autonomous" increase in capital inputs per worker and led to exceptionally strong capital intensification and large substitu-tion-related productivity increase. At the same time, it permitted real wages to be raised substantially. Although still high by international standards, the rate of increase in capital intensity has slowed down markedly since the mid-seventies, as normality began to return after the catching-up phase.

3.2.3.4   "Employment-neutral" Productivity Growth and the Real Wage
            Gap - Empirical Findings

If the change in total factor productivity is interpreted as "employ-ment-neutral" productivity growth, the behaviour of the real wage gap can be derived from the difference between real wage increases and total factor productivity growth. The following tendencies were present during the period under examination (see Table 17 and Diagram 12):

-   The behaviour of the real wage gap indicates that between 1973 and 1983 wage cost pressure was weak in the USA, considerably stronger in most EC countries and strongest in Japan. The differ-ences are even sharper if one looks at real wages and productivity per man-hour instead of the figures per worker.

-   If the early seventies are included, which seems justifiable on the grounds that effects may be lagged, the differences in the behaviour of the real wage gap between the USA on the one hand and the EC countries and Japan on the other are even more pronounced. In the early seventies, the period before the first oil crisis, the wage gap narrowed slightly in the USA but widened quite strongly in the other countries.

-   From the mid-seventies onwards pressures initially eased some-what in all the countries. In Japan and France the divergence between the rise in real wages and "employment-neutral" pro-ductivity growth widened much more slowly than in earlier years. In the Federal Republic of Germany and the USA the real wage gap stopped widening, whereas in the United Kingdom it even

Table 17   REAL WAGE GAP AND EMPLOYMENT

- total economy, average annual percentage changes -

	Real wage gap on the basis of actual values[1]		Real wage gap on the basis of "employment-neutral" productivity rise[2]		Wage and salary earners[3]
	per worker	per man-hour	per worker	per man-hour	
USA					
1970-75	-0.4	-0.4	0.4	0.6	1.2
1975-79	0.3	0.3	0.3	-0.6	3.5
1979-83	0.0	0.0	1.1	1.5	0.1
1970-83	-0.1	-0.1	0.6	0.5	1.5
1973-83	0.1	0.1	0.8	1.0	1.4
Japan					
1970-75	3.6	3.7	5.7	6.3	1.9
1975-79	-0.3	-0.3	1.0	0.6	1.7
1979-83	0.1	0.1	1.7	1.8	2.0
1970-83	1.3	1.3	3.0	3.1	1.9
1973-83	0.9	1.0	2.5	2.6	1.5
Germany					
1970-75	1.0	1.0	2.3	2.8	-0.2
1975-79	-1.2	-1.1	-0.2	-0.1	0.7
1979-83	-0.5	-0.5	0.9	1.2	-0.8
1970-83	-0.1	-0.1	1.1	1.4	-0.1
1973-83	-0.4	-0.4	0.9	1.1	-0.0
France					
1970-75	1.2	1.3	2.7	3.3	1.2
1975-79	-0.1	-0.1	1.3	1.5	0.8
1979-83	0.5	0.5	1.9	2.7	0.2
1970-83	0.6	0.6	2.0	2.6	0.7
1973-83	0.8	0.9	2.3	3.0	0.4
Italy					
1970-75	2.4	2.5	-	-	1.1
1975-79	-1.0	-1.0	-	-	1.0
1979-83	0.9	0.9	-	-	0.1
1970-83	0.9	0.9	-	-	0.8
1973-83	0.6	0.7	-	-	0.7
United Kingdom					
1970-75	1.7	1.8	2.6	3.0	0.2
1975-79	-2.5	-2.5	-1.7	-1.8	0.5
1979-83	-0.5	-0.5	0.9	1.1	-2.3
1970-83	-0.3	-0.2	0.7	0.9	-0.5
1973-83	-0.4	-0.4	0.6	0.8	-0.7

1 Rise in real wages less productivity growth. -- 2 Rise in real wages less "employment-neutral" productivity increase (see Table 16). 3 As defined for national accounting purposes.

Source: Authors' calculations using OECD and national statistics.

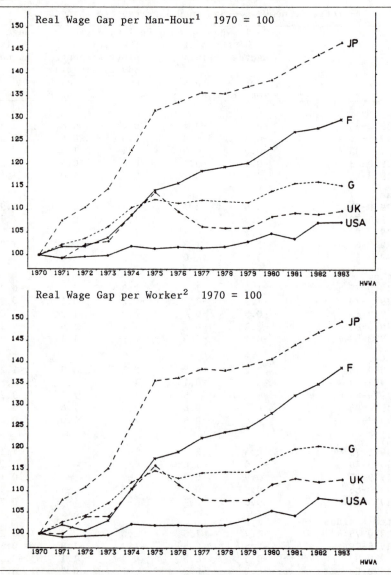

Key: USA = United States of America; JP = Japan; G = Federal Republic
of Germany;   F = France;   UK = United Kingdom.
1 On the basis of real wage and "employment-neutral" productivity increases per man-hour. -   2 On the basis of real wage and "employment-
neutral" productivity increases per worker.
Source: See Table 17.

narrowed somewhat. After the second oil crisis it widened again in all countries, though generally by not nearly as much as after the first crisis.

The differences in the behaviour of the real wage gap between 1973 and 1983 generally coincide with the differences in employment performance. In the USA, where labour cost pressures were relatively slight overall, the number of jobs continued to rise. In most EC countries, which were exposed to much greater pressure on the labour cost front, employment performance was also much less favourable.

The Special Case of Japan

Developments in Japan do not fit into this picture, however. Here, an expansion in employment was accompanied by labour cost pressures that rose steadily, easing only for a time in the second half of the seventies. This was undoubtedly partly due to the fact that economic growth in Japan was still almost twice as fast as in the other countries. Nevertheless, the question remains why a rate of growth that was still remarkable by international standards was possible despite steadily rising labour cost pressures. A possible explanation lies in the level of labour costs. At the beginning of the seventies Japanese labour costs were substantially lower than those in the other countries and the disproportionately large increases merely reduced the differential, even after exchange rate movements are taken into account.[1] Labour costs as a percentage of total costs were relatively low for an industrial country, and this could indicate that in the early seventies real wages were below the "equilibrium wage", in contrast to the situation in the other countries. The behaviour of

---

[1] Cf. Angelika ERNST, Das japanische Beschäftigungssystem - Auswirkungen auf die internationale Wettbewerbsfähigkeit, in: Ifo-Schnelldienst. Nos. 26-27/1985, pp. 27 ff., especially Table 1. Artus also points to the role of low costs. Cf. Jacques R. ARTUS, Sind die Reallöhne in Europa zu hoch? in: Finanzierung und Entwicklung, No. 4/1984, p. 13.

the real wage gap in Japan would then have to be judged differently. In addition, the figures on "employment-neutral" productivity increases are more uncertain in Japan than in the other countries owing to the high proportion of self-employed in Japan; it may have been set too low.[1]

The Japanese system of employment is also an important factor. The system of employment for life and the commitment firms assume for their employees' welfare impose an effective restraint on dismissals even when wage pressures are high; a firm that fires workers "loses face" and it may even find that loans are not renewed.[2] Direct dismissals are therefore regarded as the final resort and are avoided as long as possible. For that reason, the link between wages and employment was much looser in Japan than in other industrial countries.

EC Countries

The behaviour of labour costs is clearly much more important in explaining employment performance in the EC countries, although here too one must differentiate. The strong wage cost pressure built up mainly in the first half of the seventies. Except in France, it did not increase further for several years thereafter; only in the wake of the

---

1 To be able to determine the size of the "factor substitution element", assumptions must also be made about the level of self-employed persons' labour income (cf. equation 13a). Here it has been assumed that on average they draw the same labour income as a wage or salary earner. However, there are indications that in Japan the average income of self-employed persons was less than that of employees. (cf. Jørgen MORTENSEN, Profitability, relative factor prices and capital/labour substitution in the Community, the United States and Japan, 1960-83, in: COMMISSION OF THE EUROPEAN COMMUNITIES, European Economy, No. 20/1984, p. 45). In that case, the "factor substitution element" would be overestimated and the "technical progress element" underestimated.

2 Cf. Angelika ERNST, Das japanische Beschäftigungssystem, op. cit., pp. 28 f.

second oil crisis did it strengthen again. In the United Kingdom it actually eased on balance. The intensification came in "bursts" and the European countries' main problem lay in their failure to narrow the resulting real wage gap.[1]

There is usually a time-lag before excessive real wage increases affect employment, since the substitution of capital for labour takes time. In addition, the dismissal of workers in the European countries is made more difficult by legislation and agreements with the trade unions. The lag was obviously longer in the first half of the seventies than it was later; there were probably two main reasons for this:

- The adverse employment effects of the rising pressure of costs were obscured for a time by expansionary monetary and fiscal policies.[2]

- The experience of enduring high cost pressures fuels expectations that they will remain high; this increases firms' readiness to re-structure production. The inability to reduce wage cost pressures appears to have shortened the reaction lag.

In the Federal Republic of Germany the sharp increase in profits at the end of the sixties was a further factor. The "catching up" of wages and the consequent shortening of profit margins at the beginning of the seventies were probably regarded initially as a "normalization".

The consequences of wage behaviour for employment appear to have varied within the EC, however; they were seemingly covered up by the effects of other factors. For instance, France and Italy achieved a better employment performance than the Federal Republic of Germany, even though labour cost pressures were much stronger in those two

---

1 Cf. Jacques R. ARTUS, op. cit., p. 13.
2 See also the section on economic policy in Chapter 4 of this study.

Diagram 13   BEHAVIOUR OF REAL EXCHANGE RATES[1]

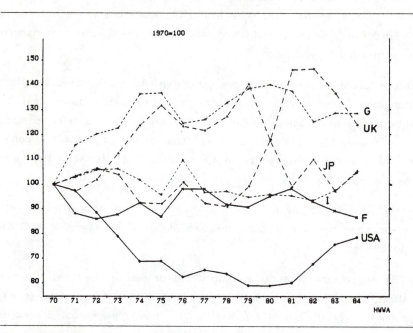

Key: USA = United States of America; JP = Japan; G = Federal Republic
       of Germany; F = France; I = Italy; UK = United Kingdom.

1   Exchange rates adjusted for difference in relative unit labour
costs in manufacturing.

Source: IMF: International Financial Statistics.

countries. In the case of France, Krugman attributes this mainly to
institutional factors such as legal and political constraints, strong
trade unions or companies' concern for their public image, which
prevented them from adjusting to changed cost conditions by dismissing labour.[1]

In the seventies, another reason may have lain in differences in
conditions for foreign trade. During this period there was a substantial real appreciation of the Deutsche Mark, whereas the French
franc and the Italian lira depreciated in real terms (see Diagram 13).

1   Cf. Paul KRUGMAN, op. cit., pp. 62 ff.

This intensified the competitive pressure on the Federal Republic of Germany, while easing the pressure on France and Italy; the effects were ultimately transmitted to employment.

All things considered, the behaviour of the real wage gap shows that clear differences developed between countries, differences that go a long way towards explaining the disparities in employment performance, at least between the USA and the EC countries. In this respect Japan is clearly a special case; the peculiarities of the Japanese system of employment mean that wages have less impact on employment there than in the other countries.

The differences in the behaviour of labour costs between the USA and the EC countries emerged primarily in the first half of the seventies. In later years the trend was broadly parallel, except in the case of France. The main difference therefore lay in the fact that the EC countries did not manage to correct the mistakes of the first half of the seventies, which remained a millstone around their necks. This accentuated the elimination of unviable jobs and led to greater rationalization and capital intensification. In the USA, on the other hand, the real wage trend was moderate, so that any need for adjustment was very slight.

3.2.4   Relative Factor Prices, Capital Intensity and Substitution

The differences in the adjustment pressure between the USA and the EC countries were also reflected in changes in capital intensity. Capital input per worker increased relatively little in the USA, but much more strongly in the EC countries (see Diagram 11). This indicates that there were also differences in the behaviour of relative factor prices between 1973 and 1983. The real wage gap concept can take only account of the employment effects flowing from a change in relative factor prices (a relative increase in the cost of labour creates an incentive to replace it by capital) since not every increase in wage cost pressures necessarily leads to a change in the ratio.

According to empirical studies by the OECD, changes in relative factor prices in a number of countries had a strong effect on employment performance. In some countries, notably the Federal Republic of Germany, the effect was patently even greater than the direct impact of an intensification of cost pressures.[1] Mortensen also sees the differences in the development of relative factor prices as an important explanation for the differences in employment trends; he concluded that there had been a relative reduction in the cost of labour in the USA but a relative increase in the EC as a whole.[2]

The degree to which a change in relative factor prices affects employment depends on the substitution elasticity. This is difficult to measure empirically, so that it is not surprising that the few studies on this topic arrive at some sharply contrasting results. Not infrequently, the problem is avoided by specifying a particular type of production function, which automatically entails a particular substitution elasticity. For example, a Leontief production function entails a substitution elasticity of nil, but a Cobb-Douglas production function an elasticity of one. The CES production function prescribes no particular substitution elasticity but assumes constancy over time.

Empirical analyses arrive at substitution elasticities of just under one over the long term for the larger EC countries. In the short run, on the other hand, the elasticity is apparently much lower; figures of between half and one-third of the long-term values have been measured.[3] The OECD has measured even lower substitution elasticities, albeit for a relatively short period.[4] The results obtained by Sneesens seem to indicate that the substitution elasticity was lower

---

1 Cf. OECD, Real Wages and Employment, op. cit., p. 50.
2 Cf. Jørgen MORTENSEN, op. cit., p. 55 f.
3 Cf. for instance Douglas TODD, op. cit., p. 21; Jørgen MORTENSEN, op. cit., Appendix I, p. 60.
4 Cf. OECD, Real Wages and Enployment, op. cit., Table 13, p. 55.

in the USA than in the EC countries.[1] Regression analysis carried out in the context of this study leads to similar conclusions.

3.2.4.1 Measuring Relative Factor Prices

It is very difficult to calculate relative factor prices empirically, since the marginal productivities of labour and capital are not known. Comparing wage and interest rate developments is a rather unsatisfactory approximation, for one is not comparing like with like; wages are costs per man-hour, while interest rates relate to developed capital input expressed in monetary units. A uniform reference base is necessary if a direct comparison is to be made; hourly labour costs must be set against hourly capital costs.

It is relatively simple to ascertain hourly capital costs for the individual enterprise; since the purchase price of the equipment and its expected service life are known, the purchase price per hour of utilization can be calculated. Financing costs must also be taken into account.[2] In simplified terms, the capital costs per working hour are given by the following equation:

$$P_{Ch} = \frac{C}{n \cdot h} \cdot (1 + i \cdot \frac{n}{2}) \tag{14}$$

Where P_{Ch} stands for capital costs per hour,

C	the purchase price of the new capital good,
n	the average service life in years,
h	the yearly usage in hours, and
i	the long-term interest rate.

---

1 Cf. Jørgen MORTENSEN, op. cit., Table I.1, p. 60.
2 The opportunity costs of self-financing must also be included, since the enterprise could have earned interest on the resources by investing them in the capital market.

The price of labour is represented by labour costs per hour. If the capital good has a service life of several years, intermediate wage increases must be included in the equation for the sake of comparability. The price of labour per working hour is therefore represented in simplified terms as follows:

$$P_{Lh} = w_h \cdot \frac{1 + (1 + dw_e)^{n-1}}{2} \tag{15}$$

where P_{Lh} stands for the price of labour per hour,

w_h	hourly wages, and
dw_e	expected wage rises.

Introducing expected wage rises brings an uncertainty into play. Actual wage rises may differ from the expected value, so that the relative factor prices assumed at the time of investment may subsequently prove wrong. However, it is the relative factor prices based on expected wage increases that are important for the decision to substitute capital for labour and hence for the employment effects.

Finally, when comparing hourly labour and capital costs directly, the output of both labour and capital must be taken into consideration and it must be ensured that both factors are used equally over the year.

It is relatively simple to calculate hourly capital costs for the individual firm, but it is a virtually insoluble problem at the macroeconomic level, for neither the "utilization reserve" inherent in new capital goods nor their average service life in years are known. In principle, all we know are the investments actually realized, capital market interest rates and the price trend for capital goods. The behaviour of capital goods prices does, however, at least provide clues as to the trend of "purchase prices" and hence that of a substantial part of the capital cost. If a specified constant service life is assumed, the trend of relative factor prices can be calculated approximately from the following equation:

Employment Trends

$$\frac{P_{Lh}}{P_{Ch}} = \frac{w_h}{P_I} \; \frac{\frac{1 + (1 + dw_e)^{n-1}}{2}}{1 + i \cdot \frac{n}{2}} \qquad (16).$$

where P_I stands for the price of capital goods.

The empirical analysis is based on the following assumptions:

- The trend of prices for gross fixed capital formation (excluding residential buildings) reflects that of the prices of all capital goods in the market.

- The average service life of all capital goods is six years.[1]

- Expected wage increases are based on those awarded on the two years prior to the investment decision.

- Utilization of capital goods over the year corresponds to the hours worked by employees.

- Investments are financed at long term; the interest rate is that prevailing in the capital market.

The GDP price deflator was used to adjust the prices of labour and capital in order to remove inflation-induced distortions.

The approach adopted here is certainly not without problems, but it seems practicable for the purposes of this study, since it is less important to record the relative factor prices exactly than to ascertain differences in their behaviour in the various countries. Since the countries considered here are all economies at a similar stage of development, international comparison is less likely to be affected by estimation errors.

---

1 Test calculations show that a slightly shorter or longer average service life does not seriously affect the results.

3.2.4.2 Trends in Relative Factor Prices - Empirical Findings

Empirical analysis of the trends in relative factor prices between 1973 and 1983 produced the following results (see Table 18 and Diagram 14):

- The price of labour increased little, if at all, in the USA but substantially in the EC countries and Japan.

- The price of labour fluctuated widely over the years. After the first oil crisis it increased more or less sharply everywhere except in the USA, but fell back temporarily thereafter. A further surge occured after the second oil crisis. The fluctuations are attributable largely to the effect of expected wage rises, which have a strong influence in times of rapid wage increases given the corporate behaviour postulated here.

- The price of capital also showed fluctuations in all the countries over time, but they were generally much less marked than those in the price of labour. Over the entire period from 1973 to 1983 the price of capital increased relatively little everywhere; the real prices of capital goods actually fell slightly in most countries.

- Relative factor prices consequently tended to shift fairly seriously in the EC countries and Japan to the detriment of capital. In the USA, by contrast, they remained largely constant and there were few notable fluctuations. In the other countries the ratio fluctuated much more widely; in France, Italy, the United Kingdom and Japan there was a substantial increase in the mid-seventies, followed by a more or less marked fall in the second half of the decade. In the Federal Republic of Germany the fluctuations were less pronounced.

The behaviour of relative factor prices therefore also differed substantially between the USA and the other countries and probably constituted a further reason for the differences in employment per-

Table 18   RELATIVE FACTOR PRICES AND CAPITAL INTENSITY
- average annual percentage changes, 1973-83 -

| | Real hourly wages[1] | Real capital goods prices[1] | Factor price ratio[2] | | Capital intensity[5] |
			variant 1[3]	variant 2[4]	
USA	0.7	-0.2	0.9	-0.3	2.3
Japan	4.1	-0.9	5.0	0.6	5.7
Germany	2.7	-0.2	3.0	1.1	4.2
France	4.8	-0.5	5.4	5.9	4.3
Italy	3.4	0.1	3.4	1.2	-
United Kingdom	1.7	-0.8	2.6	0.8	3.5

1 Deflator: GDP price index. -- 2 Ratio of the cost of labour to the cost of capital. -- 3 Ratio of hourly wages to capital goods prices. -- 4 Including expected wage changes and interest on capital. -- 5 Capital input per worker.

Source: Authors' calculations using OECD and national statistics.

formance. The divergences in factor price developments may largely explain the differences in capital intensity. Nevertheless, there were also some discordant notes; in France, for example, the rise in capital intensity was less pronounced than in Japan, despite a steeper increase in the price of labour. This may reflect inadequate measurement of factor price developments by the procedure employed here, but it may equally well be due to a higher "autonomous" rise in capital intensity in Japan.

Diagram 14   BEHAVIOUR OF RELATIVE FACTOR PRICES

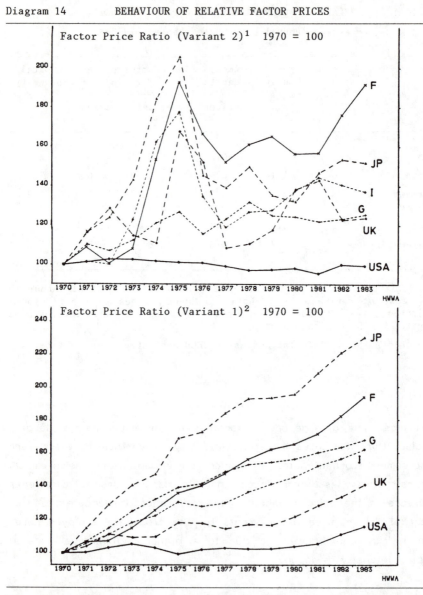

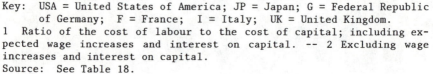

Key: USA = United States of America; JP = Japan; G = Federal Republic
      of Germany; F = France; I = Italy; UK = United Kingdom.
1 Ratio of the cost of labour to the cost of capital; including expected wage increases and interest on capital. — 2 Excluding wage
increases and interest on capital.
Source: See Table 18.

3.2.5 Nominal Wage Adjustment and Employment

The discovery of market differences in real wage behaviour between the USA, Japan and the EC countries raises the question as to their cause. In particular, the role of wage policy and monetary policy must be examined. First, however, we must briefly consider the behaviour of nominal wages and prices, the two variables from which real wages are derived mathematically.

3.2.5.1 The Behaviour of Nominal Wages and Prices in the USA, Japan and the EC

There were distinct differences in the behaviour of nominal wages in the USA, Japan and the EC between 1973 and 1983; in some cases it diverged from the behaviour of real wages (see Table 19 and Diagram 15 to 17).

- Nominal wages rose considerably in all the countries considered. The increase was smallest in the Federal Republic of Germany, slightly larger in the USA and Japan and by far the greatest in France, the United Kingdom and Italy. The ranking by country was not the same as for real wages.

- There were also differences over time. In Japan and the EC countries the already high growth rate at the end of the sixties accelerated further in the first half of the seventies, although in the Federal Republic of Germany only by a comparatively small amount. In the second half of the seventies it slowed down again everywhere; the improvement was only slight in Italy and France but more pronounced in the other countries. The second oil crisis triggered a renewed acceleration, although in Japan and the Federal Republic of Germany it was only slight. In the early eighties the rate of increase levelled off again to varying degrees in all countries. The underlying trend in the USA was similar, but

Table 19   NOMINAL WAGES, REAL WAGES AND PRICES
            - total economy, average annual percentage changes -

| | Nominal wages | | Real wages | | GDP deflator | Consumer prices |
	per worker	per man-hour	per worker	per man-hour		
USA						
1970-75	7.6	8.1	0.9	1.4	6.7	6.8
1975-79	8.1	7.8	1.2	0.9	6.9	7.8
1979-83	8.0	8.2	0.5	0.7	7.5	8.2
1970-83	7.9	8.0	0.8	1.0	7.0	7.5
1973-83	8.1	8.4	0.5	0.7	7.6	8.4
Japan						
1970-75	18.4	21.0	7.7	10.0	10.0	11.5
1975-79	8.4	6.9	3.4	2.0	4.8	6.2
1979-83	4.9	5.1	2.9	3.1	1.9	4.3
1970-83	11.0	11.5	4.9	5.4	5.9	7.6
1973-83	9.4	9.7	3.8	4.1	5.4	7.7
Germany						
1970-75	10.5	12.4	3.7	5.5	6.5	6.1
1975-79	6.5	6.6	2.6	2.7	3.8	3.8
1979-83	5.0	5.7	0.8	1.6	4.1	5.1
1970-83	7.5	8.5	2.5	3.4	4.9	5.1
1973-83	6.4	7.3	1.9	2.7	4.6	4.8
France						
1970-75	14.1	15.9	4.9	6.5	8.8	8.8
1975-79	13.3	13.6	3.3	3.6	9.7	9.7
1979-83	13.2	14.9	1.5	3.0	11.5	12.1
1970-83	13.6	14.9	3.3	4.5	9.9	10.1
1973-83	14.2	16.3	2.9	4.8	10.9	11.3
Italy						
1970-75	17.3	21.3	4.6	8.2	12.1	11.3
1975-79	19.1	18.1	2.0	1.2	16.7	15.2
1979-83	19.4	21.0	1.2	2.5	18.0	17.5
1970-83	18.5	20.2	2.8	4.3	15.3	14.4
1973-83	19.7	21.5	1.9	3.4	17.5	16.7
United Kingdom						
1970-75	17.4	19.1	3.7	5.2	13.2	13.0
1975-79	13.4	13.2	-0.2	-0.3	13.6	13.5
1979-83	12.6	13.3	1.7	2.3	10.8	10.6
1970-83	14.7	15.5	1.9	2.6	12.6	12.4
1973-83	15.3	15.8	1.3	1.7	13.9	13.6

Source: OECD, authors' calculations.

Diagram 15   NOMINAL AND REAL WAGES PER WORKER[1]

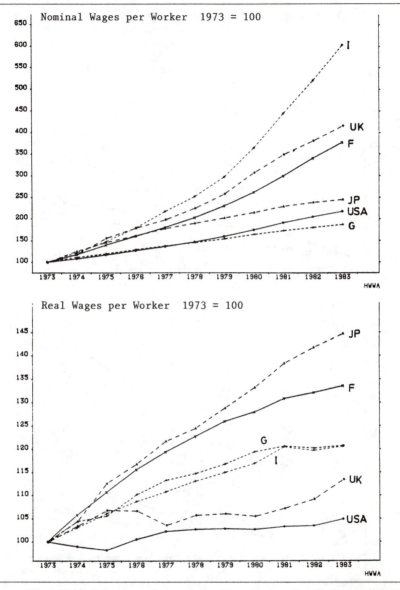

Key: USA = United States of America; JP = Japan; G = Federal Republic
      of Germany; F = France; I = Italy; UK = United Kingdom.

1 Total economy, gross income from employment worker.

Source: See Table 19.

Wage Behaviour and Labor Market Flexibility   127

Diagram 16   NOMINAL AND REAL WAGES PER MAN-HOUR[1]

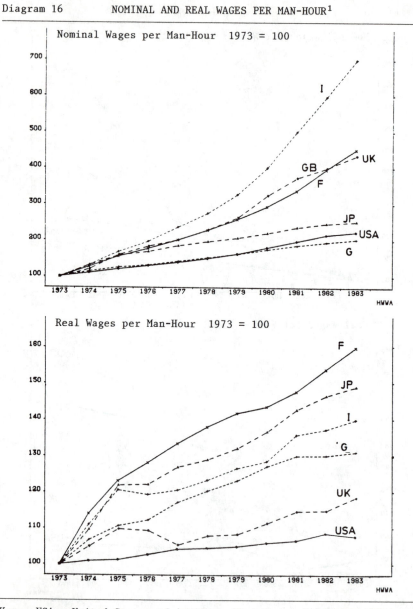

Key: USA = United States of America; JP = Japan; G = Federal Republic
       of Germany;   F = France;   I = Italy;   UK = United Kingdom.

1 Total economy, gross income from employment worker.

Source: See Table 19.

Diagram 17   NOMINAL AND REAL WAGES

- percentage changes over previous year -

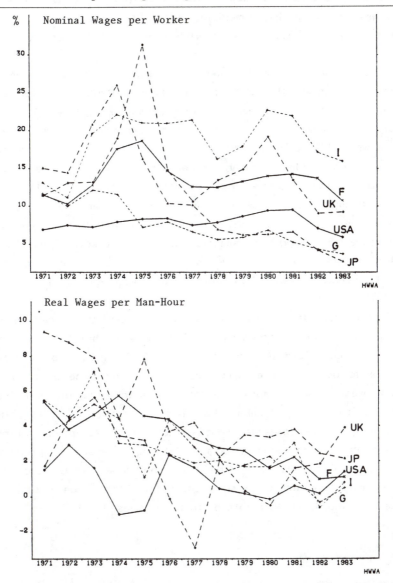

Key: USA = United States of America; JP = Japan; G = Federal Republic
of Germany;   F = France;   I = Italy;   UK = United Kingdom.

Source: See Table 19.

Wage Behaviour and Labor Market Flexibility   129

both the acceleration after the first oil crisis and the subsequent slowdown were much weaker than in the other countries; the same applies to the period immediately after the second oil crisis. In recent years the rate of increase has diminished considerably.

Price developments showed differences similar to those in nominal wages (see Diagram 18). Here too the Federal Republic of Germany put up the best performance, followed by Japan and the USA. The "record" once again went to Italy, where the price level rose five-fold between 1973 and 1983 in terms of the GDP deflator. However, there were noticeable discrepancies between countries as regards the behaviour of the deflators and consumer prices. In the USA and Japan consumer prices rose much more sharply than the GDP price index between 1973 and 1983. In the Federal Republic of Germany and France the trend was similar, but the discrepancy was much smaller. In Italy and the United Kingdom, on the other hand, the deflators increased faster than retail prices (see Diagram 19).

In all countries there were similarities between the behaviour of nominal wages and the trend in the GDP deflator, but this was only to be expected, given the definition of the deflator as a "price index of domestic output". The same was true of the general trend in nominal wages and consumer prices, although here the link was weaker in the USA and Japan than in the European countries. This might indicate that external shocks such as the oil-price induced deterioration in the terms of trade did not have such a profound effect on nominal wages in the USA and Japan as in the EC. Consequently, adjustment to such shocks would have been different in the USA and Japan than in the other countries.

Employment Trends

Diagram 18   CONSUMER PRICES AND THE GDP PRICE INDEX

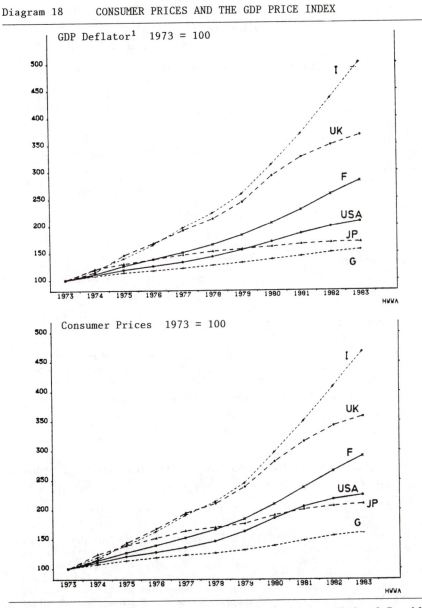

Key: USA = United States of America; JP = Japan; G = Federal Republic
       of Germany; F = France; I = Italy;   UK = United Kingdom.

1 Deflator of the gross domestic product.

Source: See Table 19.

Wage Behaviour and Labor Market Flexibility   131

Diagram 19   DIVERGENCES IN THE BEHAVIOUR OF CONSUMER PRICES
AND THE GDP PRICE INDEX[1]

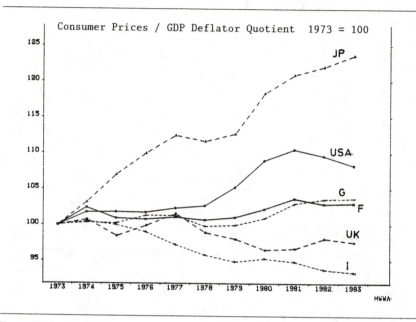

Key: USA = United States of America; JP = Japan; G = Federal Republic
of Germany; F = France; I = Italy; UK = United Kingdom.

1 Quotient of retail prices divided by the GDP price index.

Source: See Table 19.

Empirical studies strengthen this supposition; they detect a "nominal
wage rigidity" in the USA but a "real rigidity" in the EC.[1] This
implies that nominal wages in the USA react relatively slowly to

1 Cf. for example Jeffrey D. SACHS, Wages, Profits and Macroeconomic
Adjustment: A Comparative Study, in: Brookings Papers on Economic
Activity, No. 2/1979, pp. 269 ff.; Jeffrey D. SACHS, Real Wages
and Unemployment in the OECD countries, op. cit., pp. 225 ff.;
William H. BRANSON, Julio J. ROTEMBERG, International Adjustment
with Wage Rigidity, in: European Economic Review, No. 13 (1980),
pp. 309 ff.; Robert J. GORDON, Why U.S. Wage and Employment
Behaviour differs from that in Britain and Japan, in: The Economic
Journal, No. 92 (1982), pp. 13 ff.; George A. KAHN, International
Differences in Wage Behaviour: Real, Nominal, or Exaggerated? in:
AEA Papers and Proceedings, No. 74 (1984) pp. 155 ff.

shocks, whether they be due to monetary or external causes, and that they adjust to them only after a delay and often do not adjust fully. Such shocks therefore also affect real wages in the USA. In the EC countries, by contrast, nominal wages react flexibly to such shocks, so that real wages are little affected. Real wages in the EC countries are therefore relatively rigid but nominal wages virtually "indexed". Some studies also count Japan among the countries with "real wage rigidity"; however, this seems questionable in the light of the findings of this study.

The differences between the USA and the other countries in the reaction of nominal wages to shocks are attributed to differences in the effect of consumer price developments on the behaviour of nominal wages. For example, econometric analysis leads Sachs to conclude that nominal wage behaviour in the USA can best be explained in terms of a "distributed lag" in the change in consumer prices, whereas in the other countries the change is unlagged.[1] Hence in the USA consumer price movements were reflected belatedly and only partially in nominal wages, whereas in the EC countries consumer price increases led directly to higher nominal wages. Adjustment was also relatively swift in Japan, and to that extent it is often claimed that real wages are rigid there too, but the extent of the adjustment was distinctly less than in the EC countries.

The findings of the studies are to be interpreted as meaning that economies exhibiting "nominal wage rigidity" can cope with shocks such as a severe deterioration in the terms of trade better than those where nominal wages react swiftly and fully to such shocks. The differing "adjustment behaviour" would also explain why the GDP deflator (which measures increases in domestic cost factors) increased much less sharply than consumer prices in the USA and Japan, the opposite of developments in the EC countries. It might also help ex-plain differences in real wage behaviour.

1 Cf. Jeffrey D. SACHS, Real Wages and Unemployment, op. cit., p. 275.

Differences in the adjustment of nominal wages to shocks are usually attributed to differences in the degree of unionization, the nature of wage determination and the duration of wage agreements. Besides these institutional factors, wage policy also plays a role.

3.2.5.2 Wage Determination and Adjustment Behaviour

There are indeed wide differences between the various countries as regards institutional conditions such as the nature of wage determination, the length of wage agreements and the strength of trade union organization.[1] In the USA, wage agreements are usually negotiated at company level; trade unions must win a mandate from the entire workforce to be recognized as a legitimate negotiating partner.[2] The majority of wage agreements are valid for several years, generally three. Some provide for cost-of-living adjustment, but this usually applies only to the more major agreements, and even then only about half of these are indexed.[3] The importance of such indexed contracts has diminished since the end of the seventies, as they were prevalent mainly in industries with declining employment. In 1983 only around 5 million workers were covered by wage agreements that included cost-of-living adjustment clauses.[4] Trade union influence is significant mainly in traditional industries and industrial

---

1 See also the section entitled "Labour Markets and Wage Formation" in Chapter 4 of this study.

2 Cf. Günter GROSSER, Elke KURLBAUM, Wirtschaftsstruktur und Konjunkturentwicklung, in: Politik und Wirtschaft in den USA, Schriftenreihe der Bundeszentrale für politische Bildung, Vol. 208, Bonn 1984, pp. 48 ff.; with regard to the trade union system in the USA, see also Richard B. FREEMAN, James L. MEDOFF, What do Unions Do?, New York 1984.

3 Cf. John L. LACOMBE II, James R. CONLEY, Collective bargaining calendar crowed again in 1984, in: Monthly Labor Review, No. 1/ 1984, especially p. 31.

4 Ibid, p. 31.

regions and in the public sector. It is comparatively weak in the private services sector, where employment has risen fastest; here wages are negotiated more or less freely.

In Japan wage negotiations are also conducted mainly at company level. Sinse most negotiations are concentrated in the spring (the "spring wage offensive"), rates of wage increase tend to be fairly uniform.[1] Agreements run for one year, thus allowing nominal wages to adjust relatively swiftly. Wage flexibility is quite high, however, thanks largely to the nature of the Japanese system of remuneration. Pay consists of a basic wage and a bonus. The trade unions negotiate on the basic wage and the company decides on the bonus, which represents a kind of profit-sharing and is paid twice a year. Flexibility of this kind is completely different from wage indexation, for the level of the bonus does not depend primarily on the behaviour of consumer prices, as is the case with indexation, but on the profitability of the individual firm, so that the specific circumstances of the firm are taken into account.

Trade unions draw their members primarily from among workers in large companies, and then only from those employed for life; the great majority of wage agreements relate only to the wages of such workers. The wages of employees of smaller firms and "sub-contractors" (workers with fixed-term contracts) are usually negotiated between worker and employer. The desire to avoid conflict, which applies to business just as much as to other aspects of life in Japan, means that the costs of industrial disputes are lower in Japan than elsewhere.[2]

In some EC countries, such as the United Kingdom, wage negotiations are conducted at company level, while in others they are industry-wide. In most countries collective agreements run for a relatively

---

1 Cf. George A. KAHN, op. cit., p. 156.
2 Cf. Robert J. GORDON, op. cit., p. 37.

short period, one year in most cases.[1] This permits comparatively rapid adjustment. In Italy agreements are for longer periods - three years are common - but nominal wages are indexed to a high degree by the "scala mobile". That being the case, wage negotiations can only concern real wage adjustments.

Wage agreements in the EC have broader validity than in the USA; in some countries, such as the Federal Republic of Germany, they may also be declared to be generally binding for the entire industrial branch concerned, thus further extending their validity. In most countries wage bargaining is primarily in the hands of trade unions and employers' associations; wages negotiated independently between a firm and its workers are less prevalent.

3.2.5.3 Nominal and Real Wage Behaviour - the Role of Wage Policy and Monetary Policy

Differences in wage determination, in the duration of wage settlements and in the degree of unionization are certainly partly responsible for differences in wage behaviour. However, the wage policy pursued by trade unions is also an important factor. An ambitious or even aggressive wage policy will lead to higher wage increases than a moderate one, even if "institutional" and economic policy conditions are the same; this is probably true of the behaviour of real as well as nominal wages.

In these circumstances, it would not be convincing to attempt to explain international differences in real wage behaviour in terms of differences in monetary policy. It is true that there were differences in monetary policy targets and results, as evidenced by longer-term inflation differentials and by the intensity and duration of inflation. However, to see this as the decisive reason for differences in real

---

1 Cf. also the overview in Jeffrey D. Sachs, Wages, Profits, and Macroeconomic Adjustment, op. cit., pp. 317 ff.

Employment Trends

wage behaviour would ultimately mean neglecting the importance of wage policy itself for inflation. It would also assume that wage policy and the ability to enforce it were broadly identical everywhere; there are many indications that this was not the case between 1973 and 1983 and that the evident differences in real wage behaviour chiefly reflect differences in wage policies.

In the USA the nominal wage increases between 1973 and 1983 were largely eroded by price rises; real incomes - wages adjusted for increases in consumer prices - actually fell on average (see Table 14). Since nominal wage increases were relatively large, however, it is sometimes concluded that the moderate behaviour of real wages was the result not of wage restraint but of a permissive monetary policy.[1] However, that would mean either that American trade unions were suffering from money illusion or that they had relatively little influence on nominal wage behaviour.

Of course, it is absurd to suppose that the American trade unions, or their European and Japanese counterparts for that matter, laboured under money illusion for the entire past decade. It is more likely that they had comparatively little power to influence overall wage developments in the USA. The relatively low and continually falling level of unionization and the existence of non-unionized areas in important industries and regions suggest that this was one reason for the moderate behaviour of real wages.

However, this alone would not explain why real wage behaviour in those industries in the USA where trade union influence is fairly strong also remained much more moderate than in other countries. This observation tends to indicate that the trade unions pursued a

---

1 See for instance Ulrich BRASCHE, Manfred TESCHNER, Dieter VESPER, Sind die Unterschiede der Beschäftigungsentwicklung in den USA und der Bundesrepublik Deutschland in der Reallohnentwicklung begründet?, in: DEUTSCHES INSTITUT FÜR WIRTSCHAFTSFORSCHUNG (DIW), Wochenbericht, No. 33/1984, p. 408.

moderate wage policy and hence helped real wage behaviour that favoured employment.

In the EC countries, where the trade unions' influence was much greater than in the USA and even strengthened further in the early seventies,[1] the trade unions followed expansionary wage policies, albeit with national variations. Conditions in the European labour market had been good for many years, with unemployment averaging only 2.2 % of the labour force in the EC during the sixties; it was under these conditions that pay increases rocketed in France in 1968 and in Italy and the Federal Republic of Germany in 1969, partly owing to developments in the domestic political arena. Income redistribution was clearly an important objective in the years that followed. Over the short term, real wage behaviour was also affected by miscalculations of the expected rate of price increase. In the Federal Republic of Germany, for example, price rises proved to be smaller than had been assumed in wage negotiations conducted after the onset of the first oil crisis; the error was due partly to a misjudgement in monetary policy. When the unions' bargaining position began to be weakened by the deterioration in the labour market later in the decade, their objective continued to be to "safeguard what has been achieved and to share in the fruits of technological progress"; this prevented the real wage gap that had opened up from being even narrowed, let alone eliminated.

At the beginning of the eighties the pressure of rising unemployment and monetary policies directed primarily towards fighting inflation clearly caused the trade unions in many countries to pursue a more defensive wages policy, albeit reluctantly in most cases. In the EC the change of course first became apparent in the United Kingdom and the Federal Republic of Germany. In France the change did not emerge clearly until 1983, when the Government adopted a vigorous

---

1 Cf. Jeffrey D. SACHS, Wages, Profits, and Macroeconomic Adjustment, op. cit., pp. 279 f.

Employment Trends

stabilization policy that included guidelines for wages and prices. In Italy, the curtailment of automatic inflation adjustment in the last few yeras is evidence of greater moderation, although until very recently basic wage rates were rising faster than prices.

In Japan, trade union wages policy has less impact on nominal wage behaviour than in the EC countries because of the unique nature of the Japanese remuneration system. It is true that Japanese unions also managed to win substantial nominal wage raises after the first oil crisis, but the rate of increase slowed down rapidly thereafter.

From the aforegoing, it can be concluded that the differences in real wage behaviour between 1973 and 1983 had several causes:

-   Differences in wage determination, in the duration of wage agreements and particularly in the influence of the trade unions;

-   Differences in trade unions' wages policies, determined partly by the position of the trade unions and probably also partly by the consequences of monetary policies aimed at stabilization.

In the USA, not only was the trade unions' influence over wage developments weaker than in the other countries but their wage claims paid greater heed to labour market conditions; this was a key factor in keeping real wages more consistent with employment needs. To a lesser extent, the same can probably be said of Japan, subject to the unique circumstances of that country. In the EC countries, where trade union influence was noticeably stronger, the redistribution of national income was generally a more prominent objective. This was one of the main reasons why the real wage gap that had developed in the first half of the seventies could not be closed, and indeed widened further in some countries.

3.3 Wage Structure and Employment

3.3.1 Links between the Wage Structure, the General Level of Wages and Employment

The general level of wages is an average figure that may be achieved by many different wage structures. Neo-classical economists consider that the wage structure is also highly important for employment, basing this view on the notion that the labour market operates, or should operate, in fundamentally the same way as product markets. The market is cleared via the price mechanism, in other words via wages, although this does require high labour mobility. Wage fulfils two functions - first, it should channel labour into productive jobs and secondly it should highlight and ultimately eliminate labour shortage and surpluses.[1]

Labour is not a homogeneous good; workers differ as regards qualifications, ability and willingness to work. These differences must be reflected in wage differentials such as are characteristic of a market economy. Further differentiation is necessary to allow for differences in marginal productivity between firms, industries and regions and for demand and supply conditions in individual segments of the labour market. The more closely wage differentials reflect these differences, the higher will be the level of employment (other things being equal), and vice versa.

In a country that is heavily dependent on foreign trade, such as the Federal Republic of Germany, the wage structures will also be influenced by international factors. The exchange rate offsets differences in the general wage level, but not in the wage structure. For

---

1 Cf. for instance Horst GISCHER, Lohnstruktur und Beschäftigung, in: Wirtschaftsdienst, No. 12/1983, p. 610; Hans FRIDERICHS, Lohnstrukturdifferenzierung - ein Rezept zur Lösung des Beschäftigungsproblems?, in: Wirtschaftsdienst, No. 8/1985, p. 426.

Employment Trends

example, wages in the German clothing and footwear industries are below the general average, not least because of competition from low-wage countries.

If conditions that have hitherto determined the wage structure change, the wage structure must adapt. If it does not or is unduly slow in adapting, repercussions on employment performance can be expected unless the general level of wages adjusts instead. In principle, the adverse employment effects of inflexibility in the wage structure can be counteracted by general wage restraint; the wage level is adjusted instead of the wage structure. To some extent, the general wage level would then be set by wages of "marginal producers" and would be lower than if the wage structure were flexible. Adjustment of the general wage level would also lead to a different employment structure than would adjustment of the wage structure.

An examination of the possible effects of the wage structures on differences in employment performance between the USA, Japan and the EC entails comparing wage structures and changes therein and identifying differences. In addition, however, an attempt must be made to establish whether there were differences in the need for adjustment of wage structures in the various countries.

3.3.2   An International Comparison of Wage Structures - Problems and Empirical Findings

Comparative analysis of the employment effects of wage structures in the USA, Japan and the EC is made difficult by the lack of fully comparable data in this regard. It is true that statistics on earnings according to industry, occupation, sex, qualifications and region are available for many countries, but a best they are comparable only at a relatively high level of aggregation. Even the industrial classification often differs from one country to another; the finer the statistical breakdown, the greater the disparities. As a rule, the industrial sector is fairly well covered, but data on the services sector are generally rather sparse. The differences in the breakdown according to occupation and qualifications are even more serious than those at the sectoral level; here there is practically no basis of comparison at all.

If it were feasible, the construction of comparable detailed wage structures would have been so time-consuming that it would have breached the confines of this study. It was therefore necessary to limit the comparison to relatively broad sectoral wage structures. At the macroeconomic level, the available statistics allowed only the wage differentials between the ten major branches of economic activity to be compared;[1] gross income per employee was chosen as the measure of wages. France had to be left out of account, since no corresponding income data were available. (For the bilateral comparison between the USA and the Federal Republic of Germany an extended overall wage structure could be constructed on the basis of respectively 19 and 20 branches of activity.) Since the wage structures ascertained in this way merely constitute a rough grid of data, a further set of wage structures for manufacturing alone were calculated. For most countries this encompassed 19 or 20 branches of industry for which data on hourly wages were available, though only 14 in the case of Italy.[2]

The percentage deviation of earnings in individual branches from the mean - the general level of wages or average earnings in manufacturing, as appropriate - indicates the range of the wage structure and the "ranking" of individual sectors or branches of industry. The

---

1 Agriculture, mining and quarrying, manufacturing, electricity, gas and water, construction, wholesale and retail trade, transport and communication, financing, insurance and other services, social and personal services, government, as defined for national accounting purposes.

2 Branch composition according to ISIC and based on ILO earnings data; cf. INTERNATIONAL LABOUR OFFICE (ILO), Yearbook of Labour Statistics, various years.

Employment Trends

coefficient of variation, which measures the average percentage deviation, serves as the indicator for changes in wage structures. A rising coefficient indicates increasing differentiation, a falling one a narrowing of wage differentials. The calculations produced the following results for the period 1973-83[1] (see Diagram 20 in the text and Diagrams 3a to 3e, 4a and 4b in the Appendix):

- There was a clear wage gradient across the major branches in all countries. Differentials were greatest in the United Kingdom, slightly less pronounced in Italy and the USA and smallest in the Federal Republic of Germany.

- In manufacturing taken alone, the steepest gradient was in the USA, followed by Japan; in the EC countries it was much less pronounced.

- There were marked differences in the rank of individual sectors. In the USA it was mainly industrial activities that recorded above-average earnings, along with transport and communication and, in the extended sectoral breakdown, financing and insurance. The remaining service sectors, government and agriculture occupied the lower part of the wage scale. In Japan and the EC countries wage differentials between industry and services were much smaller.

- In most of the countries the wage structure changed little between 1973 and 1983. In the Federal Republic of Germany and Japan it remained fairly constant overall. If anything, there was a slight increase in differentiation in the USA, although too much significance should not be attached to this, given the relatively rough measure used. Only in the United Kingdom was there a trend towards greater differentiation, and here only since the end of the seventies. In Italy, by contrast, wage differentials narrowed.

---

1 In some cases, statistical reasons prevented including developments beyound 1982 or even 1981.

Diagram 20   DEVELOPMENTS IN WAGE STRUCTURES
                IN THE ECONOMY AS A WHOLE AND IN MANUFACTURING
                       - coefficients of variation[1] -

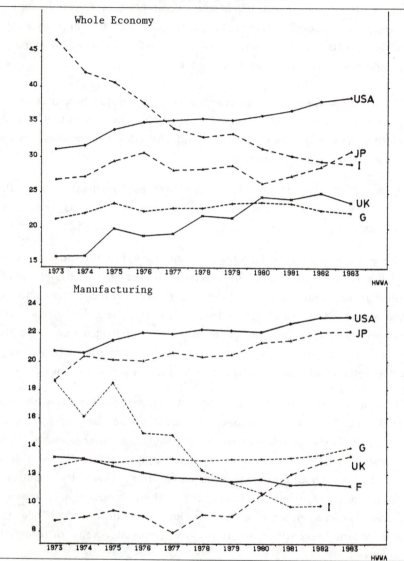

Key: USA = United States of America; JP = Japan; G = Federal Republic
        of Germany; F = France; I = Italy; UK = United Kingdom.
1 A rising coefficient of variation signifies increasing differentiation, a falling coefficient a narrowing of wage differentials.
Source: Authors' calculations using OECD and ILO data.

- A similar picture emerges in manufacturing: fairly constant wage structures in the USA, Japan and the Federal Republic of Germany, increasing differentiation since the end of the seventies in the United Kingdom, a narrowing of differentials in France and especially in Italy.

In view of the relatively coarse wage structures used, these findings should be regarded as no more than indications of the scale and possible direction of any changes. Other studies on this subject were therefore consulted as a means of cross-checking, although the problem of comparability arises again. The works in question were the structural reports by the economic research institutes for the Federal Republic of Germany,[1] a study by Saunders and Marsden for the EC,[2] and works by the Ifo-Institut,[3] the Institut der deutschen Wirtschaft (IW)[4] and the Bureau of Labor Statistics[5] for the USA. Adequate studies were not available for Japan.

1 Cf. especially DEUTSCHES INSTITUT FÜR WIRTSCHAFTSFORSCHUNG (DIW), Auswirkungen des Strukturwandels auf den Arbeitsmarkt, op. cit., pp. 91 ff.; Kurt VOGLER-LUDWIG, op. cit., pp. 71 ff.

2 See Christopher SAUNDERS, David MARSDEN, Pay Inequalities in the European Communities, Butterworths European Studies, 1981.

3 Cf. Kurt VOGLER-LUDWIG, Flexibilisierung der Lohnstrukturen, in: Ifo-Schnelldienst, No. 16/1985, pp. 18 ff.

4 Cf. Bernd HOF, Löhne, Beschäftigung und Produktivität: Sektorale Differenzierung im deutsch-amerikanischen Vergleich, in: iw-Trends, No. 2/1985, pp. 28 ff.

5 Cf. Carl B. BARKSY, Martin E. PERSONICK, Measuring wage dispersion: pay ranges reflect industry traits, in: Monthly Labor Review, No. 4/1981, pp. 35 ff.; Earl F. MELLOR, George D. STAMAS, Usual weekly earnings: another look at intergroup differences and basic trends, in: Monthly Labor Review, No. 4/1982, pp. 15 ff.; Mark SIELING, Clerical pay differentials in metropolitan areas 1961-80, in: Monthly Labor Review, No. 7/1982, pp. 10 ff.; see also Lynn E. BROWNE, How Different Are Regional Wages? A Second Look, in: New England Economic Review, March/April 1984, pp. 40 ff.

The above-mentioned works, some of which examine wage structures by qualification and regions as well as by sectors, broadly confirmed the findings of the analyses conducted in the context of this study. They too reach the conclusion that the dispersion of wages in the Federal Republic of Germany was far narrower than in the USA and in other EC countries as well, and that wage structures in Germany and the USA remained relatively stable, whereas there was a tendency for differentials to narrow in France and Italy. The following findings also appear to be relevant to the issue under examination here:

- In all countries wage disparities between men and women diminished.

- In several countries, including Germany, there was a tendency for wage differentials between employees in different qualification groups to narrow, and in some cases also those between skilled workers and employees. In Germany, however, the tendency was too weak to have a significant effect on the overall structure.

- Studies on the USA show that differences in the strength of the trade unions also affected the wage structure. In industries and firms that are highly unionized, wage differentials were narrower than in those where union influence was relatively weak or absent.[1]

The considerable changes in domestic and, above all, external conditions owing to events such as the oil price shocks and the change-over to a system of floating exchange rates have generated pressure for structural adjustment, so that it is remarkable that wage relationships remained constant in many countries. The stability of wage structures seems to refute the popular thesis that the differences in the employment performance of the USA and the EC countries were due partly to the narrowing of differentials in EC countries at a time

1 Cf. Carl B. BARSKY, Martin E. PERSONICK, op. cit., p. 37.

when wage differentiation remained high in the USA.[1] The empirical studies show that there was a tendency for wage differentials to narrow only in Italy and, to a lesser extent, in France. In the Federal Republic of Germany, where employment performed even worse than in France and Italy, no notable overall narrowing of differentials could be detected. Clearly, even the unions' policy of fixed wage increases for the lowest wage groups was only partly effective.

In interpreting the results of the empirical studies it should be borne in mind, however, that the wage structures that have been ascertained are only a very rough portrayal of reality. The wage rates are averages for large industrial branches and broad occupational groupings with different qualification requirements.[2] Hence it cannot be ruled out that differentials were eroded at levels that cannot be represented by the data used.

3.3.3 Rigid Wage Structures - Proof that they have no Relevance for Employment?

The stability of the wage structure in the Federal Republic of Germany is undoubtedly due largely to the wage bargaining policy;[3] the practice of basing wage demand on macroeconomic data and "pilot settlements" and the strategy of safeguarding real wages were key factors in perpetuating the wage structure. The same applies to the narrowing of differentials in France and Italy; in Italy in particular

---

1 Cf. for example Manfred WEGNER, The Employment Miracle in the United States, op. cit., p. 44.

2 Cf. Kurt VOGLER-LUDWIG, Flexibilisierung der Lohnstrukturen, op. cit., p. 19.

3 See for example Siegfried F. FRANKE, Der Einfluß von Lohnhöhe und Lohnstruktur auf Beschäftigungsvolumen und -struktur, in: Wirtschaftsdienst, No. 1/1983, p. 19; Erich GUNDLACH, Klaus Dieter SCHMIDT, Das amerikanische Beschäftigungswunder: Was sich daraus lernen läßt, Kiel 1985, pp. 22 f.; Horst GISCHER, op. cit., pp. 611 f.

the erosion of differentials was an important aspect of trade union strategy during a large part of the seventies.[1] Government measures also played their part, however, such as the increasing tendency to declare union wage settlements generally binding for the industries concerned in the Federal Republic of Germany, the raising of minimum wages in France and the revision of the "scala mobile" indexation system and its subsequent suspension for higher incomes in Italy.

In the Federal Republic of Germany, at least, the potential for greater differentiation was certainly there. According to the Federal Ministry of Employment there are around 43,000 collective wage agreements, of which about 15,000 are concluded at company level; around 4,500 wage and salary rates are renegotiated each year.[2] However, this potential has remained largely unexploited.

Sometimes the conclusion is drawn from this that employers also have an interest in rigid wage structures,[3] on the grounds that they increase labour market transparency, provide some protection against staff being poached by competitors and hence reduce labour turnover. It is argued that frequent changes of staff entail the risk of productivity losses and give rise to additional costs; moreover, investment staff training is worthwhile only if workers remain a fairly long time with the firm. Finally, changes in the wage structure are said to upset harmony in the workplace and to disrupt the "social consensus".[4]

---

1 Cf. Christopher SAUNDERS, David MARSDEN, op. cit., p. 348.

2 Cf. Kurt VOGLER-LUDWIG, Flexibilisierung der Lohnstrukturen, op. cit., pp. 27 f.

3 Ibid.

4 Cf. for instance Horst GISCHER, op. cit., pp. 612 f.; Hans FRIDERICHS, op. cit., pp. 431 f.; W. MIETH, Die Forderung nach flexibleren Lohnstrukturen als Entlastung der Arbeitsmarktpolitik, in: P. HERDER-DORNEICH (ed.), Arbeitsmarkt und Arbeitsmarktpolitik, Berlin 1982, pp. 171 ff.

Employment Trends

Though they certainly cannot be dismissed out of hand, arguments such as these stem from a static appraisal of the issue. Structural change requires firms to adjust constantly, and this is one of the reasons why job mobility within the firm is high. There are many indications that employers must have a strong interest in a more flexible wage structure. The fact that they have failed to achieve one is probably due in large part to the attempts of each trade union to win the "going rate" in each wage round. The result is a uniformity of wage behaviour.

The largely static wage structure in the Federal Republic of Germany does not conflict with the supposition that the nature of the wage structure has been one of the reasons for Germany's poor employment performance - unless one held the opinion that the wage structure was and still is consistent with employment needs.[1] However, this view would not be convincing, given the substantial changes that have occured in domestic and external economic conditions and the structural change that has taken place.

Up to now, published works on wage structures have dealt with employment effects more or less in passing. Most simply consider whether observed changes in wage structures had any employment effects at all. For example, in its recent report on the structure of the German economy the Deutsches Institut für Wirtschaftsforschung (DIW) examined whether the narrowing of differentials based on qualifications had harmed the employment prospects of unskilled workers. In many cases a reaction of this kind was identified, but the DIW considered that the levelling tendency was generally too slight to have had any appreciable impact on employment.[2] However, the institute does not conclude that wage relationships are irrelevant to employment.

---

1 Cf. Horst GISCHER, op. cit., p. 615.
2 Cf. DEUTSCHES INSTITUT FÜR WIRTSCHAFTSFORSCHUNG (DIW), op. cit., p. 143.

The main reason why the studies carried out so far have not generally reached satisfactory findings regarding the employment effects of wage structures - and are therefore of only limited value for the specific purposes of this study - is that it is impossible to determine empirically what wage structure would be consistent with employment needs. To that extent, it is possible only to surmise as to the need for adjustment. Nevertheless, the nature and direction of possible employment effects can be deduced from changes in domestic and external economic conditions, wage structures, wage bargaining behaviour and employment.

3.3.4 Wage Structures, Adjustment Needs and Employment - a Comparison between the USA and the Federal Republic of Germany

The question whether divergences in wage structures may have contributed to differences in employment performance will be examined below on the basis of a comparison between the Federal Republic of Germany and the USA. The decision to limit the exercise to these two countries was taken partly on statistical grounds, since the bilateral comparison can be based on more disaggregated data, and partly because many more special factors would have to be taken into account if a larger number of countries were included. This would have entailed an unacceptable increase in the effort required and would have made it much more difficult to discern underlying trends and differences.

Wage structures in both Germany and the USA remained relatively stable from the mid-seventies onwards, but the differences between them were substantial:[1]

---

1   See also Diagrams 4a and 4b in the Appendix.

- The dispersion of the sectoral wage structure, to which the comparison must be confined for statistical reasons, was significantly wider in the USA than in Germany.

- The wage differential between industry and the services sector was much larger in the USA than in Germany.

- The rank of individual branches of activity within the wage structure differed. In the USA a large part of the services sector and the government but comparatively few industrial branches fell in the lower half of the wage scale. In Germany, on the other hand, more industrial branches were in the lower half and the government was in the upper portion.

The fact that changes in the wage structure were equally minor in both the USA and Germany does not mean that they had the same effect on employment. There are indications that the Federal Republic of Germany had much greater need to adjust the wage structure to changed conditions than the USA. The change in external economic conditions as a result of the oil price crisis and the floating of exchange rates generated less pressure for adjustment of wage structures in the USA than in Germany; foreign trade accounts for a relatively small part of the American economy, the USA produces a considerable volume of oil itself and the US dollar depreciated in real terms in the seventies, whereas Germany is more heavily involved in foreign trade, is far more dependent on imported oil and other raw materials and its currency underwent a sharp real appreciation during the decade.

The behaviour of real wages provides a further indication of differing needs as regards the adjustment of wage structures. By contrast with events in Germany, the first oil price crisis did not aggravate wage cost pressures in the USA, for the reasons stated above; real wages actually fell. Overall, the general level of real wages rose only moderately in the USA in the seventies, whereas in Germany it increased much more sharply. The adjustment in the wage level in the USA therefore further reduced the need for adjustment in the wage structure, a contrast with developments in Germany.

Against this background, the virtual stability of the wage structure in the two countries between 1973 and 1983 should be judged differently. The detrimental effects that rigid wage structures have on employment under changing domestic and external conditions were clearly much less serious in the USA than in the Federal Republic of Germany. It can only be surmised that the wider range of the US wage structure was also more in keeping with employment needs than the relatively narrow spread in Germany. At any rate, the greater wage differential between industry and services in the USA was obviously good for employment, as demonstrated by the relatively rapid increase in the number of jobs in services. There is therefore much to suggest that the wage structure in the USA between 1973 and 1983 was more consistent with employment needs than that in the Federal Republic of Germany, and probably also those in the other EC countries as well.

Taking all the evidence together, there are indications that differences in wage structure contributed to differences in employment performance between the USA and the EC countries; they cannot be quantified, however. This assessment is based on an analysis of wage structures that are relatively crude and not fully comparable. The statistical material available does not permit of a more detailed examination, at least not with the limited resources that can be devoted to this study.

3.4 Labour Market Flexibility

3.4.1 Introductory Remarks

Labour markets must exhibit a high degree of flexibility if wages are to perform their function of channelling labour into jobs. The more flexible the labour market and the more smoothly supply and demand are coordinated, the more quickly the economy can make the adjustments necessitated by structural change and by substantial growth in the labour force such as occured in the seventies. The more flexible the response of the labour market, the greater the chance that the adverse employment effects of adjustment can be limited to frictional unemployment. If it does that, an efficient labour market will meet the requirements of both employers and employees, providing employers with suitably trained and qualified workers and enabling workers to find jobs that match their abilities and ambitions.[1]

Labour market flexibility is influenced by a whole range of factors, such as the regional and occupational mobility of labour, the ability and willingness of workers to adapt, companies' labour market behaviour and capital mobility. The institutional and legal framework of the market and the government's labour market policy are also extremely important, influencing labour market flexibility both directly and indirectly via other factors. There is a reciprocal relationship between wage policy and labour market flexibility; labour market conditions have an important influence on wage policy, which in turn have repercussions on the dynamics of the market.

Disruption of the process of coordination and adjustment occuring in the labour market can lead to serious frictional or structural - if it turns out to be permanent - unemployment. To this extent, labour market flexibility also has a significant influence on employment performance. This section will examine whether there were differences between the USA, Japan and the EC in this respect that can help explain the divergences in employment performance. It will aim primarily to identify differences, assess their relevance to employment and suggest possible causes. The often emotionally charged question whether American labour market conditions are a model for Europe in general and for the Federal Republic of Germany in particular will be

---

1 Cf. OECD, The Employment Outlook: Where are the Jobs in Today's Labour Market?, in: The OECD Observer, No. 130, September 1984, p. 8.

considered at a later stage. The impact of the socio-economic frame-work and labour market policy on labour market flexibility will be examined in depth in the section on economic policy in Chapter 4 of this study and will therefore be touched upon only briefly here.

For the investigations that follow, it seems expedient to concentrate on a comparison between the USA and the EC countries; the avail-ability of data means that the comparison must often be confined to the USA and the Federal Republic of Germany. The characteristics of the Japanese labour market will be described briefly at the end of the section, since labour market conditions in Japan differ in many respects from those obtaining in the USA and the EC countries; in particular, direct and indirect government influence is much stronger.

3.4.2 Labour Market Flexibility - a Comparison between the USA and the EC

There is no one universal indicator for measuring labour market flexibility; given the many factors that can influence it, a number of indicators must be examined.

3.4.2.1 Duration of Unemployment

If the "search theory" is acknowledged to be relevant to unemploy-ment and the processes taking place in the labour market, the dura-tion of unemployment is a good indicator of the degree of labour market flexibility. Unemployment of short duration would suggest intensive efforts to find work and hence high flexibility, while long duration would indicate the opposite. There are marked differences between the USA and the EC countries as regards the duration of unemployment (see Tables 20 and 21). The duration of unemployment lengthened everywhere, but it remained much shorter in the USA than in the other countries. In 1983 more than three-quarters of all unemployed in the USA were without work for no more than six

Table 20   UNEMPLOYED ACCORDING TO DURATION OF UNEMPLOYMENT

- percentages of total number of unemployed -

	1980	1981	1982	1983
Federal Republic of Germany				
less than 1 month	17.7	15.9	12.0	9.2
less than 3 months	45.2	42.3	35.4	29.2
less than 6 months	63.8	61.9	53.6	45.9
less than 12 months	83.0	83.8	78.8	71.5
12 months and longer	17.0	16.2	21.3	28.5
France				
less than 1 month	17.7	16.7	15.1	12.5
less than 3 months	44.5	41.4	39.8	37.8
less than 6 months	61.3	59.3	57.4	55.7
less than 12 months	77.7	77.8	74.8	73.4
12 months and longer	22.3	22.1	25.2	26.5
Italy				
less than 1 month	15.6	15.5	13.6	12.6
less than 3 months	34.5	33.8	31.1	27.9
less than 6 months	48.2	48.7	45.0	41.0
less than 12 months	64.4	65.6	60.2	57.0
12 months and longer	35.6	34.4	39.8	43.0
United Kingdom				
less than 1 month	16.5	11.1	9.7	11.7
less than 3 months	42.4	31.5	29.0	30.2
less than 6 months	64.4	50.7	45.3	44.6
less than 12 months	80.6	73.7	64.5	63.1
12 months and longer	19.4	26.3	35.5	37.0
USA				
less than 5 weeks	43.1	41.7	36.4	33.3
less than 14 weeks	75.5	72.4	67.4	60.7
less than 26 weeks	89.3	86.0	83.4	76.1
27 weeks and longer	10.8	14.0	16.6	23.9

Source: EUROSTAT: Employment and Unemployment 1985; US DEPARTMENT OF
LABOR: Handbook of Labor Statistics and Monthly Labor Review.

Table 21

UNEMPLOYED ACCORDING TO DURATION OF UNEMPLOYMENT
- percentage distribution -

	Federal Republic of Germany					United States of America			
	less than 1 month	from 1 to less than 3 month	from 3 to less than 6 month	from 6 to less than 12 month	1 year and longer	less than 5 weeks	from 5 to 14 weeks	from 15 to 26 weeks	27 weeks and longer
Duration of unemployment, all age groups[1]									
1973	28.4	28.8	16.1	18.2	8.5	51.0	30.2	11.0	7.8
1974	26.1	31.2	18.2	19.3	5.2	50.6	30.9	11.1	7.4
1975	16.4	25.5	21.3	27.2	9.6	37.0	31.3	16.5	15.2
1976	16.6	24.8	17.8	22.9	17.9	38.3	29.7	13.8	18.3
1977	16.0	25.6	18.1	21.8	18.6	41.7	30.5	13.1	14.8
1978	15.7	25.1	17.8	21.1	20.3	46.2	31.1	12.3	10.5
1979	16.6	25.2	18.3	20.0	19.9	48.1	31.7	11.5	8.7
1980	17.7	27.5	18.6	19.2	17.0	43.1	32.4	13.8	10.8
1981	15.9	26.4	19.5	21.9	16.2	41.7	30.7	13.6	14.0
1982	12.0	23.4	18.3	25.1	21.3	36.4	31.0	16.0	16.6
1983	9.2	19.9	16.7	25.6	28.5	33.3	27.4	15.4	23.9
Duration of unemployment by age groups 1982[2]									
under 20 years	17.4	41.2	17.1	15.0	9.3	46.5	32.2	11.7	9.5
20-24 years	12.6	26.0	18.9	24.1	18.4	36.8	29.0	14.8	19.4
25-34 years	8.9	18.4	17.7	27.8	27.2	30.1	26.3	16.8	26.7
35-44 years	7.6	15.5	16.1	27.5	33.3	27.3	25.9	16.3	30.5
45-54 years	5.8	12.4	14.1	26.3	41.4	25.4	24.9	17.0	32.5
55 years and over	4.2	11.8	14.5	27.9	41.6	27.7	22.3	16.1	34.0

1 Percentage of total unemployed. -- 2 percentage of unemployed in each age group.

Source: Amtliche Nachrichten der Bundesanstalt für Arbeit; US DEPARTMENT OF LABOR: Monthly Labor Review, Employment and Earnings.

Employment Trends

months, whereas in most EC countries the proportion was barely one-half.

The contrast is striking among the young, whose share of the total unemployed is almost twice as high in the USA as it is in the Federal Republic of Germany. In the USA almost half of them had found another job within a month and more than three-quarters within three months. In the Federal Republic of Germany the duration of youth unemployment was noticeably longer.

The distinctly shorter duration of unemployment in the USA is a first indication that labour market flexibility was much higher there than in the EC countries. Nevertheless, two features of the American employment system that limit comparability with other countries must be borne in mind in interpreting these figures, namely the use of layoffs and the system of on-the-job training.[1]

In the USA, industrial companies in particular lay workers off for short periods if sales fall temporarily or cyclical developments cause a reduction in demand; the laid-off worker is promised reinstatement when sales prospects improve.[2]

Laid-off workers are often jobless for only short periods, so that they reduce the average duration of unemployment. In the seventies they accounted for between 10 and 15 % of all unemployed; since the beginning of the eighties the proportion has risen to around one-fifth.[3] In countries such as the Federal Republic of Germany, on the

---

1 Cf. also Jürgen WARNKEN, Zur unterschiedlichen Dynamik der Arbeitsmärkte in den USA und der Bundesrepublik - ein Erklärungsversuch, in: Mitteilungen des Rheinisch-Westfälischen Instituts für Wirtschaftsforschung, Vol. 35 (1984), pp. 222 f.

2 On the definition of layoffs, see Robert W. BEDNARZIK, Layoffs and permanent job losses: workers' traits and cyclical patterns, in: Monthly Labor Review, No. 9/1983, p. 10.

3 Ibid, p. 9, Diagram 1.

other hand, employers generally put their workers on short-time work if sales slip temporarily. Workers on short-time work do not count as unemployed and therefore do not show up in the unemployment figures. This is one of the reasons why the unemployment rate in the USA is higher than in Germany.

The second difference lies in the area of job training. Germany operates a system of "dual training", with most school-leavers going on to serve an apprenticeship of several years in a company. In the USA, on the other hand, on-the-job training is the rule; apprenticeships comparable to those available in Germany do not generally exist, so that young people change firms and occupations frequently during their early working life in order to gain experience and find the most appropriate occupation. The unemployment figures obviously reflect the fact that they do not all seek or find another job immediately after leaving their last employer. This is one of the reasons for the statistically high youth unemployment and for the comparatively high percentage of short-term unemployed.

System-related differences such as these can offer only a partial explanation for the striking disparities in the duration of unemployment between the USA and the EC countries. Nor is the American system of on-the-job training quite so significant if the comparison is extended to include the other EC countries, for the German system of industrial training is not typical of the EC as a whole. On-the-job training also exists in EC countries such as the United Kingdom, and yet the average duration of unemployment there was far longer than in the USA. Instead, the shorter average duration of unemployment in the USA should be seen as a clear expression of higher labour market flexibility.

3.4.2.2 Separations, Hirings and Labour Turnover

A further indicator of labour market flexibility is provided by the development of separations and hirings. Here too there are striking differences between the USA and the EC countries (see Diagram 21).

Employment Trends

Diagram 21

EMPLOYMENT FLOWS

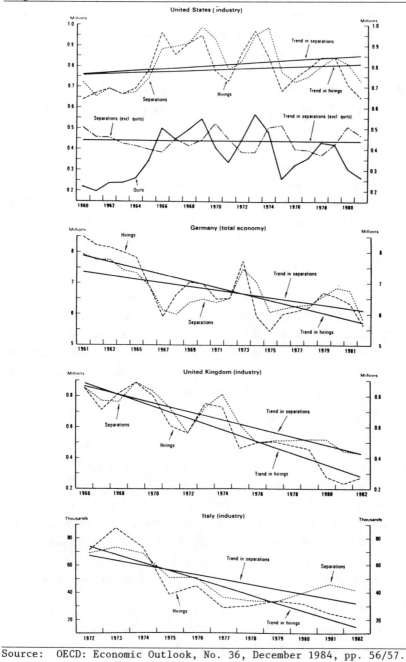

United States (industry)

Germany (total economy)

United Kingdom (industry)

Italy (industry)

Source: OECD: Economic Outlook, No. 36, December 1984, pp. 56/57.

In the USA the trend of both separations and hirings was upwards between 1973 and 1979. From this the OECD deduces that the inter-firm and regional mobility of labour was consistently high and that the turnover of labour between firms was comparatively brisk, although it also sees this as an indication of the relatively weak bargaining position of job-seekers. The continued high propensity for American firms to recruit new workers despite the recent weakening of economic growth is attributed chiefly to easy firing practices and the moderate behaviour of real wages.[1]

The development of separations and hirings in the EC countries was markedly different from that in the USA in the seventies and early eighties. In the Federal Republic of Germany the trend of both separations and hirings was distinctly downwards. The pattern was similar in the United Kingdom and Italy, at least as far as can be judged from the decline in recruitment and separations in industry. Corresponding figures for France are not available. The falling trends indicate that labour markets in the EC became less flexible, in con-trast to what was happening in the USA. This was probably due partly to declining preparedness on the part of workers to change jobs in the light of rising unemployment and growing fears for job security, and partly to greater reluctance on the part of firms to recruit owing to falling profitability, deteriorating sales prospects and increased protection against dismissal.

High labour market flexibility in the USA is also evident in the labour turnover rates in manufacturing; these show separations or hirings as a percentage of total employment. Industrial firms in the USA released an average of around 4 % of their workforce each month between 1973 and 1981; around one-third of these constituted layoffs (see Table 22). However, they also recruited workers at the same rate; around 70 % were new hirings and the remainder rehirings.[2] To

1   Cf. OECD, Economic Outlook, No. 36, December 1984, p. 54.
2   Cf. also Robert W. BEDNARZIK, op. cit., p. 10.

Table 22   LABOUR TURNOVER RATES IN MANUFACTURING IN THE USA[1]

	Separations			Hirings				Recall rate[3]
	Total	Dis-missals	Layoffs	Total	New hirings	Re-hirings	of which: recalls[2]	
1973	4.7	2.8	0.9	4.8	3.9	0.9	-	-
1974	4.9	2.4	1.5	4.2	3.2	1.0	-	-
1975	4.2	1.4	2.1	3.7	2.0	1.7	-	-
1976	3.8	1.7	1.3	3.9	2.6	1.3	1.0	0.7
1977	3.8	1.8	1.1	4.0	2.8	1.2	0.9	0.8
1978	3.9	2.1	0.9	4.1	3.1	1.0	0.7	0.8
1979	4.0	2.0	1.1	4.0	2.9	1.1	0.7	0.6
1980	4.0	1.5	1.7	3.5	2.1	1.4	1.1	0.7
1981	3.6	1.3	1.6	3.2	2.0	1.2	1.0	0.6
1973-81 average	4.1	1.9	1.4	3.9	2.7	1.2	0.9[a]	0.7[a]

1 Separations and hirings as a percentage of wage and salary earners; monthly average for each year.
2 Jobs filled by workers previously laid off.-- 3 Recalls as a percentage of layoffs.
a 1976-81 average.

Source: US DEPARTMENT OF LABOR: Handbook of Labor Statistics; Robert W. BEDNARZIK, op. cit., Table 6, p. 10.

some extent, the high turnover rates reflect the frequent changes of job among the young. Turnover was particularly rapid in the years following the first oil crisis, when considerable adjustments to the new economic conditions had to be made. The decline at the beginning of the eighties is probably above all a reflection of the effects of the recession.

Comparable figures are not available for most of the EC countries; some indication of the scale of labour turnover exists only for Germany. For example, unpublished figures from the Bundesanstalt für Arbeit on persons registering for and departing from German social security lead Warnken to conclude that in the German economy an average of only between 2 and 3 % of jobs turn over each month and that the number of registrations was smaller than that of departures in all but a very few periods in the past.[1] The figures on labour market turnover in Germany given by Willke also suggest less frequent job changes than in the USA.[2]

3.4.2.3 Mobility of Labour and Capital

Some analysts regard the brisk turnover of labour in the USA as "epidemic",[3] but this interpretation seems questionable. Rather, it suggests a high degree of labour mobility. This is also evident from

---

1   Cf. Jürgen WARNKEN, op. cit., p. 227.

2   Cf. Gerhard WILLKE: Wirtschaftspolitische Optionen gegen strukturelle Arbeitslosigkeit, in: Aus Politik und Zeitgeschichte, March 1984, Table 1, p. 13. Willke calculates a rate of unemployment turnover from data on redundancies, recruitment and the transition to and from unemployment; for 1983 he arrived at a rate of 16.6 %. However, the comparability between these annual figures and the monthly data on the USA is limited, since the monthly data cannot be converted directly to an annual basis.

3   Werner Sengenberger, op. cit., p. 402. According to Sengenberger's calculations, yearly almost every second employee in American industry left his job or moved to another company between 1972 and 1981; this would give a turnover rate of almost 50 % a year. It is not clear from Sengenberger's figures whether sufficient allowance was made for factors such as short-term layoffs.

US data on changes of occupation and residence. Measured in terms of occupational mobility rates,[1] which understate the extent of mobility, one-tenth of the men who had been employed for more than a year had changed their occupation in the course of the last year at the beginning of the eighties; the proportion was even larger in the case of women.[2] Regional mobility is also high, as demonstrated by the number of changes of residence.

As in other countries, labour mobility in the USA depends very much on age. Among the younger age groups it is considerable, not least because of on-the-job training, but it declines with increasing age. The job tenure with a particular employer lengthens accordingly. For example, in 1983 around one-third of employees in the 35 to 44 age group had worked for ten years or longer with their present employer; among those aged 45 and older the proportion was more than one-half.[3] On average, workers in this age group had spent over 12 years with the same firm; in the Federal Republic of Germany the corresponding average length of tenure was 17 years.[4]

Mobility in the USA has clearly declined somewhat since the beginning of the eighties, as indicated by the slight fall in occupational mobility rates. This was undoubtedly in part a reaction to the economic slow-down in the early part of this decade, but the possibility of a permanent reduction in mobility cannot be ruled out.[5]

---

1 The occupational mobility rate shows the percentage of all workers who had been employed for at least two years but who had changed their occupation during the year preceding the date of the survey. The survey is taken in January of each year; it does not record those who are unemployed between survey dates, workers entering the labour market or employed for less than two years or multiple changes of occupation during the year. Occupational mobility rates therefore understate the true degree of mobility.

2 Cf. Ellen SEHGAL: Occupational mobility and job tenure in 1983, in: Monthly Labor Review, No. 10/1984, p. 22, Table 6.

3 Ibid, p. 19.

4 Cf. Kurt VOGLER-LUDWIG: Flexibilisierung der Lohnstrukturen, op. cit., p. 28.

5 Cf. Joan BERGER, Edward MERVOSH, American workers don't get around much anymore, in: Business Week, 28.10.1985, pp. 48 f.

That labour mobility in the EC countries is far lower than in the USA can be deduced only indirectly from the longer duration of unemployment, the declining trend in separations and hirings and the lower turnover rates. The few studies that have dealt with this issue relate mainly to the sixties and seventies.[1] The latest EC data on occupational and regional mobility in the Community depict the situation prevailing in the mid-seventies, but they are not directly comparable with the available data on the United States. Nonetheless, they do show that there was a clear "mobility gradient" even within the EC; mobility was significantly higher in the Federal Republic of Germany than in the other major EC countries and lowest in Italy and the United Kingdom.[2]

The differences in mobility between the USA and the EC countries are undoubtedly in large part a consequence of historical, social and cultural factors.[3] In the EC countries, including Germany, workers are more "settled" than in the USA, where the "pioneer spirit" is still alive. Attitudes to work also differ, as can be seen in the fact that the "acceptability" of work - and of "bad jobs" in particular - is far less important in the USA than in the Federal Republic of Germany, for example.

Institutional differences are extremely important as well, such as differences in the social security system and in education. In the Federal Republic of Germany, for example, the differences resulting from the federal organization of the schools system tend to curb mobility. Other institutional factors affecting mobility include different mechanisms for regulating the housing market in the various countries.

1 Cf. for instance Klaus D. SIEGEL, Willi STEVENS, Manfred WERTH, Vergleichende Analyse der Mobilität in bzw. zwischen den Arbeitsmärkten der Europäischen Gemeinschaft, Nuremberg 1976.

2 Cf. EUROSTAT, Soziale Indikatoren für die Europäische Gemeinschaft 1960-75, Table II/7.

3 Cf. Janet L. NORWOOD, Labor market contrasts, op. cit., p. 7.

The comparatively high mobility of the American worker is also undoubtedly linked with the relatively high mobility of American businesses. Here too, a touch of the pioneering spirit comes to the fore. The considerable differences in wage structures, tax law, social legislation, environmental and worker protection requirements and trade union influence among the states in the USA create greater incentives for firms to relocate than in the EC countries, and not least in the Federal Republic of Germany.[1]

The large number of new company start-ups, especially the sharp increase in the number of self-employed persons, was a striking phenomenon in the USA between 1973 and 1983.[2] There is no parallel for this, especially in Germany. The American employment system and the factors determining its flexibility clearly open up a wide range of opportunities for self-employment. In this respect the differences are considerable, especially between the USA and the Federal Republic of Germany. In Germany there are many formidable restrictions on market access as a result of government influence; these inhibit an expansion of service activities in areas such as health care, legal services, restaurants, craft activities and to some extent even re-tailing.[3] Moreover, raising venture capital for new businesses seems to have been less problematical in the USA than in Germany. A large proportion of the new jobs created in the USA are in small, newly-established firms. The start-up conditions for self-employed persons therefore had a considerable impact on the employment performance of the USA.

Finally, differences in labour market flexibility between the USA and the EC countries are apparent in the supply of part-time jobs (see

---

1 Cf. also Astrid ZIMMERMANN-TRAPP, Zur Arbeitsmarktflexibilität in den USA und der Bundesrepublik Deutschland, Kreditanstalt für Wiederaufbau, July 1985, p. 13.

2 See Chapter 1, section 1.2.3.

3 Cf. Jürgen WARNKEN, op. cit., p. 234; Astrid ZIMMERMANN-TRAPP, op. cit., pp. 13 f.

Table 23). In the USA more than one-quarter of the new jobs created between 1975 and 1983 were for part-time workers, predominantly in service enterprises.[1] The proportion of part-time workers is relatively high in several branches of the services sector; in distribution, for example, it is higher than 30 %.

Data on part-time work in the EC, which are not fully comparable with those for the USA, do show that in the EC as well there was a growing trend towards part-time employment in the seventies and early eighties, particularly in the services sector; however, in several EC countries the rate of increase was less rapid in the USA and it accounted for a much smaller share of employment.

The foregoing thus shows that the American labour market was much more flexible than its European counterparts and that ultimately it was more efficient in tackling the employment problem. This is clearly a further reason for the differences in employment performance between the USA and the EC countries. The assimilation of problem groups - blacks, hispanics, the poorly qualified, the young and the older unemployed - still causes the USA considerable difficulties similar to those encountered in the EC countries, but this does not detract from the finding that the American labour market is highly flexible.[2] Problem groups in the USA accounted for a very large share of the labour force, mainly owing to the high immigration of poorly qualified workers from Mexico and Latin America. The fact that the majority of entrants to the labour market could nonetheless be assimilated is as much an indication of high flexibility as the fact that the majority of the new jobs in the services sector were filled by newcomers, and not by workers made redundant in other sectors.[3]

---

1   The period from 1975 to 1983 was chosen for purposes of comparison since comparable figures for the EC countries on part-time workers are available only from 1975 ownwards.

2   Cf. Janet L. NORWOOD, Labor market contrasts, op. cit., pp. 4 ff.

3   Cf. Werner SENGENBERGER, op. cit., p. 401.

Employment Trends

Table 23　　　　　　　PART-TIME WORK, BY SECTOR

- part-time employees as a percentage of wage and salary earners -

	1975	1983
Federal Republic of Germany		
Industry	5.9	5.9
Services	14.3	17.1
France		
Industry	2.5	3.0
Services	9.4	12.3
Italy		
Industry	3.7	2.0
Services	3.9	3.6
United Kingdom		
Industry	8.7	6.8
Services	26.5	27.1
United States of America		
Non-agricultural activities	17.9	19.3
of which: Manufacturing	7.2	7.2
Transport and public utilities	9.1	8.6
Wholesale and retail trade	29.5	32.4
Financing, insurance, other services (excluding government)	23.0	23.9

Source:　EUROSTAT: Employment and Unemployment; US DEPARTMENT OF LABOR: Employment and Earnings; authors' calculations.

The large number of women entering working life was assimilated relatively quickly, so that by 1982 the female unemployment rate was already lower than the male rate.

3.4.3   The Special Case of Japan

Japan is a special case with regard to labour market flexibility as well. Inter-firm mobility is relatively low, as can be seen from the fact that the average Japanese worker changes his job only two and a half times in his working life, compared with seven and a half in the case of his American counterpart.[1] Low "external" mobility is a consequence of the system of lifetime employment; mobility is con-fined to those who do not have a job for life - primarily workers in small and medium-sized firms, "sub-contractors" and women, who have to bear the brunt of adjustment when economic activity weakens.[2] This dual labour market structure is also apparent in wages; in large firms they are considerably higher than in small and medium-sized firms, and large firms pay their established workforce much higher wages than their sub-contractors.

Inter-firm mobility is also impeded by the various ways in which the Japanese labour market is segmented; movement occurs mainly between companies of similar size classes.[3] Highly-paid jobs are generally open only to graduates from the top schools and universities. Workers in small firms normally have little chance of moving to a much better-paid position in an "privileged" enterprise.

There are certainly also historical and social reasons for the relatively low "external" labour mobility in Japan. A close affinity between

---

1   Cf. OECD, The Employment Outlook, op. cit., pp. 8 f.

2   Cf. Robert J. GORDON, op. cit., p. 36.

3   Cf. Angelika ERNST, Das japanische Beschäftigungssystem, op. cit., p. 30.

workers and their company and a strong identification with its interests is traditional in Japan; frequent changes of employer have
been frowned upon up to now. Another factor, however, is that social
security coverage is closely tied to the job and that the state offers
only second-rate social security benefits; giving up a permanent job
therefore entails considerable risk.[1]

Part-time employment increased in Japan too between 1973 and 1983.
At the beginning of the eighties it accounted for around 13 % of
total employment. However, part-time work is to be assessed differently in Japan. It is concentrated in the "secondary" - i.e. under-
privileged - labour market, where it serves largely as a cushion
against cyclical fluctuations. It thus performs a function similar to
that of short-time working in the Federal Republic of Germany,
although in Japan it is the worker who bears the cost.

The system of lifetime employment reduces "external" mobility, but it
demands of workers a high degree of flexibility within the firm. In
exchange for a guaranteed job, the permanent workforce must be
prepared to retrain and change jobs within the company or to switch
to a subsidiary at any time; they must therefore also accept the need
to change residence, or even to move abroad. This does not entail
any loss of earnings, however, since company wage structures are
based first and foremost on the seniority principle.

Hence in Japan the relatively low inter-firm mobility constrasts with
extremely high flexibility within the company. The considerable
potential for productivity gains within companies was exploited
rigorously, especially after the first oil crisis and during the ensuing
recession, thus further helping to keep adverse employment effects
under control.

---

1 Cf. Angelika ERNST, Das japanische Beschäftigungssystem, op. cit.,
   p. 29.

Chapter 4

THE INFLUENCE OF ECONOMIC POLICY AND THE SOCIO-ECONOMIC FRAMEWORK ON EMPLOYMENT

4.1 On the Role of Economic Policy

The important part played by factor prices in causing the significant disparities in employment trends in industrial countries during the period under examination has been illustrated in the foregoing chapters. Factor prices reflect a multitude of economic and social influences that are closely interwoven. An important issue in this connection is the extent to which government economic and social policy, the socio-economic framework so formed and the ensuing behaviour of businesses and workers have exerted such distinct influences that they can be seen as contributing to differences in employment trends.

There is no need here to focus on the growth-efficiency of the respective conditions in the various countries, since the differences in growth rates between countries were small during the period under examination. More important is the question whether economic policy and the socio-economic framework had other direct or indirect effects on the supply of jobs and labour. The correlation between these variables in turn makes it difficult to establish causal relationships.

The long-term nature of the differences in employment trends - they date back to the sixties - suggest that short-term differences in the macroeconomic policies pursued in individual countries are of only minor importance for the purposes of this comparison. However, if these policies reflect differences in longer-term orientations, it must be conceded that they may have lasting effects on employment by influencing the expectations and decisions of employers and employees. Discretionary and "structural" measures only began to be more closely linked when supply-side policies came to prominence in a growing number of industrial countries from the early eighties onwards.

The many and varied effects that socio-economic conditions in the broad sense have on the employment performance of the countries examined here cannot be fully portrayed because of the difficulty of verification, in many cases due to a lack of data. The relationships have therefore been analyzed for major countries for which information is available; once again, a comparison between the Federal Republic of Germany and the USA forms the centrepiece.

4.2   The Influence of Macroeconomic Policies on Employment

4.2.1   Demand Management Predominant until the End of the Seventies

Growth and employment have been promoted in western industrial countries primarily by means of supply-side policies for some years now. Efforts to bring about a permanent improvement in the conditions for growth are aimed predominantly at modifying the underlying factors influencing companies' investment decisions over the longer term. In particular, action to reverse several decades of expansion in government activities is seen as a decisive step towards restoring greater performance incentives, achieving faster growth and solving the employment problem.[1] The most striking changes in economic policy stance were those following the change of government in the United Kingdom in 1979 and in the USA in 1981. In the Federal Republic of Germany the shift towards an improving of supply-side conditions came about with the change of government in the autumn of 1982. In France, where the socialist government had initially attempted to boost economic activity by stimulating demand, measures

---

1   Cf. Günter GROSSER, Günter WEINERT, Wirtschaftspolitische Strategien in wichtigen Industrieländern, in: Hamburger Jahrbuch für Wirtschafts- und Gesellschaftspolitik, Vol. 28 (1983), p. 159.

to improve supply-side conditions have also begun increasingly to determine economic policy since the adoption of a stabilization programme in 1983.

Up to the turning points mentioned above, and hence for the greater part of the decade under examination here, economic policy in the industrial countries was dominated by a Keynesian preoccupation with demand. Above all the rapid worldwide economic growth in the sixties, which had been interrupted by only relatively mild downturns, had strengthened the conviction that the economic cycle could be managed. The good employment performance of most countries during that period led governments to accept more or less explicit responsibility for maintaining a high level of employment. The notion of the state fine-tuning the course of economic activity was all the more seductive as the interventionism that was its inevitable accompaniment left scope for differing conceptions of the interplay between the market und the state and of the role of individual policy instruments. Underlying all this was often the notion derived for the Phillips curve that higher employment could be achieved by tolerating a faster rise in prices.

Although doubts about the success of demand management were voiced at an early stage, stop-and-go continued to dominate economic policy throughout the seventies in the USA as much as in the other industrial countries. Economic events in the middle of the decade surrounding the first oil price rise were typical. Even before oil prices rocketed, an acceleration in inflation caused the USA to adopt rigorous stabilization measures, ranging from a restrictive monetary and fiscal policy to such interventions as a temporary price freeze. The severe recession in 1974 and the rapid increase in unemployment led to another change of course in early 1975, even though inflation had slowed down only slightly. Taxes were cut, and monetary restrictions were at least eased. Economic policy in Japan and western Europe was equally erratic. Far-reaching stabilization measures, introduced either before the oil crisis - as in Germany - or in its aftermath, were followed in many industrialized countries in 1975 by packages of measures to overcome the fall in output. However, since many countries had made little progress in stemming earlier adverse developments and external constraints rapidly re-emerged, restrictions of a predominantly monetary nature were re-imposed in 1976, particularly in France, Italy and the United Kingdom.

Hence, during the critical period of accelerating inflation and steeply increasing oil prices economic policy everywhere was characterized by a rapid alternation of stop and go; the neglect of price stabilization in favour of a shortlived boost to employment was often masked by cosmetic remedies, such as prices and income controls. This was true of the USA no less than of most other industrial countries. The massive use of demand stimulation appears to have been encouraged by the fact that the scale of structural adjustment on the supply side, caused in particular by the rise in oil prices, was universally underestimated at first. The conditions for growth had worsened in most countries except the USA to such an extent that the rise in output in subsequent years remained far below the rates achieved before the 1974-75 recession, and unemployment in western Europe remained stubbornly high. Nevertheless, co-ordinated action to stimulate demand was taken yet again in 1978. But when economic growth again evaporated worldwide in the wake of the second oil price rise, the strategy of massive demand stimulus adopted in 1974-75 was not repeated, except for the 1981-82 interlude in France. After the disappointments of the seventies, economic policymakers instead recognized that lasting progress towards stabilization and adjustment was a prerequisite for an improvement in the conditions for growth.

Agreement on the fundamental causal relationships in the various countries did not produce identical policies, however. Whereas the USA attempted to strengthen the dynamism of the private sector by a massive tax reduction, particularly the Federal Republic of Germany, the United Kingdom and Japan tried to ease the burden on the capital market, reduce real interest rates and create con-

Employment Trends

fidence in a permanent improvement in growth conditions by initially reducing the public sector deficit. The difference in approach can probably be explained mainly by the fact that the USA, unlike the other countries, did not have a budget deficit of any note in the early eighties; it was also assumed that any increase in the deficit as a result of the tax cut would be only temporary.

If changes in public sector borrowing requirements are taken as a measure of the stimuli generated by government budgets, it can be seen that there were occasionally considerable differences between countries, but not over the period as a whole. In 1983 the deficits of the USA, Japan, the Federal Republic of Germany and France amounted to between 2 1/2 and 4 % of gross domestic product, corresponding to an expansionary stimulus of between 3 and 4 % compared with 1973. The stimulus was somewhat larger in Italy - where the deficit was considerably higher - but appreciably lower in the United Kingdom (see Table 24).[1]

If the "discretionary" changes estimated by the OECD are taken into consideration to characterize fiscal policy in the various countries, it emerges that in Japan, the United Kingdom and the Federal Republic of Germany there was a clear swing from predominantly deficit-increasing measures between 1973 and 1978 to deficit-reducing measures from 1979 to 1983, whereas there was a slight shift in the opposite direction in the USA - owing to the tax cuts from 1981 onwards - and in Italy. The significance of calculations of this kind is limited, however, not least because estimation of the potential path presents problems, especially after supply-side shocks such as occured in the seventies.

---

[1] Basing the calculations on the periods 1971-73 and 1982-84 to reduce the effect of chance factors affects the results only marginally.

Table 24

PUBLIC SECTOR BUDGET BALANCES, 1973-83

- Surplus or deficit (-) as a percentage of nominal GDP at market prices -

	1973	1974	1975	1976	1977	1978	1979	1980	1981	1982	1983
USA	0.5	-0.2	-4.2	-2.1	-0.9	0.0	0.6	-1.2	-0.9	-3.8	-4.1
Japan[a]	0.5	0.4	-2.6	-3.8	-3.8	-5.5	-4.8	-4.5	-4.0	-3.6	-3.5
Federal Republic of Germany	1.2	-1.3	-5.7	-3.4	-2.4	-2.5	-2.6	-2.9	-3.7	-3.3	-2.5
France	0.9	0.6	-2.2	-0.5	-0.8	-1.9	-0.7	-0.2	-1.8	-2.7	-3.1
United Kingdom	-2.7	-3.8	-4.6	-4.9	-3.2	-4.2	-3.5	-3.5	-2.8	-2.3	-3.7
Italy	-8.5	-8.1	-11.7	-9.0	-8.0	-9.7	-9.5	-8.0	-11.9	-12.6	-12.4

a) As a percentage of gross national product.

Source: Robert W.P. PRICE, Jean-Claude CHOURAQUI, Public Sector Deficits: Problems and Policy Implications, in: OECD, Occasional Studies, Paris 1983, p. 15; OECD, Economic Outlook, No. 38, Paris 1985, p. 3.

Employment Trends

However, it does not appear that there were major differences in fiscal stimuli in the industrial countries over the period as a whole, despite occasional large disparities in the behaviour of public sector borrowing requirements. Hence, the conditions influencing their employment performance should not have differed markedly on this score, although a distinction should be made as against influences that may stem from differences in the behaviour of the state's share of national product, even with similar changes in budget deficits.

Rapid switches of policy typified monetary policy as well as fiscal policy in the mid-seventies. The major countries increased their discount rates in quick succession in 1973 and reduced them substantially in 1975; the rapid expansion in the money supply that had been under way for several years slowed down drastically almost everywhere in 1973-74 but accelerated again the following year. Attempts to manage the money supply were beginning to emerge during that period, with the Federal Republic of Germany and the USA announcing money supply targets for the first time for 1975, and some countries took occasional steps to curb monetary expansion for external reasons, but the money supply grew very rapidly thereafter, especially in 1977 and 1978. The low level of interest rates - in real terms they were actually negative on short-term funds - indicated that the overall stance of monetary policy was relatively easy. However, when curbing inflation came increasingly to be regarded as a precondition for improving growth prospects in the wake of the second oil crisis, all the industrialized countries reverted to monetary restraint after 1979. The expansion in the money supply slowed down sharply almost everywhere and real interest rates rose extremely steeply. Even in the USA, where fiscal policy was very expansionary owing to the large tax reductions, the Federal Reserve Board did not ease the monetary restrictions until substantial progress towards stabilization had been made.

The industrialized countries' monetary policies were by no means always on parallel courses over the short term, especially when particular countries wanted to avoid or contain exchange rate movements triggered by external pressures. Nonetheless, monetary inter-dependence via the international financial markets clearly brought about a large measure of synchronization in monetary policy changes during the period under review.

Nevertheless, throughout the period under review there were con-siderable differences in the trend rate of money supply growth, matched to a high degree by inflation differentials. This does not mean, however, that monetary policy in individual industrial countries had an autonomous influence on real wage trends over the period as a whole and hence contributed to the differences in employment per-formance, for such a sluggish adjustment to inflation by economic agents, that monetary policy could have exploited, is unlikely to have lasted so long.

4.2.2 Labour Market Policy and Employment

In addition to monetary and fiscal policy, all the countries also had labour market instruments that could be used if necessary to reduce unemployment directly.

The level of employment had been very high in most western in-dustrialized countries during the sixties, so that labour market policy had played no significant role, but the rapid increase in unemploy-ment during the worldwide recession of 1974-75 led to a substantial expansion of measures for conserving and creating jobs. Since the deterioration in the labour market was initially diagnosed as cyclical and hence temporary, labour market policy in all the industrial countries was designed to be predominantly countercyclical. The short-term nature of the measures was particularly evident in the support given to short-time working to prevent job losses.

It was temporary employment in the state and non-profit sector that was promoted the most. In the USA the number of persons employed in this way rose from 56,000 at the end of 1974 to 350,000 at the end

178   **Employment Trends**

of 1976 and had reached 730,000 by the beginning of 1978 (0.7 % of the labour force);[1] hence the number continued to increase even when overall employment was rising strongly again. In the Federal Republic of Germany the number of workers benefiting from the job creation measures rose from 3,200 in 1974 to 51,000 in 1978, around 0.2 % of the labour force. This kind of employment promotion was on a much smaller scale in the United Kingdom and France. The impact of the measures on the labour market cannot, however, be gauged from the number of persons employed in this way, since some of the jobs would have been created in any case. This was particularly noticeable in the USA, where it appears that a considerable number of regular jobs were replaced by programme jobs, especially in local government; it has been estimated that around 35 % of the persons employed under the scheme between 1974 and 1976 fall into this category.[2] It was mainly this problem of substitution that led President Carter to impose quite severe restrictions in 1978. Interest in the programme therefore waned, and it was finally abolished shortly after the inauguration of President Reagan.

Other measures were designed to create or save jobs in industry. The instrument in this case was wage subsidies in various forms to reduce labour costs. They were introduced in the Federal Republic of Germany in 1974-75, although they were available only in certain regions and for particular groups of unemployed. In 1977 the United Kingdom introduced wage subsidies payable for a maximum of 26 months to smaller companies, again initially only in certain regions; by the end of 1979 the wages of around 170,000 workers were being subsidized. The net employment effect was put at about one-quarter of the number of subsidized jobs in both the Federal Republic of Germany and the United Kingdom.[3] Still lower net employment effects

---

1 Cf. Gert BRUCHE, Bernard CASEY, Arbeitsmarktpolitik unter Stagflationsbedingungen, in: Mitteilungen aus der Arbeitsmarkt- und Berufsforschung, No. 3/1982, p. 237.

2 Ibid., p. 240.

3 Ibid., p. 238.

were achieved in France under the 1975 and 1977 "employment pacts", which provided for a 50 % reduction in employers' social security contributions if they took on additional young people, women and long-term unemployed. A further variant of this were the national "solidarity" arrangements in 1981, whereby employers' social security contributions were waived for additional staff engaged in connection with a reduction in the working week from 37 to 36 hours. No such conditions were imposed in Italy, where the state took over part of employers' social security contributions on several occasions, such as in the spring of 1979, in order to dampen the rise in labour costs. In Japan employers were paid premiums if they hired persons from problem groups in the working population, although the amounts offered were too small to make a discernible impact on labour costs.[1]

Marginal wage subsidies were used as an employment promotion instrument in the USA as well. The "New Jobs Tax Credit Program" in 1977 and 1978 even included a very comprehensive variant of this instrument; firms that increased their workforce by more than 2 % over the level of the preceding year received a lump-sum tax rebate equal to between 20 and 25 % of the average annual wage for every additional worker they hired. In 1977 firms filed claims for 795,000 man-years. However, a large proportion of the jobs would probably have been created in any case, and the net employment effect is put at only 10 %.[2] The programme that replaced it, the "Targeted Jobs Tax Credit Program", provided for tax rebates declining over a two-year period and only in respect of jobs created for young people, handicapped persons and social security recipients. It was used especially by branches of activity with relatively low pay, but here again many of the new jobs would have been created irrespective of the scheme.

1 Cf. Angelika ERNST, Japans unvollkommene Vollbeschäftigung, Hamburg 1980, p. 307.

2 Gert BRUCHE, Bernard CASEY, op. cit., p. 238.

In some cases labour market objectives were linked with regional and structural policy objectives. This "grey area" included schemes such as Germany's special programme to support the construction industry in areas of above-average unemployment in 1974 and the $ 4 billion increase in US government expenditure on public construction in 1977, which was to be distributed in accordance with the regional pattern of unemployment. Japan had several schemes under which firms jeopardized by structural change or creating additional jobs in rural areas could obtain wage subsidies. In addition, from 1978 onwards emphasis was placed on labour market criteria in designating problem regions for the purposes of managing structural economic change.[1]

In the second half of the seventies it gradually became clear that unemployment was structural, and labour market policy changed accordingly in many industrialized countries. In France and the United Kingdom, in particular, the emphasis shifted away from short-term employment promotion; in view of rising youth unemployment, attention focussed instead on improving occupational qualifications, a neglected area for a long time in these two countries. For example, in the United Kingdom the number of persons benefiting from work creation schemes aimed at young people and the older unemployed fell from 43,000 in 1979 to 11,000 in 1980, while the number partici-pating in youth training programmes increased over the same period from 25,000 to 150,000; by 1981 it had risen to 360,000.[2] In the Federal Republic of Germany, too, efforts to improve the employment prospects of the unemployed by improving their occupational qualifi-cations were intensified. Finally, labour market policy in the USA concentrated on training for marginal groups, young people, "poor" sections of the community and eventually those affected by mass dismissals. The funds provided under the Comprehensive Employment

---

1 Cf. Angelika ERNST, Japans unvollkommene Vollbeschäftigung, op. cit., p. 300 ff.

2 Cf. Gert BRUCHE, Bernard CASEY, op. cit., p. 239; OECD, Positive Adjustment Policies, Paris 1982, p. 88.

and Training Act - $ 4 billion, only half the sum made available in 1980 - were used from 1983 onwards exclusively to finance measures to promote training and job-finding.

The overall impact of labour market policy[1] on employment in individual countries can hardly be quantified reliably. Substitution effects and the inclusion of jobs that would have been created anyway mean that the net gain was certainly less than expenditure on the measures might suggest; however, estimates of the effect of the measures differ widely. But since the USA and the EC countries provided a broadly similar level of support it cannot be assumed that the differences in employment performance were due in any significant degree to differences in labour market policy. In recent years there has been a tendency in the USA to curtail employment programmes as a matter of principle, whereas in the EC countries they have continued to expand, though with the accent shifting towards training.

4.3 The Socio-Economic Framework

The legal conditions laid down by the government for the conduct of economic activity constitute what we call the "socio-economic framework". In recent years, discussion of the employment problem has once again focussed attention on issues of the socio-economic order in western industrialized countries, after the period of demand management had ended with slow growth and high unemployment. Our concern here is whether this framework influenced the "employment efficiency" of economic growth.

The countries examined here have a dual economic order consisting of a state sector and a competitive sector, in which prices - and hence resource allocation - are determined in principle by the market.

---

1 Measures aimed at reducing the supply of labour have not been taken into account here.

The state affects the economic process by a variety of means, ranging from indirect influence, such as the regulation of activities in the private sector, to the direct redistribution of income and the appropriation of real resources; there are considerable differences between countries in the nature and scale of state involvement.

Trade unions and employers' associations have a special place in the economic and social order, since they generally have a dominant influence over the negotiation of pay and working conditions. The state, for its part, is concerned with maintaining order in the dense network of economic, social and political interests active in the labour market, though the methods it uses differ from country to country.

4.3.1   Differences in the Size of the Public Sector

There is no universal yardstick by which to assess the position of the state in a particular economy. The size of the public sector, however, measured in terms of total government expenditure as a percentage of gross domestic product, may be taken as an indication of the extent to which market forces are overlaid by governmental decision-making. Throughout the period under examination the relative size of the public sector was far lower in Japan and the USA than the average for the EC countries; in 1983 it stood at 35 and 38 % respectively in those two countries, as against an average of 51 % for the EC countries.[1] On the assumption that competition is at least significantly keener in the non-state sector than it is in the public sector, the figures suggest that free market criteria play a different role in the process of macroeconomic coordination that determines income distribution and resource allocation.

Against this background, the stronger expansion in employment in both the USA and Japan by comparison with most EC countries may

[1] Cf. OECD, Economic Outlook, Historical Statistics, 1960-1983, p. 64.

be linked with the smaller size of the public sector, which reflects the lighter constraints imposed on market forces by the state. Such a supposition is not confirmed, however, if changes in the relative size of the public sector over the period under examination are compared. In the case of Japan, the public sector rose from 22 % in 1973 to 35 % in 1983, a particularly unfavourable development under the hypothesis stated above. There were also marked inconsistencies among the EC countries. The public sector increased the most in Italy, from 38 % to 57 %. In the United Kingdom and the Federal Republic of Germany it rose by "only" 7 percentage points to 47 % and 49 % respectively. Despite this, Italy's employment performance was much better than that of the other EC countries. It is an open question how much this was due to the "natural vitality" of the Italian economy or to a continued sustainment of output over this period by the steady expansion in Italy's public sector, despite the fact that at the same time the conditions for growth were steadily deteriorating as the necessary adjustment measures were postponed and inflation remained rapid. From these examples it is clear that differences in the size or rate of growth of the public sector, which are themselves probably due to a variety of causes, can hardly explain the effect that a varying dosage of free market forces has on employment trends.

4.3.2 Differences in the Degree of Competition

The extent to which economies diverge from the model of perfect competition as a result of direct and indirect state intervention and restraints on competition fostered or tolerated by government can be illustrated in more concrete terms. Here too, the nature and strength of these influences differ widely from one country to another, so that there are marked differences in the competitive systems achieved. The principles of competition law concerning market behaviour or market structures restricting or jeopardizing competition are very similar everywhere, but there are differences in the severity of the legislation and the way in which it is implemented. This often reflects general differences in the legal systems of the various countries.

184   **Employment Trends**

Court rulings may considerably narrow the differences but may also accentuate them, so that reality may differ significantly from the codified order. The role of differences in the intensity of competition cannot be examined here, however, since there is no suitable yardstick for measuring the degree of competition in individual economies.

In these circumstances, only analysis of government intervention in individual markets can throw light on the question. The type of government intervention involved here is primarily state regulation in areas where market mechanisms are thought to be deficient, such as those involving a natural monopoly, the danger of cut-throat competition or the supply of public goods. With the importance of services steadily growing, attention has focussed increasingly on regulation of this sector as an explanation for employment trends.

Despite broad consensus on fundamentals, there are differences between countries as regards the aims, methods and instruments of regulation, reflecting different shades of economic and social ideology, especially on the relative roles of the state and the market. The tendency towards state regulation was less pronounced in the USA than in the western European countries, but there were also considerable differences among the latter. Comparing other countries with Japan is very difficult; the Japanese principle of "administrative guidance" based on close co-operation between the state and business in effect leads to a form of regulation that is less obvious than elsewhere.[1]

---

1 On the relationship between politics and business in Japan, see Willy KRAUS, Japan, Wirtschaftspolitik jenseits von Markt und Plan, in: D. CASSEL (ed.), Wirtschaftspolitik im Systemvergleich, Munich 1984, pp. 348 ff.; Gerhard LUNTKE, Zusammenhänge zwischen Industrie und Administration in Japan, in: Fortschrittliche Betriebsführung und Industrial Engineering, No. 6/1984, pp. 319 ff. On administrative guidance, Luntke writes that without invoking sovereign powers or the law, an administrative body persuades an economic agent to adopt a particular line of conduct voluntarily (p. 321).

The areas subject to state regulation are typically public utilities, transport, telecommunications, banking and insurance. In western Europe but not in the USA, they also include mining, production of basic materials and house and apartment rental. If market forces were thought to have failed, western European countries had a strong preference to turn production over to state-owned enterprises, but the tendency in the USA was to make private companies subject to supervision by commissions that operated on the basis of legislation and precedents. The commissions[1] are controlled in turn by the political system, that is to say Congress and the Government. In the western European economies, connections between state-owned enterprises operating in regulated industries and the political sphere are much closer.

Apart from differences in the prevalence of state-owned enterprises - and, in the Federal Republic of Germany, socially-oriented non-profit enterprises - regulation often takes similar forms: restrictions on market entry including authorization requirements for investment leading to an expansion in capacity, volume and price regulations including controls on profits and costs, obligations on monopolies to supply goods or services, and regulations governing quality and conditions of services (banking and insurance). Some specific forms of regulation, such as the Industrial Code and the compulsory closing time in the Federal Republic of Germany, also apply to branches other than those listed above.

The differences in the extent of the regulated sector, the combination of instruments used and the strength of official intervention undoubtedly meant that the degree of "market correction" differed, though it is, similar to the problem of measuring the intensity of competition, almost impossible to quantify the effect adequately. Several studies

1 Such as the Federal Energy Regulatory Commission, the Interstate Commerce Commission, the Federal Communications Commission and the Securities and Exchange Commission.

Employment Trends

relating to the USA have concluded that the American system for overcoming market deficiencies was not successful either, but tended to lead to greater inefficiency owing to accompanying policy deficiencies.[1] Many of the studies looked at the impact of measures to regulate profitability, a form of intervention that is rare in the Federal Republic of Germany. Their conclusions concerning the effects on allocation decisions, however, are open to dispute, so that an international comparison would have little meaning.

Though it is not possible to quantify the employment effects of regulations of this kind directly, certain conclusions can be drawn from developments observed after the removal of restrictions on competition. In the USA in particular, deregulation was a key element in the change in course of economic policy in the late seventies and early eighties. The sectors most affected were oil production and processing as well as transport by road, by rail and by air. The telecommunications, banking and natural gas industries were also deregulated.

The removal of obstacles to competition in the transport field led to marked reductions in charges and a diversification of supplied services. In trucking, where regulations began to be eased in 1977, the number of vehicles deployed by existing carriers and new enterprises increased strongly from 1979 onwards, a period during which economic growth was slowing down. This meant an increase in jobs in this area, although its impact on employment in later years is difficult to quantify since then the recession and the subsequent recovery were dominating influences.[2]

---

1 Cf. Jürgen MÜLLER, Ingo VOGELSANG, Ist eine Effizienzsteigerung der öffentlichen Verwaltung durch Anwendung des Instrumentariums der amerikanischen "Public Utility Regulation" möglich?, in: Ernst HELMSTÄDTER (ed.), Neuere Entwicklungen in den Wirtschaftswissenschaften, Schriften des Vereins für Socialpolitik, Vol. 98 (new series), Berlin 1978, p. 778.

2 Cf. Thomas G. MOORE, Deregulating Ground Transportation, in: Herbert GIERSCH (ed.), New Opportunities for Entrepreneurship, Tübingen 1984, especially pp. 150 and 153.

Another example was the deregulation of aviation on domestic routes in the USA. Between 1977 and 1983 restrictions on fares and market access were removed in stages. After deregulation was enacted in 1978, the number of airline companies increased from 36 to 98 within three years; the new carriers were mainly small operators, as shown by the fact that the number of aircraft flying increased by only 8 %. Employment also rose sharply at first, although staff numbers were reduced again in 1981 and 1982 as a result of the weakness of economic activity and the rise in aviation costs due to the increase in oil prices. Though overlaid by these influences, deregulation clearly led to a diversification of air transport services and a reduction in tariffs; adjustments in staff costs played an important part in this.[1]

There are many indications that the cost reduction and supply improvements in deregulated industries since the end of the seventies set processes in motion that had a fundamentally beneficial effect on employment. The adjustment of factor incomes to changes in relative profitability, though obscured by cyclical fluctuations, tended to create new jobs or save those under threat. However, the macroeconomic effects of deregulation were not identical with the benefits it brought to individual sectors. For example, deregulation of the aviation industry had some adverse substitution effects on other forms of transport. On the other hand, the impact of deregulation on resource allocation, which was undoubtedly linked with more rapid introduction of technical progress over the longer term, tended to enhance the dynamism of the economy as a whole. Nevertheless, the effects of deregulation were small by comparison with the differences in employment performance between the USA and western Europe.

---

1 In some smaller non-unionized companies workers received salaries that were up to two-thirds lower than those paid by the major airlines. At the same time, business concepts were introduced that provided for worker participation in the capital and profits of their companies and for staff's employment in various tasks as required. See Klaus-Werner SCHATZ, Markt über den Wolken, in: Wirtschaftswoche, No. 30, 19.7.1985, p. 55.

Other differences in socio-economic conditions also affected employment performance in the various countries. Particular mention should be made here of foreign trade policy (degree of liberalization or protection),[1] taxation policy (especially concessions such as preferences or privileges) and policy regarding subsidies in the strict sense. In the last-mentioned field too, the predominant effect is to preserve the status quo and to distort resource allocation. There are probably marked differences here between the various economies, but comparison is extremely difficult.[2] This is clearly the reason why no exhaustive studies have been made into the effects of such differing parameters on employment performance.

4.3.3 The Social Security System, Wage Costs and Flexibility

Restrictions on competition resulting from state regulation of business activity are confined to a few areas of the economy, albeit major ones, but welfare provisions apply to all fields of activity. The remarks made above with regard to the socio-economic framework also apply to the social field in a strict sense: the objectives, approaches and instruments are broadly of the same kind in industrial countries, but there are appreciable differences in the actual shape of the social order and especially in the degree of state intervention, owing chiefly to the different weights attached to the principles of solidarity and "subsidiarity"[3]. The associated differences in the scale of social

---

1 The OECD believes that the employment effects of protectionist measures are very small compared with the effects of changes in macroeconomic conditions. See Costs and Benefits of Protection, in: OECD Observer, May 1985, p. 20.

2 See for example Frank STILLE, Subventionen in den USA, in: DEUTSCHES INSTITUT FÜR WIRTSCHAFTSFORSCHUNG, Vierteljahreshefte zur Wirtschaftsforschung, H. 1/1985, pp. 5-20. Stille concludes that subsidies and tax concessions seem to play a more significant role in the USA than in the Federal Republic of Germany.

3 "Subsidiarity" means that the individual and his family, respectively, bear responsibilities to the limit of their ability, before responsibility passes to society.

security transfers and government consumption - including benefits in kind provided by statutory health insurance schemes - account for a large part of the differences in the size of the public sector. In 1973 social security benefits accounted for 5 % of GDP in Japan, 9 % in the USA and an average of 14 % in the EC. By 1983 the figures for Japan and the USA had risen to around 12 % and that for the EC to 19 %.[1] As stated in discussing the size of the public sector, no hard and fast conclusions regarding employment performance can be drawn from these differences, given that economic growth in the countries concerned was approximately the same.

The link is clearer from the effect that the shape of the social order has on the relative price of labour and on other conditions relevant to the establishment and dissolution of employment contracts. Social expenditure in the form of non-wage labour costs are an important and widely varying element in the costs incurred by firms when they employ workers.[2] However, the weight of the individual items is very difficult to estimate. Since firms calculate on the basis of the total cost of the labour input, the level of contracutally agreed direct pay is partly determined by the level of non-wage labour costs.[3] The extent to which this occurs in turn depends on the general conditions affecting wage determination.

The picture is even more complicated when viewed in macroeconomic terms. For example, a country in which a relatively small proportion of social security benefits is paid by employers may have relatively low labour costs, despite the direct wage being relatively high; other things being equal, however, the general level of taxation or employees' contributions must be correspondingly higher. Since the range of possibilities here is very broad, it is almost impossible to

1   Cf. OECD, Economic Outlook, Historical Statistics 1960-1983, p. 63.
2   See Chapter 3, section 2.1.
3   See OECD, The Role of the Public Sector, OECD Economic Studies, No. 4, Paris 1985, pp. 172 ff.

attribute employment effects to the financing arrangements of the social security system.[1]

The configuration of the system of social security contributions and benefits can have an appreciable effect on employment and on labour flexibility, even leaving aside the incentives it may create to transfer activities to the shadow economy. Of particular importance here are differences in unemployment insurance, especially between the USA and the western European economies. There is no uniform arrangement in the USA, since unemployment insurance is a matter for the individual state, but the available data do show that unemployment contributions and benefits are much lower than in western Europe.

According to an international comparison relating to 1979,[2] in other words more or less in the middle of the period under examination, the rate of unemployment insurance contribution in the USA, which is borne solely by the employer in that country, was 3.4 %, similar to the rate in France (3.6 %) and in the Federal Republic of Germany (3.2 %) but much higher than in the United Kingdom (1.6 %) and Italy (1.3 %); however, the maximum contribution was clearly lower in the USA than in most European countries. On the other hand unemployment benefits, differing substantially from one state to another, were noticeably lower than in western Europe and the period of benefit was much shorter. Depending on the length of the preceding period of employment, benefits were paid for up to 39 weeks in the USA, whereas the maximum period was a year or longer - depending on age - in France, up to a year in the Federal

---

1 The effect of the burden of tax and social insurance contributions on employees' willingness to work poses a special problem. In as far as social security contributions are concerned, the extent to which the individual can perceive the link between contributions and entitlement to state benefits is the deciding factor. Here there are undoubtedly considerable differences, determined mainly by the form the social system actually takes.

2 Cf. Jürgen B. DONGES, Dean SPINANGER, Interventions in Labour Markets, Kiel 1983, p. 19.

Republic of Germany and Italy and up to 312 days in the United Kingdom.

The relatively low income ceiling for unemployment contributions in the USA tends to raise the cost of employing low-paid, poorly qualified workers in relation to higher salary earners; contribution and benefit ceilings are much higher in western Europe. The low ceiling means that contributions take on the character of fixed costs per employee.[1] In itself, this has the short-term effect that American firms seek to adjust the volume of labour by dismissing or laying off workers rather than by reducing working hours, particularly as the state provides no financial support for short-time working.

Since unemployment benefits in the USA are relatively small and short-lived and welfare benefits are also low, unemployed workers are under particularly strong pressure to look for a job and to accept employment that does not necessarily accord with their preferences as regards location or quality of work. This increases the flexibility of the labour supply and tends to dampen wage inflation.

A comparison of the possible employment effects of unemployment insurance systems must also encompass any arrangements for partial unemployment in the form of short-time working. In the Federal Republic of Germany, France and Italy, for example, firms are "dissuaded" from dismissing staff in the event of temporary cuts in production, in that the state compensates workers if working hours in the firm are reduced generally.[2] This does not obviate long-term adjustment of employment but it does at least reduce short-term job

---

1 Cf. R.A. HART, Unemployment Insurance and the Firm's Employment Strategy: A European and United States Comparison, in: Kyklos, Vol. 35 (1982), p. 657.

2 Cf. OECD, Positive Adjustment in Manpower and Social Policies, op. cit., Paris 1984, p. 65. In the United Kingdom there is less incentive to opt for short-time working rather than dismissals. Cf. OECD, Lay-offs and Short-time Working, Paris 1983, pp. 15 f.

losses. In the Federal Republic of Germany, for instance, an annual average of 675,000 persons were on short time in 1983. The lack of corresponding arrangements in the USA undoubtedly contributes to the fact that a large part of unemployment in that country is due to temporary layoffs.[1]

Labour costs comprise not only wage costs but also one-off payments to which employees in many countries are entitled in the event of dismissal. Many statutory or contractual arrangements that limit the scope for adjusting employment to changing requirements and for laying down working hours or determining the organization of work also affect costs.[2] The resulting loss of flexibility impairs labour productivity.

Since there are also substantial differences between the countries' legal arrangements governing job contracts, it is reasonable to suppose that they significantly affect their employment performance. Here again, Japan constitutes a special case. The principle of life-long employment practiced in a large part of the Japanese economy, and which in other countries is to be found only in the public administration, reduces the flexibility with which firms can adjust the size of their workforce, but as a quid pro quo it demands very high flexibility on the part of workers as regards deployment.[3] It

1 Between 1966 and 1971 about half of the unemployment due to the loss of a job was due to this factor. Cf. Martin S. FELDSTEIN, The Importance of Temporary Layoffs: An Empirical Analysis, in: Brookings Papers on Economic Activity, No. 3/1975, p. 729.

2 In the Federal Republic of Germany more than 80 % of 800 firms surveyed recently by the Arbeitsgemeinschaft selbständiger Unternehmer cited legal impediments to the dismissal of staff as the greatest obstacle to recruitment, 11 % the continued payment of wages during illness and 9 % the "social plan" mechanism. A liberalization of labour legislation was considered to be a more effective way to reduce unemployment than a curb on labour costs. See 'Die Tarifhoheit sollte künftig mit den Betriebsräten geteilt werden', in: Handelsblatt, 17.10.1985, p. 7.

3 Cf. Angelika ERNST, Japans unvollkommene Vollbeschäftigung, op. cit., p. 27.

was probably thanks partly to the principle of lifelong employment that the slowdown in economic growth in Japan from the mid-seventies translated to such a large extent into a slowdown in productivity growth and less into a slackening of the rise in employment.

In the western European economies and the USA, on principle, employees can generally be dismissed. However, whereas in the USA employment has remained primarily a matter for "contractual" agreements, in western Europe employment law has given workers ever greater job security and progressively limited employers' rights.

In the USA a contract of employment can be terminated by either side on the same terms. Around 70 % of contracts fall into the employment-at-will category, which permits the employer to end the arrangement as he likes even for non-economic causes. Only in recent years the courts have restricted the employment-at-will doctrine.[1] In around 20 states dismissals are void if they result from a refusal to commit an illegal act, from performing an important public duty or from exercise of a statutory right or privilege. In 13 states dismissal is possible only on "just grounds" if the employee's conduct and work record can be shown to have been satisfactory.

Overall, employers in the USA retained wide powers in personnel matters. Agreements between trade unions and employers enabling a dismissed worker to call in an assessor if the grounds for dismissal relate to the personality of the employee cover only about one-fith of the labour force. In more than half of the cases reviewed the reasons for dismissal were held to be insufficient and the worker was reinstated. Only three states have passed legislation requiring prior notification of factory closures and compensation for the workers affected.[2]

---

1 Cf. Jack STIEBER, Most U.S. workers still may be fired under the employment-at-will doctrine, in: Monthly Labor Review, Vol. 107, No. 5/1984, pp. 34 f.

2 Cf. Beyond Unions, in: Business Week, 8.7.1985, p. 47.

Although the courts have strengthened the position of employees vis-à-vis their employers, personnel decisions in the USA are still far less hampered by social regulations than in western Europe. The differences become clear if one compares the situation in the USA with the provisions obtaining in the Federal Republic of Germany, which does not appear to be in the vanguard in Europe. In Germany staff can be dismissed for a variety of reasons that may or may not be related to their plant. However, if more than five workers are employed in the plant in question a comprehensive assessment of interests must be made; dismissal must be "socially justified". This condition is met only if dismissal does not breach an agreement with the works council, if the employee cannot be transferred to another post within the works and if labour representatives do not oppose dismissal.[1] Court rulings have extended the social aspect beyond the works level to the private sphere. In one form or another, all western European economies have similar regulations that give employees much greater protection against dismissal than in the USA. The obstacles to dismissal in France and Italy seem to have been even greater than in Germany, owing partly to political pressure on firms; this is also suggested by the fact that employment changes were less marked for a good part of the period of weak growth in the early eighties.

It is not just legal hurdles that make dismissals much more difficult in western Europe than in the USA - it is also often much more costly to fire workers, since the law or previous court judgements require employers to pay compensation. In the Federal Republic of Germany, where compensation is mandatory if dismissal is not socially justified, severance payments are now becoming increasingly common. Depending on age and length of service, it can amount to up to 18 months' salary.

---

1 Employees' rights of participation in social and business decisions within the firms that employ them go much further in western Europe than in the USA, thus reflecting the differences in economic and social orders. The attempt to arrive at a broad consensus necessarily entails restricting business flexibility.

In addition to individual compensation of this kind, a number of western European countries also operate a "social plan" mechanism; the only comparable arrangements in the USA are the compensation schemes established in three states, as mentioned above. If asked to do so by the works council, German firms with more than 20 employees must draw up a "social plan" providing for compensation for workers who lose their jobs as a result of plant reorganisation or closure. While arrangements of this kind often do delay dismissals and hence tend to sustain formal employment for a time, they raise the threshold for new recruitment by comparison with the USA on account of the costs involved, which are difficult to predict and are usually incurred when economic activity is slack.

Overall, the different accents of the social orders in important industrialized countries - liberal in the USA, social in western Europe, paternalistic in Japan - translate into wide differences in the principles for entering into and terminating job contracts. In the USA there has been a noticeable tendency to place greater emphasis on social aspects in recent years, but this has not yet narrowed the gap appreciably. The labour costs involved - even if they may only be contingent liabilities - are still higher in western Europe and there is less scope for adjusting employment to production requirements, which ultimately gives rise to costs. The increase in companies' costs and risks has certainly induced the substitution of capital for labour in western Europe. To that extent, the attempt to provide better social security for the individual worker has ultimately reduced the opportunities for increasing employment in the economy as a whole.

4.3.4 Labour Markets and Wage Formation

Differing wage trends, as measured by the real wage gap, obviously go a long way towards explaining the differences in employment performance between the USA and the EC countries.[1] However, inasmuch as the level and behaviour of wages were influenced by the socio-economic framework, it was ultimately the latter that caused the associated employment effects.

Wage behaviour is a key variable for economic policy, not only because of the allocation effects under discussion here but also from the points of view of income distribution and stabilization policy. Priorities in this respect differ between countries, at least over the short term, and some countries are more inclined than others to influence developments by institutional and discretionary means. Changes in domestic policy also affect the intensity and nature of state intervention.

In all the countries under consideration here, wage determination is left essentially to the parties involved, that is to say employers and employees or their representative bodies. Direct state intervention was either temporary or limited in scope. In particular, the setting of minimum wages comes under this heading. Attempts to protect persons whose bargaining position is weak because they are poorly qualified normally raise the cost of employment above the market level and thus tend to reduce their chances of obtaining a job. Minimum wages can generate different employment effects in different countries, depending on the method adopted and the level set.

The most common form is a statutory absolute minimum wage. Such an arrangement exists in the USA, where the minimum wage amounted to 43 % of average hourly pay in manufacturing in 1983. Although exemptions apply to 20 % of the labour force, the employment prospects of young people in particular are impaired since they enter

1 See Chapter 3.

working life with the barest of qualifications, the more so as they have not received the kind of occupational training provided in the Federal Republic of Germany. Most studies on this issue have concluded that minimum wage legislation has significantly prejudiced the employment of such groups in the USA. It is estimated that between 80,000 and 200,000 more teenagers would have found a job in 1979 had it not been for the legislation. On the other hand, studies of various other sections of the labour force have not revealed such strong adverse employment effects of minimum wages.[1]

In France the minimum wage (SMIC) amounted to 48 % of a worker's average monthly earnings in 1981; it also applies to apprentices, young people and handicapped persons at a slightly lower rate. In the seventies between 4 and 5 % of the labour force were paid SMIC rates, a proportion that rose to around 8 % after the substantial increase in minimum wages in July 1981. Econometric studies indicate that here, too, the legislation makes it more difficult for young people to find work, although the impact is slight.[2] It was to reduce effects of this kind that the United Kingdom abolished the minimum wage regulations for young people in 1985.

The above examples therefore show that the employment-reducing effect of setting - what in both cases are relatively low - minimum wages has been limited and has not therefore significantly influenced the overall employment performance; this is particularly evident with respect to differences between the EC countries and the USA.

In the Federal Republic of Germany there is no statutory minimum wage, although it is sometimes said that the wide coverage of wage agreements produces a similar effect owing to the law on collective bargaining, "outsider" clauses and the declaration of collective agree-

---

1 Cf. John P. MARTIN, Effects of the Minimum Wage on the Youth Labour Market in North America and France, in: OECD Economic Outlook, Occasional Studies, June 1983, p. 47.

2 Ibid, p. 59.

Employment Trends

ments as generally binding. The ability to negotiate wages freely when concluding contracts of employment is severely restricted; collective agreements apply to industries employing around 90 % of all workers, compared with estimates of 70 % in the United Kingdom and 50 % in France.[1] The extensive coverage of settlements in Germany effectively fixes the agreed wage structure as the minimum wage for particular ranges of qualifications or types of employment, so that the wage system is much more rigid than in the USA. The same applies to the practice of concluding collective agreements on an industry-wide basis. For example, the wage scale for the metalworking industry applies to branches with very different productivity and profitability. In the USA, by contrast, many wage agreements are concluded with individual firms, so that there is greater scope for wage differentials between firms within the same industry. Firms fighting to survive have even adopted the practice of paying different wages and salaries for the same activities, in that newly recruited workers receive less pay than existing staff, despite doing equivalent work. In the Federal Republic of Germany it is debatable whether a firm belonging to the Employers' Association could pay a non-unionized worker less than a union member, even if no generally binding wage agreement existed and no "outsider" clause applied, or whether such action would violate the constitutional principle of equal treatment.

In a number of countries the high degree of indexation of wages to price movements appears to have had a lasting effect on wage trends. In some cases wage indexation became a cornerstone of the general system of wage determination, even where it was introduced under collective wage agreements. Italy is the prime example of this, although the de facto wage indexation in France had a similar effect. In particular, it made the adjustment of real wages to the reduced scope for domestic income distribution more difficult in both countries

1 Cf. Der Bundesminister für Arbeit und Sozialordnung (ed.), Bundes-
   arbeitsblatt, No. 3/1985, p. 5; Kate BARKER, Andrew BRITTON, Robin
   MAJOR, Macroeconomic Policy in France and Britain, in: National
   Institute Economic Review, No. 4/1984, p. 71.

at the time of the acceleration in inflation caused by the rise in oil prices. Some collective agreements in the United Kingdom and the USA also included similar clauses, although they did not gain such a lasting influence over wage behaviour.

Besides introducing institutional arrangements - such as minimum wage legislation, declaring collective agreements to be generally binding and tolerating and encouraging wage indexation - governments have repeatedly taken discretionary action to influence wage determination, usually to curb pay increases as part of their stabilization efforts. Income policy measures of this kind were introduced both in the USA, where Presidents Nixon and Carter imposed wage freezes and wage guidelines in the seventies, and in major western European economies, such as the United Kingdom in the mid-seventies and Italy and France until quite recently. In some cases governments were even themselves party to negotiations between employers and unions.[1] In the Federal Republic of Germany, by contrast, the government stayed out of pay negotiations even when the battle over income distribution became intense. However, comparing income policy activities of governments with observed differences in wage trends does not reveal any systematic correlation.

The conditions for wage determination are affected particularly strongly by the position of the trade unions within society. Legislation, history and current lines of thinking combine in a way specific to each country. The trade unions' innate pay objectives and their ability to achieve them, which is determined by numerous factors, are well-nigh impossible to separate. The differences in the behaviour of real wages in the USA on the one hand and in western Europe on the other seem to have mirrored at least in part the differences in trade union objectives.[2] One factor could have been that American trade unions identify closely with the existing economic order in

1 Cf. for example OECD, Italy, Paris 1977, p. 37.
2 See Chapter 3, section 2.5.3.

Employment Trends

the USA, whereas in many western European countries, such as the United Kingdom and to a large extent Italy and France, the unions have close ties with political parties that have serious reservations about the existing economic system and the results it produces.

The trade unions' ability to achieve their objectives also differed. This is only inadequately reflected in the statistics on trade union membership. Kendall calculates that between 15 and 25 % of all workers belonged to a trade union in France and Italy in the late sixties, the start of the phase of particularly sharp divergences in wage trends.[1] In the USA and the United Kingdom the degree of unionization was 30 and 40 % respectively, while in the Federal Republic of Germany it stood at 37 %, including civil servants. The low level of unionization in France and Italy was clearly more than offset by the strong concentration of members in three trade unions or trade union confederations organized along political lines and by the particularly high proportion of active members, which was probably a corollary of such concentration.[2]

The trade unions in the USA steadily lost ground during the seventies, with unionization falling to 23 % in 1980 and 19 % in 1984.[3] This was due partly to the structural shift in employment at the expense of more heavily unionized industrial workers and the above-average rate of economic growth in the southern states, where the "psychological and social resistance to worker organization"[4] is

---

1 See Walter KENDALL, Gewerkschaften in Europa, Hamburg 1977, p. 325. In his calculations, Kendall tried to make allowance for the un-reliability of data in some countries.

2 For France, see David MARSDEN, Industrial Democracy and Industrial Control in West Germany, France and Great Britain, Research Paper No. 4, Department of Employment, London, September 1978, p. 63.

3 See Hugo MÜLLER-VOGG, Gewerkschaften am kurzen Hebel, in: Frankfurter Allgemeine Zeitung, 21.9.1985, p. 15.

4 Cf. Carl LANDAUER, Sozial- und Wirtschaftsgeschichte der Vereinigten Staaten von Amerika, Stuttgart 1981, p. 204.

greater than in the North and compulsory union membership as a result of working in "union shops" is generally forbidden. Hence trade union influence further declined, having already been considerably curtailed by the Labor-Management Relations Act of 1947 (the Taft-Hartley Act). In western Europe, similar attempts were made only in the United Kingdom, where the trade unions enjoyed considerable freedom of action. In accordance with shifts in domestic policy, restrictions were introduced in 1971, in particular on compulsory union membership under "closed shop" agreements, but were lifted again in 1974. In the eighties new legislation on industrial disputes - the 1980 and 1982 Employment Acts and the 1984 Trade Union Act - again curbed the trade unions' freedom of action. Towards the end of the period under examination there was a decline in the frequency of strikes in the EC countries as well as in the USA and Japan. This may be seen as an indication that the slowdown in growth in the eighties and the deterioration in the employment situation tended to weaken the bargaining position of the trade unions everywhere.

Overall, there appears to be some connection between the conditions governing wage determination and the observed trend of wage increases. The relatively moderate increase in wage costs in the USA matched the relatively weak position of trade unions there, while the relatively strong, in part politically determined power of trade unions in Italy and France was accompanied by a particularly rapid rise in wages. On the other hand, measured in terms of the real wage gap, wage behaviour in Germany and the United Kingdom over the period as a whole was very similar, despite the fact that the countries' processes of wage determination and - connected with this - strike records, too, were markedly different, mainly on account of differences in trade union organization. Finally, the pronounced widening of the real wage gap in Japan reflected neither particularly strong union power nor wage determination mechanism biased in favour of workers. This reinforces the assumption that the behaviour of the real wage gap in Japan should be viewed against the background of the very low level of wages at the beginning of the period under examination.

Comparing institutional and discretionary conditions for wage formation teaches us little about their impact, since other conditions, including economic policy, differed between the various economies. Deep-rooted differences of opinion between trade unions, employers and governments on the role of market mechanisms, the conditions under which they may operate and thus the assessment of the scope for income distribution seem to have been more important than differences in the formal regulatory framework.

All in all, the employment effects of socio-economic conditions are scarcely quantifiable, given their interaction with other factors, the many interdependent relationships and not least the structural and cyclical developments that have overlaid them. Nevertheless, there are many indications that differences in the socio-economic framework were an important cause of differences in employment behaviour, especially between the USA and the EC countries. For example, developments following the deregulation of certain industries in the USA show that increased competition triggered a dynamic increase in the range of goods or services offered and induced greater elasticity in the use of inputs, thereby increasing employment opportunities. Company flexibility was also less hampered by labour and social legislation than in the EC countries and the willingness of American firms to enagage additional staff therefore tended to be greater. Finally, the lower level of employers' social security contributions in the USA was accompanied by relatively restrained behaviour on the part of the trade unions, favouring a moderate rise in wage costs and maintaining a comparatively strong incentive to increase employment. Hence, differences in the preferred mix between competition and regulation and in the emphasis laid on economic and social factors contributed to differences in employment trends.

Chapter 5

SUMMARY OF FINDINGS AND CONCLUSIONS

The aim of this study was to explain differences in the employment performance of major industrialized countries, an undertaking involving an extremely broad spectrum of facts and relationships. The time and resources available were scarce by comparison with the task, and for that reason some issues could not be fully explored. The paucity of the available information created further difficulties. A number of reasons for differences in employment performance between the USA, Japan and the EC countries could be identified, but some points could not be clarified satisfactorily.

The difficulty of identifying universally valid causes increases considerably as the number of countries in the comparison rises. The more countries involved, the greater the number of special factors obscuring and distorting the theoretically relevant relationships. The problems are compounded by statistical deficiencies. In some areas there are considerable gaps, particularly in the case of Italy, and all too often the comparability of data is seriously impaired by differences of definition, collection and processing. The lower the level of aggregation, the more serious the divergences. Hence in many cases comparisons can only be made at a relatively high level of aggregation or entail disproportionately heavy efforts. Many plausible hypotheses are impossible to verify empirically for lack of adequate statistical material or can only be tested indirectly. This applies especially to such factors as labour market flexibility or the effect of the socio-economic framework and of economic policy measures. These constraints should be borne in mind when assessing the findings of the study.

5.1 Summary of Findings

5.1.1 Diagnosis: Differences in Employment Trends between the USA, Japan and the EC

Unemployment was on a sharply rising trend in the industrialized countries over the last ten years; unemployment rates rose appreciably everywhere. To that extent, there are similarities between the USA, Japan and the EC countries, but on the other hand there are marked differences in employment trends, both in the economy as a whole and at the sectoral level.

The number of persons in employment rose by an average of 1.7 % a year between 1973 and 1983 in the USA and by 0.9 % a year in Japan but declined slightly on average in the EC, although there were also appreciable differences between the major EC countries. In Italy employment continued to rise, but it virtually stagnated in France and fell in the United Kingdom and the Federal Republic of Germany, especially the latter. Over the period in question, Germany recorded the worst employment performance of all the countries examined.

Employment differences were also pronounced at the sectoral level, except in agriculture and forestry, where they were minor. The employment share of industry diminished in all countries; in absolute terms, industrial employment nearly stagnated in the USA and continued to rise slightly in Japan but in most of the major EC countries it decreased distinctly, in Italy slightly. The proportion of employment provided by the services sector (including government) increased in all the countries considered between 1973 and 1983. The number employed in such activities rose sharply everywhere, with the largest increases occurring in the USA and Italy and the smallest in the Federal Republic of Germany.

Detailed analysis of employment trends within the services sector had to be confined to a comparison of developments in the USA and the Federal Republic of Germany for statistical reasons. In both countries the number of wage and salary earners increased in many branches of services, but the extent of the expansion often differed considerably. Fundamental differences also emerged with regard to the importance of the government as a creator of jobs. In Germany more than two-thirds of all new jobs in the services sector were in "science, the arts and advertising" - and mainly in education within that group - in the health services and in public authorities. In the USA, by contrast, these branches accounted for less than one-third.

In many countries the behaviour of employment led to problems in the labour market, but these were aggravated everywhere by developments on the supply side. The working-age population increased everywhere between 1973 and 1983, in some countries more strongly than in others. By far the largest percentage increase was recorded by the USA, where unemployment rose despite the creation of many new jobs. In the Federal Republic of Germany, on the other hand, the labour force grew much more slowly than in the other countries and the increase began later.

The expansion of the labour force had essentially two causes: population growth and changes in working habits. The population of working age increased considerably in all countries as a result of the "baby boom" of the fifties and sixties; there has even been an acceleration in the EC since the mid-seventies. In the USA the participation rate also rose sharply as a result of much increased participation by women; there were also slight increases in Japan and Italy, but the downward trend in the other EC countries was accentuated.

5.1.2 Reasons for Differences in Employment Trends

Since all the economies in question are essentially market-oriented, it can be assumed that the same fundamental employment determinants apply. The reasons for differences in employment performance are therefore to be sought in differences in the importance and/or developments of these determinants in individual countries.

The following factors were examined:

- differences in economic growth and in the structure of growth;

- differences in the behaviour of wages and wage structures;

- differences in the flexibility and efficiency of the labour market, and

- differences in the socio-economic framework and in fundamental conceptions of economic policy.

5.1.2.1 Growth, the Growth Process and Productivity

Measured in terms of developments in real GDP, there were many similiarities in the growth rates recorded by the USA, Japan and the EC countries between 1973 and 1983. Growth slowed down considerably from the rates recorded in the sixties and early seventies and there was little difference between rates in most of the countries. In the USA real GDP increased by an average of 1.9 % a year over the period, barely faster than in the EC, which recorded an annual rate of 1.7 %. As in earlier years, Japan was an exception. Growth slowed down considerably here too, but it was still almost twice as high as in the USA or the EC. Hence the differences in employment performance between the USA and the EC, at least, cannot be explained in terms of differences in the pace of economic growth.

Differences in the structure of growth are sometimes seen as a cause of divergences in employment performance. It is thus postulated that growth is more labour-intensive in countries with a large and/or more rapidly expanding services sector, such as the USA, than in those where services account for a smaller share of the economy and/or are expanding more slowly. Behind this lies the belief that the level of productivity and the rate of productivity growth are generally lower in services than in industry. However, no evidence was found for a distinct "productivity gradient" between industry and services between 1973 and 1983. It was greatest in the USA, but even there the level of productivity of the services sector was only around one quarter lower than in industry. Moreover, average productivity increases in the American services sector were only slightly lower than in industry, while in most of the other countries there were greater differences. Further, economic growth in the services sector was no stronger in the USA than in the EC countries between 1973 and 1983. This all suggests that little importance should be attached to structural factors such as the different relative size of the services sector to explain differences in employment performance, particularly between the USA and the EC countries.

It should be borne in mind, however, that productivity is extremely difficult to measure in the services sector. Calculating output is fraught with difficulty and deflating the results poses further problems. It is also questionable whether the level of productivity can be adequately expressed by the usual measure, that is to say real gross output per person employed. At any event, a comparison of productivity levels is more uncertain than a comparison of changes in productivity over time.

The argument that the increase in employment in the USA was due mainly to a sharp increase in the resident and working-age populations and in female participation rates also relies ultimately on differences in the structure of the growth process, that is to say a disproportionately large increase in private demand for services. There was no evidence to confirm this claim either, for the increase in the consumption of services in the USA was only slightly faster than in Germany and was actually slower than in France and Japan. Here too, problems of definition made comparison difficult.

Since by definition there is a close ex post correlation between growth, productivity and employment, the differences in employment performance were reflected in productivity trends. In the USA, Japan and Italy increases in productivity slowed down more sharply than economic growth, but in most EC countries the reverse was the case. Put another way, production became more labour-intensive in the USA but more capital-intensive in most EC countries despite a pronounced simultaneous increase in the supply of labour.

Ex post identities do not, however, shed any light on how the observed configuration of growth, productivity changes and employment changes came about. They tell us nothing about the nature or course of these processes or about causal relationships. None of the three variables is exogenous, not even productivity growth, which is influenced by a whole series of factors. Analysis of the factors determining productivity changes suggests that the differences in productivity between the USA, Japan and the EC were due largely to the same factors that caused the differences in employment performance.

5.1.2.2 Wage Behaviour and the Structure of Wages

It is not only neo-classical economists who consider that wage behaviour - or more precisely the behaviour of real wages - is of great importance for employment. For that reason particular attention was paid to this aspect. The following hypotheses were examined:

- Wage cost pressure, and hence the threat to the profitability of jobs, differed from one country to another owing to differences in real wage behaviour.

- Differences in real wage behaviour contributed to disparities in relative factor prices. Hence, the extent of capital intensification and capital/labour substitution differed.

- The extent to which wage structures were consistent with employment requirements differed from one country to another.

On the whole, the study confirms the plausibility of the hypotheses.

The wage cost pressure hypothesis was tested using the "real wage gap" concept, which states that wage cost pressure develops if the rise in the overall real wage level exceeds the "employment-neutral"

Employment Trends

productivity growth; this in turn has a negative impact on the profitability of jobs and hence on employment. The "employment-neutral"
productivity growth was calculated by adjusting the measured productivity growth for "substitution-related" productivity increases,
which could be deduced approximately from changes in capital
intensity.

The substitution-related rise in productivity is that part of the
measured productivity growth resulting from a change in the ratio of
factor inputs. It showed distinct differences between countries over
the period from 1973 to 1983; it was lowest in the USA, much higher
in the EC (though differing from one country to another) and highest
in Japan.

Measured in terms of changes in the real wage gap, wage cost
pressure in the USA was slight in the seventies and early eighties,
despite only modest "employment-neutral" productivity growth, since
real wages also rose little. It was much stronger in the EC countries
and Japan, since real wage increases far exceeded the employment-
neutral productivity growth, especially in the first half of the
seventies and more particularly after the first oil crisis. Subsequently, the behaviour of the real wage gap was similar to that in
the USA, but these countries did not manage to correct the adverse
tendencies created in the first half of the seventies; they remained
an impediment to employment.

The differences in real wage behaviour were reflected in changes in
relative factor prices, which can be reproduced only approximately,
however. In the USA the factor price ratio remained virtually unchanged between 1973 and 1983, but in the EC countries and Japan
the cost of labour rose in relation to that of capital. This goes a
long way towards explaining the differences in capital intensification
and in the level of substitution-related productivity increases.

The differences in real wage behaviour raised the question as to their
cause. On the basis of developments in nominal wages and prices, it

was concluded that there was some delay before nominal wages in the USA adjusted to a rise in retail prices induced by monetary or external shocks and that adjustment was less than complete ("nominal wage rigidity"); the impact was therefore also reflected in real wages. In the EC countries, on the other hand, nominal wages reacted relatively quickly to such shocks, at least during the seventies, so that real wages were little affected ("real wage rigidity"). Adjustment was fairly rapid in Japan too, although less so than in the EC countries.

Differences in nominal wage adjustment were due to differences in wage determination, in the nature and duration of collective wage agreements, in the influence of trade unions and in the wage policy. There are many indications that American trade unions, and probably those in Japan as well, took greater account of employment require-ments than did their European counterparts.

The question whether wage structures displayed differences that were relevant to employment was difficult to answer, since no suitable yardstick was available; a wage structure consistent with employment needs could not be determined empirically. However, clues as to a possible need for adjustment of the wage structure could be gleaned from the range and development of wage structures and from changes in domestic and external economic parameters. Relatively rough sectoral wage structures had to be used, however, and in some respects the comparison had to be restricted to the USA and the Federal Republic of Germany owing to the inadequacy of the statistical material available.

Analysis revealed market differences in the spread of wage struc-tures, especially between the Federal Republic of Germany and the other countries. Movement was minor in most countries between 1973 and 1983; only in France and Italy was there a fairly strong tendency towards a reduction of differentials. The virtual stability in the wage structure in Germany is to be assessed differently from that in the USA, where the need for adjustment of the wage structure as a result

212   **Employment Trends**

of changes in domestic and external conditions was less marked than in Germany, at least in the seventies, since American foreign trade contributes relatively less to national product and the US dollar was depreciating in real terms, whereas the Deutsche Mark was appreciating. Differences in the behaviour of the real wage level in the two countries also led to differences in the need for adjustment of the wage structure.

It can only be surmised that the wider wage range in the USA took better account of employment needs than the relatively narrow dispersion of wages in the Federal Republic of Germany. The wider wage differential between industry and services in the USA undoubtedly benefited the creation of new jobs; that is at least the implication of the strong growth in employment in the US services sector.

All things considered, there is therefore much evidence to suggest that the American wage structure was more consistent with employment needs than Germany's. Whether the same is true in relation to the other EC countries cannot be established with sufficient certainty owing to the inadequacy of the statistical material available. A comparison with Japan has little meaning, owing to the peculiarities of the Japanese system of employment and remuneration.

5.1.2.3 Labour Market Flexibility

An efficient labour market that can adequately perform its guidance and co-ordination functions requires a high degree of flexibility. This depends upon a whole range of factors, such as the regional and occupational mobility of labour, the mobility and labour market behaviour of firms and to a large extent also the socio-economic framework and the influence of the government over the labour market.

A international comparison of labour market flexibility must therefore take account of a multitude of factors. There is no all-embracing measure that can encapsulate the situation in all countries equally well, and analysis is further complicated by the fact that indicators of labour market flexibility are few and often are not comparable. Nevertheless, the information available does allow conclusions to be drawn about this aspect of the labour market in the countries in question.

One indication is the degree of regulation and governmental influence; this was significantly less in the USA than in the EC countries. The average duration of unemployment also has an indicative value. Between 1973 and 1983 it was much shorter in the USA than in the EC. However, the figures were also affected by on-the-job training and the American practice of laying off labour temporarily in times of falling sales, which would lead to the introduction of short-time working in Germany. The trend of separations and hirings was slightly upwards in the USA but distinctly downwards in the EC countries; this too suggests considerable differences in labour market flexibility. Since it is relatively easy to fire workers in the USA, the propensity to hire new staff also remained consistently high. In the EC countries, by contrast, the increasing difficulties in dismissing workers and the cost of doing so had a marked dampening effect on recruitment.

The brisk turnover of labour in the USA suggests that inter-firm labour mobility is higher there than in the EC. However, average job tenure increases with age in the USA as well. In the USA businesses also proved more mobile, and the climate for business start-ups, which are extremely important from the point of view of employment, was also more favourable than in the EC countries.

The conclusion to be drawn from these various indicators is that the labour market was much more flexible in the USA than in the EC countries. It proved more efficient at coping with structural adjustment problems and assimilating the large number of new entrants to the labour market.

Employment Trends

As in many other respects, Japan occupies a special position as far as labour market conditions are concerned. The Japanese labour market is much more segmented than those of the other countries. Inter-firm mobility is relatively low, but mobility and flexibility within the firm are extremely high. For Japan, the system has proved appropriate to its employment needs.

5.1.2.4 Economic Policy and the Socio-Economic Framework

High employment is the more or less explicit central aim of economic policy in the industrialized countries. This is especially true of short term economic policy, which was uniformly Keynesian-oriented in all the countries for most of the period from 1973 to 1983. The differences that emerged, particularly towards the end of the period, can hardly explain the poor employment performance and rising unemployment in the EC countries by comparison with the USA at more or less the same rates of growth.

On the other hand, the socio-economic framework, which influences the matching of supply and demand in the goods and factor markets differently in the countries considered, clearly played an important role. A multitude of factors are at work here, and their effects on employment are virtually impossible to quantify individually owing to the many tiers of interaction and the lack of detailed information. Comparisons with Japan are subject to reservations in view of the specific legal and behavioural norms in that country.

Processes set in motion by the deregulation of certain industries in the USA also suggest a positive correlation between competition and employment. The strengthening of competition and the reduction of charges in trucking and aviation led to dynamic growth that created new jobs; the more flexible adjustment of activities and remuneration to changing conditions of profitability in these industries was also a factor. The United States has always shown a lesser tendency to regulate competition in important industries or to restrict it by expanding other governmental activities, and this probably favoured the growth in employment.

Differences in labour and social legislation are more important in this connection, however. They affect labour costs directly and indirectly by preventing businesses from adjusting labour inputs to changing production requirements as flexibly as they would wish. For example, less individual protection of workers in the USA against dismissal and unemployment clearly encourages employers to recruit additional staff, whereas in the EC countries the high direct and indirect costs associated with dismissals make employers less willing to recruit. In Japan, however, the widespread practice of lifetime employment does not impair employers' flexibility, partly because only the core work-force enjoys such protection and partly because the high proportion of profit-related pay transfers a considerable share of the risk to employees.

It is not easy to determine the extent to which differences in the level of social security contributions caused divergences in labour costs over the longer term and hence affected employment indirectly, since this will depend ultimately on whether such contributions are taken into account in setting other components of pay. The position of the trade unions within the labour market structure is important in this respect. There are many indications that labour organizations in the USA and Japan behaved with greater restraint than their counterparts in Western Europe during the period under examination and hence avoided increasing labour costs to the detriment of employment.

The effect of differing socio-economic frameworks on employment trends cannot be adequately portrayed through the impact of a multitude of individual factors; instead it is a question of forming a global impression of differences in countries' willingness to accept market forces and their effect on goods and factor markets, and especially the latter. Attemps to "adjust" in favour of labour, even at the cost of impairing its competitiveness in relation to other inputs, may probably have been less prevalent in the USA and Japan because these countries had not experienced the long period of labour shortage that had afflicted Europe in the sixties.

The study concludes that the reasons for the differences in employment performance between the USA and the EC countries between 1973 and 1983 are to be found primarily in differences in the behaviour of labour costs, in wage structures and in labour market flexibility; Japan constitutes a special case, to which we shall return later. Differences in the socio-economic framework also played an important role, and the individual factors were interdependent.

5.1.2.5 Differences within the EC

Although the employment differential between the USA and the EC as a whole can be explained quite satisfactorily in terms of the factors outlined above, differences in employment performance within the EC appear to have been due to other factors as well. In France and Italy, for example, wage cost pressures and the relative increase in the cost of labour were more pronounced than in the Federal Republic of Germany and the United Kingdom; nevertheless, the employment performance of the first two countries, and especially Italy, was far better. Wage behaviour must have been covered up by other factors.

The poorer employment performance of the United Kingdom may have been due partly to the fact that economic growth was much weaker than in the other countries. However, differences in growth rates were not a significant cause of the differences in employment performance between the Federal Republic of Germany on the one hand and France and Italy on the other. Differences in external conditions in the seventies offer a possible explanation here, for whereas the Deutsche Mark appreciated strongly during that period the real external value of the French franc and the Italian lira declined. In Germany businesses therefore found their profits being squeezed from two sides - by increasing competition and rising labour costs. This made jobs unprofitable sooner and accelerated the substitution of capital for labour. In France and Italy, meanwhile, the falling real external value of the currency tended to ease the pressure of competition, so that wage cost pressures had less of an impact on employment, even though in themselves they were stronger than in Germany. A further reason may have been that the effects of an expansionary monetary and fiscal policy, which entailed tolerating rising inflation rates, masked the adverse impact of real wage behaviour on employment for longer in France and Italy than in Germany.

In Italy employment was probably also boosted by the fact that public enterprises could operate without regard to profitability. The practice of taking unviable, near-bankrupt private companies under the wing of public enterprises and continuing to run them on employment grounds had the same effect. The fact that productivity growth in the Italian economy slowed down considerably in the seventies and actually came to a standstill in the early eighties accords with this supposition. Many questions remain unanswered, however, since the statistical material on Italy is very deficient und unreliable and is revised frequently. Moreover, it is almost impossible to assess the impact that the widespread Italian practice of holding a second job had on employment.

5.1.2.6 The Special Case of Japan

Japan is a special case in many respects. The period from 1973 to 1983 witnessed an expansion in employment coupled with steadily rising wage cost pressures that only abated sporadically in the second half of the seventies. Undoubtedly this should be seen in conjunction with the fact that growth in Japan was still almost twice as fast as in the other countries. (This nevertheless begs the question why growth at such a remarkable rate by international standards should have been possible while wage cost pressures were steadily increasing.) One possible explanation lies in the level of

Employment Trends

wage costs, which were considerably lower than in the other countries in the early seventies, so that the subsequent large wage increases merely narrowed the differential appreciably, even after taking account of exchange rate developments. For an industrial country, Japan's labour costs accounted for a relatively small proportion of total costs, which could indicate that real wages were below the "equilibrium wage" at the beginning of the seventies, in contrast to the situation in the other countries; if that were so, the sharp increase in real wages should be assessed differently from that in the other countries from the point of view of employment.

The system of remuneration in Japan is also different. Pay consists of a basic wage and a twice-yearly bonus, which constitutes a form of profit-sharing. The bonus system takes account of features peculiar to the firm, providing another reason for assessing the rapid wage increases in Japan differently from those in the EC countries.

The Japanese system of employment is another extremely important factor. The system of lifetime employment and the firms' social commitment to their workforce act as an effective brake on dismissals, even in times of high wage cost pressure. Direct dismissal is regarded as a last resort and is avoided as long as possible. This was undoubtedly one of the reasons why productivity growth slowed down so markedly between 1973 and 1983. The link between wages and employment is clearly looser in Japan than in the other countries.

The system of lifetime employment, which is to be found primarily in large enterprises, requires employees to be highly flexible within the firm. This potential for flexibility was rigorously exploited by employers in the years following the first oil crisis when they had to adjust to changed conditions. However, a considerable part of the burden of adjustment was shifted to suppliers, subcontractors, and so forth - and hence onto the "secondary" labour market. Workers in small and medium-sized firms and subcontractors enjoy a much lower level of social protection and status than "privileged" workers in major enterprises, but even in these areas dismissals are generally the last resort, so that employers often use other methods first, such as reduced working hours or lay-offs; laid-off workers do not count as unemployed.

Hence the reasons for the relatively good employment performance in Japan were different from those that applied to the USA; developments in the two countries are therefore scarcely comparable.

5.2 Some Conclusions

Employment trends over the period under examination have shown that the American system of employment was more efficient than that in the EC countries in coping with employment problems, not least the assimilation of the large number of new entrants to the labour market. The same applies to the Japanese system, although the special conditions applying there mean that it is not comparable with those in the EC or the USA. The example of the United States also shows that moderate economic growth need not be associated with stagnating or declining employment, as is frequently assumed in the Federal Republic of Germany; this would appear to be the case only if at the same time other factors were detrimental to employment.

The comparison with the USA reveals weak points in the employment systems of the EC countries, not least in that of the Federal Republic of Germany. Learning lessons from this does not imply a desire to introduce "American ways", as some critics seem to assume. This would not be possible, since the employment systems in the USA and the European countries have been shaped by different historical, social, political and cultural developments. The differences in social systems, in labour legislation and in attitudes towards business and the state should also be viewed in this light. Although both employment systems are market oriented, they each display characteristics that cannot necessarily be reproduced elsewhere.

All that is needed to eradicate the weaknesses in the employment system is to reactivate mechanisms that are already present and which had successfully led to full employment relatively quickly in the Federal Republic of Germany in the early post-war years. The high degree of flexibility and adaptability evident then has been greatly reduced over the years by the increasing cartelization of markets, ever more comprehensive social security provisions and the transfer of more and more responsibility to the state. In view of the adverse consequences these developments had for employment, it is time for a change of thinking. Precisely what this would entail cannot be set out in detail here, and an attempt to do so would go beyond the terms of reference of this work; only the broad outlines can be sketched.

Wage claims must allow sufficient differentiation of wages and salaries between industries, companies, qualifications and regions and they must be linked to "employment-neutral" productivity growth, rather than to the productivity increases that are actually realized. In principle, much of this is possible within the framework of the traditional system of wage determination, although ways must be found to prevent wage scales negotiated for relatively large and heterogeneous sectors from becoming rigid and binding norms. Upward divergence from agreed rates is already possible in the existing system and is actually practised, but downward divergence is an impossibility on principle, so that the standard wage is effectively a fixed minimum wage. It would be better if individual industries and firms had some leeway to take account of their own specific characteristics.

Markets should be as free from regulation as possible, especially in the potentially fast-growing services sector. Among other things, that requires the dismantling of restrictions on market entrance. Where state influence is deemed necessary, it should use market-related instruments as far as possible. Opening of the markets means not only the removal of regulation in existing markets, however; it also entails creating favourable conditions for the emergence of new markets. This ultimately also requires the acceptance of new technology. All of these changes would facilitate the establishment of new firms and would have a multiplier effect on employment.

An efficient labour market that adequately performs its guidance function needs to be highly flexible. A more flexible wage policy would help here too. Equally important, however, is a reduction in institutional obstacles; a modest reduction in the high "dismissal barrier" and its associated costs would undoubtedly foster a greater willingness to recruit staff, especially in small and medium-sized companies. More flexible working hours and easier arrangements for part-time work would also contributed to greater flexibility.

Labour market flexibility presupposes occupational and regional mobility of labour and a willingness to retrain. Changing occupations and gaining new qualifications requires a high degree of adaptability on the part of workers. Here again, the wage system and the socio-economic framework create serious barriers and negative incentives.

The opportunities for increased employment will lie primarily in service industries in the Federal Republic of Germany too. It is often claimed publicly that the consequences of this will be of dubious value. It is widely held that American experiences show that a large number of the new jobs in services are "bad jobs" with low pay, poor working conditions and inadequate protection against dismissal; jobs of that kind would not be acceptable on social grounds in Germany and would break the social consensus. It has already been demonstrated that these characteristics do not apply to a substantial part of the new jobs in the American services sector,[1] apart from the low degree of protection against dismissal, which is not unique to that sector of the American economy. One must also ask what the alternative would be. If it is "no jobs", as is to be feared, then jobs

---

1 See Chapter 1, section 1.2.4.

of a lower quality would undoubtedly be better than none at all. Long-term unemployment with a substantial "wage differential" vis-à-vis those who have a job cannot be regarded as more desirable than low-paid "inferior" jobs.

Finally, another point about which reservations are voiced in Germany concerns productivity. In the USA the increase in employment in the period under examination was accompanied by a marked slowdown in productivity growth. From this it is sometimes concluded that Germany could not go the "American way" because a country so heavily dependent on foreign trade could not afford a further slowdown in productivity growth. Germany must certainly raise its productivity to remain competitive in international markets, but it is the "quality" of the productivity gain that is decisive. From the point of view of competitiveness, what is needed primarily is a rapid implementation of technical innovations, in other words an increase in total factor productivity. The same does not apply to productivity increases due to the substitution of capital for labour induced by a rise in relative labour costs. A slowdown in productivity growth stemming from an abatement of wage cost pressures would be perfectly tolerable. No adverse effects on international competitiveness need be expected, as the slowdown would be matched by wage cost developments consistent with sustained competitiveness.

BIBLIOGRAPHY

Addison, John T.
   The Evolving Debate on Unions and Productivity, in: The Journal of Industrial Relations, Sept. 83

Albert, Michael
   Wachstum, Investition und Beschäftigung in Europa in den 80er Jahren, in: A. Heertje (Ed.): Investieren in die Zukunft Europas, Oxford 1983

Alvarez, Donato; Cooper, Brian
   Productivity trends in manufacturing in the U.S. and 11 other countries, in: Monthly Labor Review, Jan. 1984

Andersen, P.S.
   The Productivity Slowdown and its Policy Implications, in: Bank for International Settlements, Monetary and Economic Department, Basel: BIS Working Papers No. 8, March 1983

Arndt, Helmut
   Vollbeschäftigung: Einführung in Theorie und Politik der Beschäftigung, Berlin 1984

Artus, Jacques R.
   Sind die Reallöhne in Europa zu hoch?, in: Finanzierung und Entwicklung, No. 4, Dec. 1984

Atkinson, A.B.
   Unemployment, Wages and Government Policy, in: The Economic Journal 92, March 1982

Bade, Franz-Josef
   Produktionsorientierte Dienste - Gewinner im wirtschaftlichen Strukturwandel, in: Deutsches Institut für Wirtschaftsforschung, Berlin (DIW), Wochenbericht, No. 16, 1985

Bailey, Elizabeth E.
   Deregulation and Regulatory Reform of U.S. Air-Transportation Policy, in: Bridger M. Mitchell; Paul R. Kleindorfer (Eds.): Regulated Industries and Public Enterprise, Brüssel 1979

Baily, Martin Neil
   The Productivity Growth Slowdown, in: Martin Neil Baily; Arthur M. Okun (Eds.): The Battle against Unemployment and Inflation, 3rd Ed., New York, London 1982

Barker, Kate; Britton, Andrew; Major, Robin
   Macroeconomic Policy in France and Britain, in: National Institute Economic Review, No. 4, 1984

Barsky, Carl B.; Personick, Martin E.
   Measuring wage dispersion: pay ranges reflect industry traits, in: Monthly Labor Review, April 1981

Becker, Eugene H.
Self-employed workers: an update to 1983, in: Monthly Labor Review, July 1984

Bednarzik, Robert W.
Layoffs and permanent job losses: workers' traits and cyclical patterns, in: Monthly Labor Review, Sept. 1983

Bell, David
Labour Utilization and Statutory Non-wage Costs, in: The London School of Economics and Political Science (Ed.): Economica, Vol. 49, 1982

Berekoven, Ludwig
Der Dienstleistungsmarkt in der Bundesrepublik Deutschland, Vol. 1 and 2, Göttingen 1983

Berger, Joan; Mervosh, Edward
American Workers don't get around much anymore, in: Business Week, Oct. 28, 1985

Berk, Allan J.
The impact of Government Deregulation on Collective Bargaining, in: M. David Vaughn (Ed.): Collective Bargaining in a Changing Environment, Practising Law Institute 1982

Birch, David L.
Dynamik der Kleinen, in: Wirtschaftswoche, No. 19, 1984

Black, Stanley W.
Politics versus Markets. International Differences in Macroeconomic Policies, in: American Enterprise Institute: Contemporary Economic Problems, William Fellner, Project Director, Washington 1982

Blankart, Charles Beat; Faber, Monika (Eds.)
Regulierung öffentlicher Unternehmen, Königstein/Ts. 1982

Blattner, Niklaus; Mordasini, Bruno
Die Arbeitsproduktivität in der Schweiz 1960-1980: Entwicklung und Versuche der Erklärung, in: Die Volkswirtschaft, Vol. 55, 1982

Bosch, Gerhard
Kündigungsschutz und Kündigungspraxis in der Bundesrepublik Deutschland, in: Arbeitskreis Sozialwissenschaftliche Arbeitsmarktforschung (SAMF) (Ed.): Paper No. 5, 1983

Boyer, Robert; Petit, Pascal
Employment and productivity in the EEC, in: Cambridge Journal of Economics, No. 5, 1981

Branson, William H.; Rotemberg, Julio J.
International Adjustment with Wage Rigidity, in: European Economic Review, Vol. 13, 1980

Brasche, Ulrich; Teschner, Manfred; Vesper, Dieter
Sind die Unterschiede der Beschäftigtenentwicklung in den USA und der Bundesrepublik Deutschland in der Reallohnentwicklung begründet?, in: DIW-Wochenbericht No. 33, 1984

Brown, Charles; Gilroy, Curtis; Kohen, Andrew
The Effect of the Minimum Wage on Employment and Unemployment, in: Journal of Economic Literature, Vol. XX, June 1982

Browne, Lynn E.
How Different Are Regional Wages? A Second Look, in: New England Economic Review, March/April 1984

Bruche, Gert
Zwischen antizyklischer Beschäftigungspolitik und Förderung benachteiligter Gruppen, in: Mitteilungen aus der Arbeitsmarkt- und Berufsforschung, No. 3, 1984

Bruche, Gert; Casey, Bernard
Arbeitsmarktpolitik unter Stagflationsbedingungen, in: Mitteilungen aus der Arbeitsmarkt- und Berufsforschung, No. 3, 1982

Bruno, Michael
Raw materials, profits, and the productivity slowdown, in: The Quarterly Journal of Economics, Vol. XCIX, No. 1, Feb. 1984

Buiter, Willem H.; Miller, Marcus H.
The macroeconomic consequences of a change in regime: the U.K. under Mrs. Thatcher, in: Centre for Labour Economics, London School of Economics (Ed.): Discussion paper No. 179, Nov. 1983

Bundesanstalt für Arbeit
Amtliche Nachrichten der Bundesanstalt für Arbeit, selected volumes

Bundesanstalt für Arbeit (Ed.)
Wirtschafts- und Arbeitsmarktentwicklung in den USA und in der Bundesrepublik Deutschland, Beiträge zur Arbeitsmarkt- und Berufsforschung, No. 96, 1986

Der Bundesminister für Arbeit und Sozialordnung (BMA) (Ed.)
Bundesarbeitsblatt, No. 3, 1985

Capdevielle, Patricia; Alvarez, Donato
International comparisons of trends in productivity and labor costs, in: Monthly Labor Review, Dec. 1981

Capdevielle, Patricia; Alvarez, D.; Cooper, B.
International trends in productivity and labor costs, in: Monthly Labor Review, Dec. 1982

Carey, Max L.
Occupational employment growth through 1990, in: Monthly Labor Review, Aug. 1981

Carruthers, J.B.
Labour Market Services in Britain and Germany - Employer and Trade Union Participation, in: Anglo-German Foundation for the Study of Industrial Society (Ed.): Monograph Series, No. B 779, 1979

Christensen, Andrea S.
The impact of Deregulation on Collective Bargaining in the Transportation Industry, in: M. David Vaughn (Ed.): Collective Bargaining in a Changing Environment, Practising Law Institute, 1982

Clark, Kim B.; Summers, Lawrence H.
Labor Market Dynamics and Unemployment: A Reconsideration, in: Brookings Papers on Economic Activity No. 1, 1979

Congressional Quarterly Inc.
Employment in America, Washington, D.C., 1983

Crandall, Robert W.
Regulation and Productivity Growth, in: The Decline in Productivity Growth: Proceedings of a Conference held at Edgartown, Mass., June 1980

Crystal, Graef S.
The Re-emergence of Industry Pay Differentials, in: Compensation Review, Third Quarter 1983

Denison, Edward F.
Accounting for Slower Economic Growth, Washington, D.C., 1979

Deutsches Institut für Wirtschaftsforschung (DIW)
Auswirkungen des Strukturwandels auf den Arbeitsmarkt, Anforderungen des Strukturwandels an das Beschäftigungssystem, Schwerpunktthema im Rahmen der Strukturberichterstattung 1983, Berlin 1983

Dickens, William T.; Leonard, Jonathan S.
Accounting for the Decline in Union Membership, in: National Bureau of Economic Research (Ed.): Working Paper No. 1275, Cambridge, Feb. 1984

Dobrzynski, Judith H., u.a.
Small is beautiful. A New Survey of Hot Growth Companies, in: Business Week, May 27, 1985

Donges, Jürgen B.; Spinanger, Dean
Interventions in Labour Markets, Kiel 1983

Dooley, Martin D.; Gottschalk, Peter
Earnings Inequality among Males in the United States: Trends
and the Effect of Labor Force Growth, in: Journal of Political
Economy, Vol. 92, No. 1, 1984

Ernst, Angelika
Arbeitslosigkeit und Unterbeschäftigung in Japan, in: Mitteilungen aus der Arbeitsmarkt- und Berufsforschung, No. 1, 1978

Beschäftigungsprobleme und Beschäftigungspolitik in Japan, in:
Mitteilungen aus der Arbeitsmarkt- und Berufsforschung, No. 2,
1981

Das japanische Beschäftigungssystem - Auswirkungen auf die
internationale Wettbewerbsfähigkeit, in: Ifo-Schnelldienst,
No. 26/27, 1985

Japans unvollkommene Vollbeschäftigung, Hamburg 1980

Farber, Henry S.
Right-to-Work Laws and the Extent of Unionization, in: National
Bureau of Economic Research (Ed.): Working Paper No. 1136,
Cambridge, June 1983

Federal Reserve Bank of Boston (Ed.)
The Decline in Productivity Growth, Proceedings of a Conference held in June 1980, Conference Series Nr. 22

Federal Reserve Bank of St. Louis, The
Annual U.S. Economic Data 1965-1984, St. Louis, May 1985

Monetary Trends, St. Louis, Sept. 1985

Feldstein, Martin S.
The Importance of Temporary Layoffs: An Empirical Analysis,
in: Brookings Papers on Economic Activity, No. 3, 1975

Fels, Gerhard; Seffen, Achim; Vogel, Otto (Eds.)
Soziale Sicherung: Von der Finanzkrise zur Strukturreform,
Köln 1984

Franke, Siegfried F.
Der Einfluß von Lohnhöhe und Lohnstruktur auf Beschäftigungsvolumen und -struktur, in: Wirtschaftsdienst, No. 1, 1983

Freedman, David
Employment and unemployment in the 1980s: Economic dilemmas
and socio-political challenges, in: International Labour Review,
Vol. 123, No. 5, Sept./Oct. 1984

Freeman, Richard B.
Individual Mobility and Union Voice in the Labor Market, in: The American Economic Review, Vol. 66, No. 2, 1976

Union Wage Practices and Wage Dispersion within Establishments, in: Industrial and Labor Relations Review, Vol. 36, No. 1, Oct. 1982

Freeman, Richard B.; Medoff, James L.
What Do Unions Do?, New York 1984

Friderichs, Hans
Lohnstrukturdifferenzierung - ein Rezept zur Lösung des Beschäftigungsproblems?, in: Wirtschaftsdienst, No. 8, 1985

Geary, Patrick T.; Kennan, John
The Employment - Real Wage Relationship: An International Study, in: Journal of Political Economy, 90, No. 4-6, 1982

Gershuny, Jonathan I.; Miles, Ian D.
The New Service Economy, London 1983

Giebel, Ulrich J.
Unternehmensgröße und Belastung durch Sozialleistungen, in: Wirtschaftsdienst, No. 5, 1985

Giersch, Herbert
Arbeit, Lohn und Beschäftigung, in: Weltwirtschaftliches Archiv, No. 119, 1983

Produktivität und Beschäftigung. Der volkswirtschaftliche Aspekt, in: Produktivität, Eigenverantwortung, Beschäftigung. Eds.: Verband Deutscher Maschinen- und Anlagenbau (VDMA) and Institut der deutschen Wirtschaft (IW), 1983

Giersch, Herbert; Wolter, Frank
On the recent slowdown in productivity growth in advanced economies, in: Institut für Weltwirtschaft an der Universität Kiel: Kieler Arbeitspapiere No. 148, July 1982

Giezen, Robert W. van
A new look at occupational wages within individual establishments, in: Monthly Labor Review, Nov. 1982

Gischer, Horst
Lohnstruktur und Beschäftigung, in: Wirtschaftsdienst, No. 12, 1983

Gordon, Robert J.
Why U.S. Wage and Employment Behaviour differs from that in Britain and Japan, in: The Economic Journal, Vol. 92, 1982

Gottschalk, Peter
United States of America: U.S. Labor Market Policies Since the
1960s - A Survey of Programs and their Effectiveness, in:
K. Gerlach; W. Peters; W. Sengenberger (Eds.): Public Policies to Combat Unemployment in a Period of Economic Stagna-
tion. An International Comparison, Frankfurt/M. - New York
1984

Greene, Richard
Tracking job growth in private industry, in: Monthly Labor
Review, Sept. 1982

Großer, Günter; Kurlbaum, Elke
Wirtschaftsstruktur und Konjunkturentwicklung, in: Politik und
Wirtschaft in den USA, Schriftenreihe der Bundeszentrale für
politische Bildung, Vol. 208, Bonn 1984

Großer, Günter; Weinert, Günter
Wirtschaftspolitische Strategien in wichtigen Industrieländern,
in: Hamburger Jahrbuch für Wirtschafts- und Gesellschaftspolitik, Vol. 28, 1983

Guger, Alois
Internationaler Arbeitskostenvergleich nach Industriebranchen,
in: Österreichisches Institut für Wirtschaftsforschung (Wifo):
Monatsberichte, No. 6, 1985

Gundlach, Erich; Schmidt, Klaus-Dieter
Das amerikanische Beschäftigungswunder: Was sich daraus lernen läßt, Kiel 1985

Hamada, Koichi
Lessons from the Macroeconomic Performance of the Japanese
Economy, in: Australia - Japan Research Centre: Paper
No. 107, Canberra, Dec. 1983

Hamermesh, Daniel S.
Subsidies for Jobs in the Private Sector, in: Palmer, John L.
(Ed.): Creating Jobs, Washington 1979

Hardes, Heinz-Dieter
Arbeitsmarktstrukturen und Beschäftigungsprobleme im internationalen Vergleich, in: Schriften zur angewandten Wirtschaftsforschung, No. 44, Tübingen 1981

Hart, R.A.
Unemployment Insurance and the Firm's Employment Strategy:
A European and United States Comparison, in: Kyklos, Vol. 35,
1982

Hecker, Gundolf F.
Die Produktivität in der Bundesrepublik, Japan und den USA
im Vergleich, in: Wirtschaftsdienst, No. 9, 1982

Heitger, Bernhard
Die Theorie stimmt, in: Wirtschaftswoche, No. 45, Nov. 2, 1984

Hof, Bernd
Beschäftigungsschwellen und Reallohnentwicklung im Verarbeitenden Gewerbe ausgewählter Industrieländer, in: IW-Trends, No. 1, 1984

Löhne, Beschäftigung, Produktivität: Sektorale Differenzierung im deutsch-amerikanischen Vergleich, in: IW-Trends, No. 2, 1985

Produktivitätsdynamik international, in: Beiträge zur Wirtschafts- und Sozialpolitik, No. 114, March 1983

Sektorale Beschäftigungsentwicklung in den Vereinigten Staaten und in der Bundesrepublik Deutschland, in: IW-Trends, No. 2, 1984

Unternehmensbesteuerung im internationalen Vergleich, in: IW-Trends, No. 2, 1985

Hönekopp, Elmar; Ullmann, Hans
Auf dem Weg zur Dienstleistungsökonomie?, in: Mitteilungen aus der Arbeitsmarkt- und Berufsforschung, No. 2, 1980

Hort, Peter
Amerika, hast Du es besser? Das "Job-Wunder" und was dahintersteckt, in: Frankfurter Allgemeine, No. 147, June 29, 1985

HWWA-Institut für Wirtschaftsforschung-Hamburg
Analyse der strukturellen Entwicklung der deutschen Wirtschaft, Strukturbericht 1980, Materialband 1, Hamburg 1980

Internationale Wettbewerbsfähigkeit und strukturelle Anpassungserfordernisse, Ergänzungsband 3 zum HWWA-Strukturbericht 1983, Hamburg 1984

Immenga, Ulrich
Wettbewerbsbeschränkungen auf staatlich gelenkten Märkten, Tübingen 1967

Institut der deutschen Wirtschaft
Internationale Wirtschaftszahlen, selected volumes

International Labour Organisation (ILO)
Labour force, employment, unemployment and underemployment, in: Report II, ICLS/13/II, Geneva 1982

International Labour Office (ILO)
Yearbook of Labour Statistics, selected volumes

Japan Institute of Labour, The
    Wages and Hours of Work, in: Japanese Industrial Relations,
    Series 3, Tokyo 1984

Jungblut, Michael
    Die kleinen Riesen. Kleine und mittlere Unternehmen schlagen
    die Großindustrie, in: Die Zeit, No. 13, March 22, 1985

Kalmbach, Peter
    Lohnhöhe und Beschäftigung: Ein Evergreen der wirtschafts-
    politischen Debatte, in: Wirtschaftsdienst, No. 7, 1985

Kaufman, Roger T.; Woglom, Geoffrey
    The effects of Expectations on Union Wages, in: The American
    Economic Review, Vol. LXXIV, No. 74, 1984

Kayser, Gunter; Friede, Christina
    Wirkungsanalyse der Sozialgesetzgebung, in: Institut für Mittel-
    standsforschung, ifm-Materialien No. 24, Dec. 1984

Kearton, Lord
    Where are the jobs coming from, in: London Business School
    Journal, Vol. 3, No. 2, 1978

Keller, Dietmar
    The International Competitiveness of Europe, the USA and Ja-
    pan, in: Intereconomics, No. 2, 1985

Kendall, Walter
    Gewerkschaften in Europa, Hamburg 1977

Kendrick, John W.
    International Comparisons of Recent Productivity Trends, in:
    American Enterprise Institute: Essays in Contemporary Economic
    Problems: Demand, Productivity, and Population, Washington
    1981

    Productivity Trends and the Recent Slowdown: Historical Per-
    sepctive, Causal Factors, and Policy Options, in: American
    Enterprise Institute: Contemporary Economic Problems, Washing-
    ton 1979

Kendrick, John W.; Vaccara, Beatrice N. (Eds.)
    New Developments in Productivity Measurement and Analysis,
    Chicago/London 1980

Keynes, John M.
    The General Theory of Employment, Interest and Money, Lon-
    don, Melbourne, Toronto 1967

Klasen, Fred; Winter, Gabriele
Der staatlich organisierte "graue Arbeitsmarkt", in: Veröffentlichungsreihe des Internationalen Instituts für Vergleichende Gesellschaftsforschung (IIVG)/Arbeitspolitik des Wissenschaftszentrums Berlin, Berlin, June 1984

Klodt, Henning
Lohnquote und Beschäftigung - Die Lohnlücke, Institut für Weltwirtschaft an der Universität Kiel (ed.), Kieler Arbeitspapiere No. 230, Kiel 1985

Klodt, Henning
Produktivitätsschwäche in der deutschen Wirtschaft, Institut für Weltwirtschaft an der Universität Kiel (ed.), Kieler Studien No. 186, Tübingen 1984

Vor der Trendwende?, in: Wirtschaftswoche, No. 16, 1984

Kahn, George A.
International Differences in Wage Behaviour: Real, Nominal, or Exaggerated?, in: AEA Papers and Proceedings, No. 74, 1984

Kommission der Europäischen Gemeinschaften
Der europäische Arbeitsmarkt. Neue Studien über Arbeitsmarktfragen in der Europäischen Gemeinschaft. Sammlung Aktuelle Fragen, Reihe Sozialpolitik, No. 42, Brüssel 1981

Kraus, Willy
Japan, Wirtschaftspolitik jenseits von Markt und Plan, in: D. Cassel (Ed.): Wirtschaftspolitik im Systemvergleich, München 1984

Kroker, Rolf
Deregulierung und Entbürokratisierung, Institut der deutschen Wirtschaft (Ed.), Beiträge zur Wirtschafts- und Sozialpolitik, No. 130, Jan. 1985

Krugmann, Paul
The real wage gap and employment, in: Annales de L'Insee, No. 47-48, 1982

Kutscher, Ronald E.; Mark, Jerome A.
The service-producing sector: some common perceptions reviewed, in: Monthly Labor Review, April 1983

Lacombe II, John J.; Conley, James R.
Collective bargaining calendar crowded again in 1984, in: Monthly Labor Review, Jan. 1984

Landauer, Carl
Sozial- und Wirtschaftsgeschichte der Vereinigten Staaten von Amerika, Stuttgart 1981

Lederer, Klaus G.
Produktionsstrategien in Japan, USA und Deutschland, in: Fortschrittliche Betriebsführung und Industrial Engineering, No. 6, 1984

Leon, Carol Boyd
Occupational winners and losers: who they were during 1972-80, in: Monthly Labor Review, April 1982

Lewis, H.G.
Unionism and Relative Wages in the United States, Chicago/London 1963

Luntke, Gerhard
Zusammenhänge zwischen Industrie und Administration in Japan, in: Fortschrittliche Betriebsführung und Industrial Engineering, No. 6, 1984

Malinvaud, Edmund
Wages and Unemployment, in: The Economic Journal, No. 92, 1982

Marsden, David
Industrial Democracy and Industrial Control in West Germany, France and Great Britain, Research Paper, No. 4, Department of Employment (London), Sept. 1978

Martin, Jack K.; Lichter, Daniel T.
Geographic Mobility and Satisfaction with Life and Work, in: Social Science Quarterly, Vol. 64, No. 3, Sept. 1983

Martin, John P.
Effects of the Minimum Wage on the Youth Labour Market in North America and France, in: OECD: Economic Outlook, Occasional Studies, June 1983

Medoff, James L.
U.S. Labor Markets: Imbalance, Wage Growth, and Productivity in the 1970s, in: Brookings Papers on Economic Activity, No. 1, 1983

Mellor, Earl F.; Stamas, George D.
Usual weekly earnings: another look at intergroup differences and basic trends, in: Monthly Labor Review, April 1982

Mieth, W.
Die Forderung nach flexibleren Lohnstrukturen als Entlastung der Arbeitsmarktpolitik, in: P. Herder-Dorneich (Ed.): Arbeitsmarkt und Arbeitsmarktpolitik, Berlin 1982

Momigliano, F.; Siniscalco, D.
　　The Growth of Service Employment: A Reappraisal, in: Banca
　　Nazionale del Lavoro (Hrsg.): Quarterly Review, Vol. 35, No.
　　142, Sept. 82

Moore, Thomas G.
　　Deregulating Ground Transportation, in: Herbert Giersch (Ed.):
　　New Opportunities for Entrepreneurship, Tübingen 1984

Mortensen, Jørgen
　　Profitability, relative factor prices and capital/labour substitu-
　　tion in the Community, the United States and Japan, 1960-83,
　　in: Commission of the European Communities, European Economy
　　No. 20/1984

Mounts, Gregory J.
　　Labor and the Supreme Court: significant decisions of 1979-80,
　　in: Monthly Labor Review, April 81

Moy, Joyanna
　　Recent labor market developments in the U.S. and nine other
　　countries, in: Monthly Labor Review, Jan. 1984

Müller, Gernot
　　Das "Beschäftigungswunder" in den USA, in: Wirtschafts- und
　　Sozialwissenschaftliches Institut des Deutschen Gewerkschafts-
　　bundes (ed.), WSI-Mitteilungen, No. 9, 1984

Müller, Jürgen; Vogelsang, Ingo
　　Ist eine Effizienzsteigerung der öffentlichen Verwaltung durch
　　Anwendung des Instrumentariums der amerikanischen "Public
　　Utility Regulation" möglich?, in: Ernst Helmstädter (Ed.):
　　Neuere Entwicklungen in den Wirtschaftswissenschaften, Schrif-
　　ten des Vereins für Socialpolitik, NF Vol. 98, Berlin 1978

　　Staatliche Regulierung, Baden-Baden 1979

Müller-Vogg, Hugo
　　Gewerkschaften am kurzen Hebel, in: Frankfurter Allgemeine,
　　Sept. 21, 1985

Norsworthy, J.R.; Harper, Michael J.; Kunze, Kent
　　The Slowdown in Productivity Growth: Analysis of Some Con-
　　tributing Factors, in: Brookings Papers on Economic Activity,
　　No. 2, 1979

Norwood, Janet L.
　　Jobs and Prices in a Recovering Economy, in: U.S. Department
　　of Labor/Bureau of Labor Statistics, Report No. 704, April 1984

　　Labor market contrasts: United States and Europe, in: Monthly
　　Labor Review, Aug. 1983

Norwood, Janet L.
    Arbeitsplatzbeschaffung als Herausforderung im wirtschaftlichen
    Wandel, in: Bundesanstalt für Arbeit (ed.): Wirtschafts- und
    Arbeitsmarktentwicklung in den USA und in der Bundesrepublik
    Deutschland, BeitrAB No. 96

OECD
    Italy, Paris 1977

    Economic Outlook, No. 36, Dec. 1984 u. June 1985

    Economic Outlook, Historical Statistics, 1960-1983

    The Employment Outlook: Where are the Jobs in Today's Labour
    Market?, in: The OECD Observer, No. 130, Sept. 1984

    Flows and Stocks of Fixed Capital, 1955-1980, Paris 1983

    Labour Force Statistics, selected volumes

    Lay-offs and Short-time Working, Paris 1983

    National Accounts, Vol. II, div. Jgg.

    Positive Adjustment in Manpower and Social Policies, Paris 1984

    Positive Adjustment Policies, Paris 1982

    Productivity Trends in the OECD Area, Working Party No. 2 of
    the Economic Policy Committee, Paris 1980

    Real Wages and Employment, Working Party No. 1 of the Eco-
    nomic Policy Committee, Paris 1982

    The Role of the Public Sector, OECD Economic Studies, No. 4,
    Paris 1985

    Unemployment compensation and related employment policy mea-
    sures, Paris 1979

Okita, Saburo
    Labor Productivity and Economic Development; the Japanese
    Experience, in: Australia-Japan research centre: Research paper
    No. 83, Canberra, May 81

Perlman, Mark
    Collective Bargaining and Industrial Relations: The Past, the
    Present, and the Future, in: American Enterprise Institute:
    Essays in Contemporary Economic Problems: Disinflation, 1983-
    1984 Edition

Pettenati, P.
The Labour Market and Inflation in Transitional Growth: Lessons from the Italian Experience, in: Banca Nazionale del Lavoro (Ed.): Quarterly Review, Vol. 35, No. 141, June 1982

Price, Robert W.R.; Chouraqui, Jean-Claude
Public Sector Deficits: Problems and Policy Implications, in: OECD: Occasional Studies, June 1983

Pugel, Thomas A.
Japan's Industrial Policy: Instruments, Trends, and Effects, in: Journal of comparative economics, No. 8, 1984

Rau, Jes
Amerikas neue Kapitalisten. Junge Unternehmer haben in den USA nahezu unbegrenzte Möglichkeiten, in: Die Zeit, No. 23, May 31, 1985

Reincke, Helmut
Amerikas Arbeitsmarktdynamik im Prüfstand, in: Arbeitslosigkeit - Schicksal der achtziger Jahre? Ed.: Wirtschaftsredaktion der "Neue Zürcher Zeitung", Zürich 1983

Riche, Richard W.; Hecker, Daniel E.; Burgan, John U.
High technology today and tomorrow: a small slice of the employment pie, in: Monthly Labor Review, Nov. 1983

Ries, John C.
Unemployment in 1982: Beyond the Official Labor Force Statistics, in: New England Economic Review, May/June 1984

Robertson, J.A.S. e.a.
Structure and Employment Prospects of the Service Industries, in: Department of Employment, Research Paper No. 30, London, July 1982

Roda, Siegfried; Spörl, Franz
Japans Automobilindustrie, in: Fortschrittliche Betriebsführung und Industrial Engineering, No. 6, 1984

Rohwer, Bernd
Wachstum, Produktivität und Beschäftigung, in: Jahrbuch der Sozialwissenschaft, Vol. 34, 1983, No. 1

Rose, Klaus
Produktivität, in: Handwörterbuch der Sozialwissenschaften, Vol. 8, Göttingen 1964

Rubery, J. u.a.
EEC Labour Market Studies, in: University of Cambridge: Programme of Research and Actions on the Development of the Labour Market, No. 23, 1981

Rüthers, Bernd
Der Schutz wird zur Strafe. Wenn das Arbeitsrecht die Arbeit-
nehmer wendet, in: Frankfurter Allgemeine, No. 92, April 1985

Sachs, Jeffrey D.
Real Wages and Unemployment in the OECD Countries, in:
Brookings Papers on Economic Activity, No. 1, 1983

Wages, Profits, and Macroeconomic Adjustment: A Comparative
Study, in: Brookings Papers on Economic Activity, No. 2, 1979

Salowsky, Heinz
Personalzusatzkosten in westlichen Industrieländern, in: Institut der deutschen Wirtschaft (Ed.), Beiträge zur Wirtschafts-
und Sozialpolitik, No. 1/2, Köln 1977

Saso, Mary
The Roots of Japanese Manufacturing's Competitive Edge, in:
The Economist Intelligence Unit (EIU): Multinational Business,
No. 3, 1984

Saunders, Christopher; Marsden, David
Pay Inequalities in the European Communities, Butterworths
European Studies, 1981

Scharpf, Fritz W.
Strukturen der post-industriellen Gesellschaft oder: Verschwin-
det die Massenarbeitslosigkeit in der Dienstleistungs- und In-
formationsökonomie? In: Internationales Institut für Management
und Verwaltung/Arbeitsmarktpolitik (Ed.): discussion papers
No. 23, Berlin 1985

Schatz, Klaus-Werner
Markt über den Wolken, in: Wirtschaftswoche, No. 30, 1985

Schatz, Klaus-Werner; Wolter, Frank
International Trade, Employment and Structural Adjustment:
The Case Study of the Federal Republic of Germany, in: Inter-
national Labour Office: World Employment Programme Research:
Working Papers, Genua, Oct. 1982

Schlumpf, Roland
Der Anschein der Vollbeschäftigung in Japan, in: Arbeitslosigkeit - Schicksal der achtziger Jahre? Ed.: Wirtschaftsredaktion
der "Neue Zürcher Zeitung", Zürich 1983

Schmitt-Rink, Gerhard
Reallohnniveau und unfreiwillige Arbeitslosigkeit. Neoklassische
und neokeynesianische Erklärungsansätze, in: WISU, No. 1,
1985

Schulze, Günther C.
Der japanische Erfolg, in: Fortschrittliche Betriebsführung und Industrial Engineering, No. 6, 1984

Sehgal, Ellen
Occupational mobility and job tenure in 1983, in: Monthly Labor Review, Oct. 1984

Sekscenski, Edward S.
The health services industry: a decade of expansion, in: Monthly Labor Review, May 1981

Sengenberger, Werner
Das amerikanische Beschäftigungssystem - dem deutschen überlegen? In: Wirtschaftsdienst, No. 8, 1984

Zur Flexibilität im Beschäftigungssystem. Ein Vergleich zwischen den USA und der Bundesrepublik Deutschland, München 1984

Sengenberger, Werner; Köhler, Christoph
Beschäftigungselastizität und Arbeitsmarktstruktur - Ein Vergleich interner Arbeitsmärkte in der deutschen und amerikanischen Automobilindustrie, in: Haller, Max; Müller, Walter (Ed.): Beschäftigungssystem im gesellschaftlichen Wandel, Frankfurt/M./New York 1983

Siegel, Klaus D. e.a.
Vergleichende Analyse der Mobilität in bzw. zwischen den Arbeitsmärkten der Europäischen Gemeinschaft, Institut für Arbeitsmarkt- und Berufsforschung der Bundesanstalt für Arbeit, Beiträge zur Arbeitsmarkt- und Berufsforschung No. 11, 1976

Sieling, Mark S.
Clerical pay differentials in metropolitan areas, 1961-80, in: Monthly Labor Review, July 1982

Silvestri, George T.; Lukasiewicz, John M.; Einstein, Marcus E.
Occupational employment projections through 1995, in: Monthly Labor Review, Nov. 1983

Sorrentino, Constance
Japan's low unemployment: an in-depth analysis, in: Monthly Labor Review, March 1984

Spinanger, Dean
Wage Rigidities, Barriers to Entry and the Welfare State - their Impact on Labor Markets in Industrialized Countries, in: Institut für Weltwirtschaft an der Universität Kiel (Ed.): Kieler Arbeitspapiere, No. 188, Oct. 1983

Statistisches Amt der Europäischen Gemeinschaften (EUROSTAT)
Beschäftigung und Arbeitslosigkeit

Statistisches Amt der Europäischen Gemeinschaften (EUROSTAT)
Soziale Indikatoren für die Europäische Gemeinschaft 1960-1975

Statistisches Bundesamt, Wiesbaden
Ausbau der Konzentrationsstatistiken im Produzierenden Gewerbe, Feb. 1985

Fachserie 14, R.6: Personal des öffentlichen Dienstes, selected volumes

Fachserie 18: Volkswirtschaftliche Gesamtrechnungen, selected volumes

Wirtschaft und Statistik, selected volumes

Stieber, Jack
Most U.S. workers still may be fired under the employment-at-will doctrine, in: Monthly Labor Review, May 1984

Stille, Frank
Subventionen in den USA, in: Deutsches Institut für Wirtschaftsforschung (DIW): Vierteljahreshefte zur Wirtschaftsforschung, No. 1, 1985

Swedish Employers' Confederation
Wages and total labour costs for workers, International Survey 1971-1981, 1984

Taira, Koji
Japan's low unemployment: economic miracle or statistical artifact?, in: Monthly Labor Review, July 1983

Todd, Douglas
Some aspects of industrial productivity performance in the European Community: an appraisal, in: Commission of the European Communities, European Economy, Nr. 20/1984

Upjohn Institute for Employment Research, The W.E. (Ed.)
What's Happening to American Labor Force and Productivity Measurements?, Kalamazoo, Michigan, 1982

Urquhart, Michael
The employment shift to services: where did it come from?, in: Monthly Labor Review, April 1984

The services industry: is it recession-proof?, in: Monthly Labor Review, Oct. 1981

U.S. Department of Commerce
Statistical Abstract of the United States 1985

U.S. Department of Labor
Employment and Earnings, selected volumes

U.S. Department of Labor
Handbook of Labor Statistics, selected volumes

Monthly Labor Review, selected volumes

Vajna, Thomas
Langfristige Entwicklung der intersektoralen Lohnstruktur in der Industrie, in: Institut der deutschen Wirtschaft (ed.), IW-Trends, No. 3, 1983

Vogler-Ludwig, Kurt
Auswirkungen des Strukturwandels auf den Arbeitsmarkt, Ergänzungsband zur Ifo-Strukturberichterstattung 1983, München 1983

Flexibilisierung der Lohnstrukturen. Ein Patentrezept der Beschäftigungspolitik? In: ifo-Schnelldienst, No. 16, 1985

Wagner, Joachim
Mangelnde Faktormobilität - eine Ursache der Arbeitslosigkeit? in: HWWA (Hrsg.): Wirtschaftsdienst, No. 6, 1985

Walsh, Brendan M.
Employment and Competitiveness in the European Community, in: The World Economy, Vol. 7, No. 1, March 1984

Warnken, Jürgen
Zur unterschiedlichen Dynamik der Arbeitsmärkte in den USA und der Bundesrepublik - Ein Erklärungsversuch, in: Mitteilungen des Rheinisch-Westfälischen Instituts für Wirtschaftsforschung, Vol. 35, 1984

Wartenberg, Erwin
Entwicklung der Produktion, Beschäftigung und Arbeitsproduktivität in der Bundesrepublik Deutschland im internationalen Vergleich, in: Statistisches Bundesamt (ed.), Wirtschaft und Statistik, No. 10, 1984

Waschke, Hildegard
Amerikas Arbeitsbeziehungen sind anders, in: Institut der deutschen Wirtschaft (Ed.): Beiträge zur Gesellschafts- und Bildungspolitik, No. 11, 1980

Großbritanniens Arbeitsbeziehungen im Wandel, in: Institut der deutschen Wirtschaft (Ed.): Beiträge zur Gesellschafts- und Bildungspolitik, No. 3, 1983

Japans Arbeitsbeziehungen zwischen Tradition und Moderne, in: Institut der deutschen Wirtschaft (Ed.): Beiträge zur Gesellschafts- und Bildungspolitik, No. 1, 1982

Weder, Dietrich Jörn
Das "US-Beschäftigungswunder" und Europa oder: Wie billig müssen sich Arbeitssuchende verkaufen? In: Die Neue Gesellschaft, No. 11, 1984

Wegner, Manfred
Erklärungen für das Arbeitsplatzwunder in den USA und für die stagnierende Beschäftigung in der EG, in: Ifo-Studien, No. 2, 1983

The employment Miracle in the United States and Stagnating Employment in the European Community, Commission of the European Communities, Economic Papers, No. 17, July 1983

Die Schaffung von Arbeitsplätzen im Dienstleistungssektor, in: ifo-Schnelldienst, No. 6, 1985

Werner, Heinz
Die Leistungsgewährung bei Arbeitslosigkeit in den Ländern der Europäischen Gemeinschaft, in: Mitteilungen aus der Arbeitsmarkt- und Berufsforschung, No. 4, 1984

Werner, Josua
Beziehungen zwischen Beschäftigungspolitik und Arbeitsvolumen, in: WISU, No. 5, 1985

Willke, Gerhard
Wirtschaftspolitische Optionen gegen strukturelle Arbeitslosigkeit, in: Aus Politik und Zeitgeschichte, March 1984

Wilson, George W.
Regulating and Deregulating Business, in: Indiana University Graduate School of Business: Business Horizons, Vol. 25, No. 4, July/Aug. 1982

Winkler-Büttner, Diana
Die Beschäftigungsentwicklung in den USA und in der Bundesrepublik. Unterschiede und Gemeinsamkeiten, in: Wirtschaftsdienst, No. 7, 1984

Wohlers, Eckhardt
Beschäftigungsfeindlicher Produktivitätsfortschritt? in: Wirtschaftsdienst, No. 1, 1985

Wollny, Hubert; Schoer, Karl
Entwicklung der Erwerbstätigkeit 1970 bis 1981. Ergebnis einer Revision der Erwerbstätigenzahlen, in: Statistisches Bundesamt (ed.), Wirtschaft und Statistik, No. 11, 1982

Wragg, Richard; Robertson, J.
Post-war trends in employment, productivity, output, labour costs and prices by industry in the United Kingdom, in: Department of Employment, Research Paper No. 3, London, June 1978

Zimmermann-Trapp, Astrid
Zur Arbeitsmarktflexibilität in den USA und der Bundesrepublik Deutschland, in: Kreditanstalt für Wiederaufbau (Ed.): Analysen-Meinungen-Perspektiven, Frankfurt/M., July 1985

Anon.
Beschäftigungswunder Vereinigte Staaten - heute und in den siebziger Jahren, in: Citibank AG: Weltwirtschaft aktuell, No. 40, Frankfurt, Dec. 1984

Beyond Unions, in: Business Week, July 1985

Costs and Benefits of Protection, in: OECD Observer, May 1985

Das Beschäftigungswunder in den USA, in: WISU, No. 8-9, 1984

Der Produktivitätsfortschritt in der Bundesrepublik und seine Bestimmungsfaktoren, in: Monatsberichte der Deutschen Bundesbank, No. 1, 1980

Die neuen Arbeitsplätze in den USA sind meist nicht besonders hochwertig, in: Handelsblatt, March 12, 1985

Die Tarifhoheit sollte künftig mit den Betriebsräten geteilt werden, in: Handelsblatt, Oct. 17, 1985

How the U.S. is able to create so many jobs, in: Business week, July 16, 1984

Jahreswirtschaftsbericht der EG 1984-85, in: Europäische Wirtschaft, No. 22, 1984

Judicial decisions in the field of labour law, in: International Labour Review, March-April 1984

Judicial decisions in the field of labour law, in: International Labour Review, January-February 1985

Employment Trends

APPENDIX

Appendix   249

Table 1a: POPULATION AND EMPLOYMENT: UNITED STATES

- thousands -

	1973	1974	1975	1976	1977	1978	1979	1980	1981	1982	1983

POPULATION AND EMPLOYMENT

	1973	1974	1975	1976	1977	1978	1979	1980	1981	1982	1983
TOTAL POPULATION	211909	213854	215973	218035	220239	222585	225056	227738	230019	232309	234496
POPULATION, FROM 15 TO 64 YEARS	134224	136589	138916	141381	143749	146128	148467	150736	152499	154096	155524
MALES, FROM 15 TO 64 YEARS	66006	67186	68355	69589	70782	71969	73140	74290	75209	76046	76801
FEMALES, FROM 15 TO 64 YEARS	68217	69403	70560	71792	73968	74159	75327	76446	77288	78048	78723
TOTAL LABOUR FORCE	91756	94179	95755	98302	101142	104368	107050	109042	110812	112384	113749
CIVILIAN LABOUR FORCE	89428	91949	93775	96158	99009	102251	104962	106940	108670	110204	111550
MALES	54624	55739	56299	57174	58396	59620	60726	61453	61974	62450	63047
FEMALES	34804	36211	37475	38983	40613	42631	44235	45487	46696	47755	48503
UNEMPLOYED	4365	5156	7929	7406	6991	6202	6137	7637	8273	10678	10717
CIVILIAN EMPLOYMENT	85064	86794	85846	88752	92017	96048	98824	99303	100397	99526	100834
AGRICULTURE	3572	3613	3507	3453	3425	3549	3509	3529	3519	3571	3541
INDUSTRY	28225	28194	26288	27354	28401	29887	30918	30315	30190	28257	28253
SERVICES	53265	54987	56049	57944	60189	62610	64394	65457	66688	67701	69037

CIVILIAN EMPLOYMENT BY SECTORS (ISIC)

	1973	1974	1975	1976	1977	1978	1979	1980	1981	1982	1983
ALL ACTIVITIES	85064	86794	85846	88752	92017	96048	98824	99303	100397	99526	100834
AGRICULTURE	3572	3613	3507	3453	3425	3549	3509	3529	3519	3571	3541
MINING AND QUARRYING	642	671	752	794	842	859	900	979	1118	1028	921
MANUFACTURING	21054	21026	19457	20261	20889	21784	22458	21942	21817	20286	19946
ELECTRICITY, GAS AND WATER	967	980	986	1044	1058	1078	1123	1179	1195	1187	1237
CONSTRUCTION	5562	5517	5093	5255	5612	6166	6437	6215	6060	5756	6149
TRADE, RESTAURANTS AND HOTELS	17929	18458	18708	19356	20141	20746	21238	21339	21721	22028	22444
TRANSPORT, COMMUNICATION	4933	5138	5032	4993	5168	5464	5677	5619	5673	5594	5302
FINANCING, INSURANCE AND BUSINESS SERVICES	6190	6431	6427	6672	7095	7686	8149	8351	8651	9066	9738
COMMUNITY, SOCIAL AND PERSONAL SERVICES	24213	24960	25882	26923	27785	28714	29330	30148	30643	31013	31553

WAGE EARNERS AND SALARIED EMPLOYEES IN MANUFACTURING (ISIC)

	1973	1974	1975	1976	1977	1978	1979	1980	1981	1982	1983
MANUFACTURING, TOTAL	20154	20077	18323	18997	19682	20505	21040	20285	20170	18781	18497
FOOD, BEVERAGES AND TOBACCO	1792	1784	1733	1766	1782	1795	1803	1777	1741	1705	1691
TEXTILE, WEARING APPAREL AND LEATHER IND.	2732	2599	2359	2500	2481	2488	2435	2345	2305	2129	2115
WOOD, WOOD PRODUCTS	1266	1202	1032	1124	1186	1249	1265	1157	1130	1030	1104
PAPER, PAPER PROD., PRINTING, PUBLISHING	1815	1817	1725	1775	1833	1891	1942	1945	1955	1934	1957
CHEMICALS, PETROLEUM AND PLASTIC PRODUCTS	1923	1952	1817	1881	1990	2058	2101	2032	2060	1973	1960
NON-METALLIC MINERAL PRODUCTS	716	708	629	644	669	698	709	662	638	577	573
BASIC METAL INDUSTRIES	1259	1289	1139	1155	1182	1215	1254	1142	1122	922	838
FABR. METAL PROD., MACHINERY AND EQUIPMENT	8196	8275	7482	7724	8122	8660	9088	8809	8810	8129	7887
OTHER MANUFACTURING INDUSTRIES	454	452	407	429	438	452	445	418	408	382	371

Table 1a: POPULATION AND EMPLOYMENT: UNITED STATES

– percentage change –

	1973	1974	1975	1976	1977	1978	1979	1980	1981	1982	1983
POPULATION AND EMPLOYMENT											
TOTAL POPULATION	0.96	0.92	0.99	0.95	1.01	1.07	1.11	1.19	1.00	1.00	0.94
POPULATION, FROM 15 TO 64 YEARS	1.82	1.76	1.70	1.77	1.67	1.65	1.60	1.53	1.17	1.05	0.93
MALES, FROM 15 TO 64 YEARS	1.85	1.79	1.74	1.81	1.71	1.68	1.63	1.57	1.24	1.11	0.99
FEMALES, FROM 15 TO 64 YEARS	1.78	1.74	1.67	1.75	3.03	0.26	1.57	1.49	1.10	0.98	0.86
TOTAL LABOUR FORCE	3.27	2.64	1.89	2.45	2.89	3.19	2.57	1.86	1.62	1.42	1.21
CIVILIAN LABOUR FORCE	2.75	2.82	1.99	2.54	2.96	3.27	2.65	1.88	1.62	1.41	1.22
MALES	2.00	2.04	1.00	1.55	2.14	2.10	1.86	1.20	0.85	0.77	0.96
FEMALES	3.96	4.04	3.49	4.02	4.18	4.97	3.76	2.83	2.66	2.27	1.57
UNEMPLOYED	-10.59	18.12	53.78	-6.60	-5.60	-11.29	-1.05	24.44	8.33	29.07	0.37
CIVILIAN EMPLOYMENT	-3.54	2.03	-1.09	3.39	-3.68	-4.38	-2.89	0.48	1.10	-0.87	1.31
AGRICULTURE	-0.72	1.15	-2.93	-1.54	-0.81	3.62	-1.13	0.57	-0.28	1.48	-0.84
INDUSTRY	5.62	-0.11	-6.76	4.06	-3.83	5.23	3.45	-1.95	-0.41	-6.40	-0.01
SERVICES	2.76	3.23	1.93	3.38	3.87	4.02	2.85	1.65	1.88	1.52	1.97
CIVILIAN EMPLOYMENT BY SECTORS (ISIC)											
ALL ACTIVITIES	3.54	2.03	-1.09	3.39	3.68	4.38	2.89	0.48	1.10	-0.87	1.31
AGRICULTURE	-0.72	1.15	-2.93	-1.54	-0.81	3.62	-1.13	0.57	-0.28	1.48	-0.84
MINING AND QUARRYING	6.12	4.52	12.07	5.59	6.05	2.02	4.77	8.78	14.20	-8.05	-10.41
MANUFACTURING	5.57	-0.13	-7.46	4.13	3.10	4.28	3.09	-2.30	-0.57	-7.02	-1.68
ELECTRICITY, GAS AND WATER	2.98	1.34	0.61	5.88	1.34	1.89	4.17	4.99	1.36	-0.67	4.21
CONSTRUCTION	5.36	-0.81	-7.69	3.18	6.79	9.87	4.40	-3.45	-2.49	-5.02	6.83
TRADE, RESTAURANTS AND HOTELS	2.42	2.95	1.35	3.46	4.06	3.00	2.37	0.48	1.79	1.41	1.89
TRANSPORT, COMMUNICATION	0.71	4.16	-2.06	-0.78	3.50	5.73	3.90	-1.02	0.96	-1.39	-5.22
FINANCING, INSURANCE AND BUSINESS SERVICES	6.28	3.89	-0.06	3.81	6.34	8.33	6.02	2.48	3.59	4.80	7.41
COMMUNITY, SOCIAL AND PERSONAL SERVICES	2.77	3.09	3.69	4.02	3.20	3.34	2.15	2.79	1.64	1.21	1.74
WAGE EARNERS AND SALARIED EMPLOYEES IN MANUFACTURING (ISIC)											
MANUFACTURING, TOTAL	5.24	-0.38	-8.74	3.68	3.61	4.18	2.61	-3.59	-0.57	-6.89	-1.51
FOOD, BEVERAGES AND TOBACCO	-1.54	-0.45	-2.86	1.90	0.91	0.73	0.45	-1.44	-2.03	-2.07	-0.82
TEXTILE, WEARING APPAREL AND LEATHER IND.	2.55	-4.87	-9.23	5.98	-0.76	0.28	-2.13	-3.70	-1.71	-7.64	-0.66
WOOD, WOOD PRODUCTS	4.71	-5.06	-14.14	8.91	5.52	5.31	1.28	-8.54	-2.33	-8.85	7.18
PAPER, PAPER PROD., PRINTING, PUBLISHING	1.79	0.11	-5.06	2.90	2.92	3.16	2.70	0.15	0.51	-1.07	1.19
CHEMICALS, PETROLEUM AND PLASTIC PRODUCTS	4.80	1.51	-6.92	3.52	5.79	3.42	2.09	-3.28	1.38	-4.22	-0.66
NON-METALLIC MINERAL PRODUCTS	5.60	-1.12	-11.16	2.38	3.88	4.33	1.58	-6.13	-3.63	-1.07	-0.69
BASIC METAL INDUSTRIES	7.33	2.38	-11.64	1.40	2.34	2.79	3.21	-8.93	-1.75	-17.83	-9.11
FABR. METAL PROD., MACHINERY AND EQUIPMENT	8.48	0.96	-9.58	3.23	5.15	6.62	4.94	-3.07	0.01	-7.73	-2.98
OTHER MANUFACTURING INDUSTRIES	4.85	-0.44	-9.96	5.41	2.10	3.20	-1.55	-6.07	-2.39	-6.37	-2.88

Table 1b:

POPULATION AND EMPLOYMENT: JAPAN

- thousands -

	1973	1974	1975	1976	1977	1978	1979	1980	1981	1982	1983
POPULATION AND EMPLOYMENT											
TOTAL POPULATION	108660	110160	111520	112770	113880	114920	115880	116800	117650	118450	119260
POPULATION, FROM 15 TO 64 YEARS	74250	74970	75640	76250	76840	77400	77970	78700	79180	79860	80670
MALES, FROM 15 TO 64 YEARS	36810	36830	37180	37550	37920	38180	38510	38920	39190	39550	40010
FEMALES, FROM 15 TO 64 YEARS	37900	38200	38460	38720	38920	39220	39470	39790	40000	40310	40660
TOTAL LABOUR FORCE	53260	53100	53230	53780	54520	55320	55960	56500	57070	57740	58880
MALES	32790	33110	33360	33660	33810	34060	34370	34650	34980	35220	35640
FEMALES	20470	19990	19870	20100	20700	21250	21600	21850	22090	22520	23240
UNEMPLOYED	680	730	1000	1080	1100	1240	1170	1260	1260	1360	1560
CIVILIAN EMPLOYMENT	52590	52370	52230	52710	53420	54080	54790	55360	55810	56380	57330
AGRICULTURE	7050	6750	6610	6430	6340	6330	6130	5770	5570	5480	5310
INDUSTRY	19570	19380	18730	18880	18890	18930	19140	19560	19700	19650	19930
SERVICES	25970	26240	26890	27400	28190	28820	29520	30030	30540	31250	32090
CIVILIAN EMPLOYMENT BY SECTORS (ISIC)											
ALL ACTIVITIES	52590	52370	52230	52710	53420	54080	54790	55360	55810	56380	57330
AGRICULTURE	7050	6750	6610	6430	6340	6330	6130	5770	5570	5480	5310
MINING AND QUARRYING	130	140	160	180	190	150	120	110	100	100	100
MANUFACTURING	14430	14270	13460	13450	13400	13260	13330	13670	13850	13800	14060
ELECTRICITY, GAS AND WATER	340	330	320	330	310	310	300	340	310	340	360
CONSTRUCTION	4670	4640	4790	4920	4990	5200	5360	5480	5440	5410	5410
TRADE, RESTAURANTS AND HOTELS	10850	10970	11270	11510	11930	12100	12280	12480	12740	12960	13130
TRANSPORT, COMMUNICATION	3370	3310	3330	3410	3410	3420	3490	3500	3440	3490	3500
FINANCING, INSURANCE AND BUSINESS SERVICES	1570	1630	1700	1730	1790	1800	3100	3170	3320	3490	3660
COMMUNITY, SOCIAL AND PERSONAL SERVICES	10060	10220	10510	10660	10950	11400	10560	10740	10920	11170	11640
WAGE EARNERS AND SALARIED EMPLOYEES IN MANUFACTURING (ISIC)											
MANUFACTURING, TOTAL	8153	7915	7547	7402	7195	7028	7193	7255	7317	7416	7430
FOOD, BEVERAGES AND TOBACCO	597	616	633	640	652	650	657	642	637	732	737
TEXTILE, WEARING APPAREL AND LEATHER IND.	970	890	850	841	773	741	764	741	727	715	688
WOOD, WOOD PRODUCTS	334	313	291	279	268	264	254	252	243	216	205
PAPER, PAPER PROD., PRINTING, PUBLISHING	500	484	466	477	466	459	463	455	447	458	461
CHEMICALS, PETROLEUM AND PLASTIC PRODUCTS	751	752	745	679	657	632	640	639	636	614	608
NON-METALLIC MINERAL PRODUCTS	374	363	338	332	331	334	339	334	326	309	299
BASIC METAL INDUSTRIES	637	633	607	591	572	548	542	540	532	529	514
FABR. METAL PROD., MACHINERY AND EQUIPMENT	3691	3574	3349	3290	3207	3134	3232	3345	3453	3533	3598
OTHER MANUFACTURING INDUSTRIES	299	290	268	273	269	266	302	308	316	310	320

Table 1b:

POPULATION AND EMPLOYMENT: JAPAN

- percentage change -

	1973	1974	1975	1976	1977	1978	1979	1980	1981	1982	1983
POPULATION AND EMPLOYMENT											
TOTAL POPULATION	2.34	1.38	1.23	1.12	0.98	0.91	0.84	0.79	0.73	0.68	0.68
POPULATION, FROM 15 TO 64 YEARS	1.92	0.97	0.89	0.81	0.77	0.73	0.74	0.94	0.61	0.86	1.01
MALES, FROM 15 TO 64 YEARS	1.73	1.15	0.95	0.94	1.04	0.71	0.84	1.06	0.69	0.92	1.16
FEMALES, FROM 15 TO 64 YEARS	2.18	0.79	0.68	0.68	0.52	0.77	0.64	0.81	0.53	0.77	0.87
TOTAL LABOUR FORCE	2.44	-0.30	0.24	1.03	1.38	1.47	1.16	0.96	1.01	1.17	1.97
MALES	1.93	0.98	0.76	0.96	0.39	0.74	0.91	0.81	0.95	0.69	1.19
FEMALES	3.28	-2.14	-0.60	1.16	2.99	2.66	1.65	1.16	1.10	1.95	3.20
UNEMPLOYED	-6.85	7.35	36.99	8.00	1.85	12.73	-5.65	-2.56	10.53	7.94	14.71
CIVILIAN EMPLOYMENT	2.59	-0.42	-0.27	0.92	1.35	1.24	1.31	1.04	0.81	1.02	1.68
AGRICULTURE	-6.62	-4.26	-2.07	-2.72	-1.40	-0.16	-3.16	-5.87	-3.47	-1.62	-3.10
INDUSTRY	5.16	-0.97	-3.35	0.80	0.05	0.21	1.11	2.19	0.72	-0.25	1.42
SERVICES	3.47	1.04	2.48	1.90	2.88	2.23	2.43	1.73	1.70	2.32	2.69
CIVILIAN EMPLOYMENT BY SECTORS (ISIC)											
ALL ACTIVITIES	2.59	-0.42	-0.27	0.92	1.35	1.24	1.31	1.04	0.81	1.02	1.68
AGRICULTURE	-6.62	-4.26	-2.07	-2.72	-1.40	-0.16	-3.16	-5.87	-3.47	-1.62	-3.10
MINING AND QUARRYING	-18.25	7.69	14.29	12.50	5.56	-21.05	-20.00	-8.33	-9.09	0.00	0.00
MANUFACTURING	4.34	-1.11	-5.68	-0.07	-0.37	-1.04	0.53	2.55	1.32	-0.36	1.88
ELECTRICITY, GAS AND WATER	17.24	-2.94	-3.03	3.11	-6.06	3.23	3.13	-9.09	3.33	9.68	5.88
CONSTRUCTION	7.85	-0.64	3.23	2.71	1.42	4.21	3.08	2.24	-0.73	-0.55	0.00
TRADE, RESTAURANTS AND HOTELS	3.83	1.11	2.73	2.13	3.65	1.42	1.49	1.63	2.08	1.73	1.31
TRANSPORT, COMMUNICATION	3.06	-1.78	0.30	2.71	0.00	0.29	2.05	0.29	-1.71	1.45	-0.29
FINANCING, INSURANCE AND BUSINESS SERVICES	5.37	3.82	4.29	1.76	3.47	0.56	72.22	2.26	4.73	5.12	4.87
COMMUNITY, SOCIAL AND PERSONAL SERVICES	3.18	1.59	2.84	1.43	2.72	4.11	-7.37	1.70	1.68	2.29	4.21
WAGE EARNERS AND SALARIED EMPLOYEES IN MANUFACTURING (ISIC)											
MANUFACTURING, TOTAL	3.14	-2.92	-4.65	-1.92	-2.80	-2.32	2.35	0.86	0.85	1.35	0.19
FOOD, BEVERAGES AND TOBACCO	-12.21	3.18	2.76	1.11	1.88	-0.31	1.08	-2.28	-0.78	14.91	0.68
TEXTILE, WEARING APPAREL AND LEATHER IND.	1.46	-8.25	-4.49	-1.06	-8.09	-4.14	3.10	-3.01	-1.89	-1.65	-3.78
WOOD, WOOD PRODUCTS	-0.60	-6.29	-7.03	-4.12	-3.94	-1.49	-3.79	-0.79	-3.57	-11.11	-5.09
PAPER, PAPER PROD., PRINTING, PUBLISHING	5.71	-3.20	-3.72	2.36	-2.31	-1.50	0.87	-1.73	-1.76	2.46	0.66
CHEMICALS, PETROLEUM AND PLASTIC PRODUCTS	4.74	0.13	-0.93	-8.86	-3.24	-3.81	1.27	-0.16	-0.47	-3.46	-0.98
NON-METALLIC MINERAL PRODUCTS	5.35	-2.94	-6.89	-1.78	-0.30	-0.91	1.50	-1.47	-2.40	-5.21	-3.24
BASIC METAL INDUSTRIES	2.58	-0.63	-4.11	-2.64	-3.21	-4.20	-1.09	-0.37	-1.48	-0.56	-2.84
FABR. METAL PROD.; MACHINERY AND EQUIPMENT	6.99	-3.17	-6.30	-1.76	-2.52	-2.28	3.13	3.50	3.23	2.12	1.84
OTHER MANUFACTURING INDUSTRIES	-5.68	-3.01	-7.59	1.87	-1.47	-1.12	13.53	1.99	2.60	-1.90	3.23

Table 1c:

POPULATION AND EMPLOYMENT: EC

- thousands -

POPULATION AND EMPLOYMENT

	1973	1974	1975	1976	1977	1978	1979	1980	1981	1982	1983
TOTAL POPULATION	256709	257707	258243	258594	258854	259549	260208	261064	261777	262229	262564
POPULATION, FROM 15 TO 64 YEARS	162577	163685	164366	165133	166094	167267	168602	170047	171833	173733	175488
TOTAL LABOUR FORCE	108294	108854	109279	109911	110728	111410	112656	113581	114315	115003	115390
CIVILIAN LABOUR FORCE	106019	106610	107076	107694	108504	109193	110451	111359	112059	112743	113140
CIVILIAN EMPLOYMENT	103018	103385	102394	102193	102635	103218	104451	104889	103470	102578	101827
AGRICULTURE	9400	9087	8757	8508	8216	8044	7837	7587	7291	7008	6951
INDUSTRY	43159	42910	41422	40665	40564	40367	40480	40181	38644	37455	36275
SERVICES	50459	51389	52215	53020	53854	54806	56126	57122	57532	58115	58602

Table 1c:

POPULATION AND EMPLOYMENT: EC

- percentage change -

POPULATION AND EMPLOYMENT

	1973	1974	1975	1976	1977	1978	1979	1980	1981	1982	1983
TOTAL POPULATION	0.57	0.39	0.21	0.14	0.10	0.27	0.25	0.33	0.27	0.17	0.13
POPULATION, FROM 15 TO 64 YEARS	0.70	0.68	0.42	0.47	0.58	0.71	0.80	0.86	1.05	1.11	1.01
TOTAL LABOUR FORCE	1.04	0.52	0.39	0.58	0.74	0.62	1.12	0.82	0.65	0.60	0.34
CIVILIAN LABOUR FORCE	1.08	0.56	0.44	0.58	0.75	0.63	1.15	0.82	0.63	0.61	0.35
CIVILIAN EMPLOYMENT	1.31	0.36	-0.96	-0.20	0.43	0.57	1.18	0.43	-1.35	-0.86	-0.73
AGRICULTURE	-3.50	-3.33	-3.63	-2.84	-3.43	-2.09	-2.57	-3.19	-3.90	-3.88	-0.81
INDUSTRY	-0.76	-0.58	-3.47	-1.83	-0.25	-0.49	0.28	-0.74	-3.83	-3.08	-3.15
SERVICES	2.75	1.84	1.61	1.54	1.57	1.77	2.41	1.77	0.72	1.01	0.84

Table 1d:

POPULATION AND EMPLOYMENT: GERMANY
- thousands -

	1973	1974	1975	1976	1977	1978	1979	1980	1981	1982	1983
POPULATION AND EMPLOYMENT											
TOTAL POPULATION	61976	62054	61829	61531	61400	61327	61359	61566	61682	61638	61423
POPULATION, FROM 15 TO 64 YEARS	39509	39654	39606	39593	39732	39945	40287	40828	41427	41973	42390
MALES, FROM 15 TO 64 YEARS	19262	19370	19344	19356	19471	19635	19883	20251	20603	20892	21104
FEMALES, FROM 15 TO 64 YEARS	20247	20284	20262	20236	20261	20310	20404	20577	20824	21081	21286
TOTAL LABOUR FORCE	27195	27147	26884	26651	26577	26692	26915	27191	27373	27465	27445
CIVILIAN LABOUR FORCE	26684	26620	26359	26119	26044	26162	26383	26660	26838	26933	26907
MALES	16651	16511	16300	16098	16056	16162	16266	16362	16409	16429	16363
FEMALES	10034	10110	10060	10022	9988	10030	10117	10298	10429	10504	10544
UNEMPLOYED	273	582	1074	1060	1030	993	876	889	1272	1833	2258
CIVILIAN EMPLOYMENT	26411	26038	25285	25059	25014	25169	25507	25771	25566	25100	24649
AGRICULTURE	1924	1842	1773	1682	1589	1536	1479	1436	1405	1381	1371
INDUSTRY	12554	12158	11480	11258	11176	11182	11313	11383	11123	10721	10352
SERVICES	11933	12038	12032	12119	12249	12451	12715	12952	13038	12998	12926
CIVILIAN EMPLOYMENT BY SECTORS (ISIC)											
ALL ACTIVITIES	26411	26038	25285	25059	25014	25169	25507	25771	25566	25100	24649
AGRICULTURE	1924	1842	1773	1682	1589	1536	1479	1436	1405	1381	1371
MINING AND QUARRYING	398	374	356	358	332	345	338	340	359	329	323
MANUFACTURING	9697	9479	9010	8807	8770	8751	8810	8849	8597	8318	8002
ELECTRICITY, GAS AND WATER	206	217	237	216	232	224	227	237	238	248	245
CONSTRUCTION	2253	2088	1877	1877	1842	1862	1938	1957	1929	1826	1782
TRADE, RESTAURANTS AND HOTELS	3899	3838	3773	3766	3799	3842	3880	3896	3868	3775	3703
TRANSPORT, COMMUNICATION	1607	1613	1576	1539	1522	1519	1534	1548	1545	1538	1519
FINANCING, INSURANCE AND BUSINESS SERVICES	1298	1330	1336	1347	1335	1372	1441	1507	1551	1569	1582
COMMUNITY, SOCIAL AND PERSONAL SERVICES	5129	5257	5347	5467	5593	5718	5860	6001	6074	6116	6122
WAGE EARNERS AND SALARIED EMPLOYEES IN MANUFACTURING (ISIC)											
MANUFACTURING, TOTAL	9211	9000	8555	8375	8340	8340	8389	8433	8193	7914	7598
FOOD, BEVERAGES AND TOBACCO	745	718	702	707	732	736	747	757	766	747	717
TEXTILE, WEARING APPAREL AND LEATHER IND.	1060	952	882	852	829	822	809	794	722	659	633
WOOD, WOOD PRODUCTS	512	489	489	464	478	480	483	501	481	466	448
PAPER, PAPER PROD., PRINTING, PUBLISHING	556	535	500	467	458	489	486	483	481	478	464
CHEMICALS, PETROLEUM AND PLASTIC PRODUCTS	999	1003	1011	979	934	922	955	963	956	914	877
NON-METALLIC MINERAL PRODUCTS	347	322	279	290	295	286	297	283	292	279	268
BASIC METAL INDUSTRIES	610	608	578	488	622	521	542	483	693	566	543
FABR. METAL PROD., MACHINERY AND EQUIPMENT	4298	4297	4043	4061	3927	4019	4003	4095	3730	3742	3589
OTHER MANUFACTURING INDUSTRIES	84	76	71	67	65	65	67	74	72	62	59

Table 1d:

POPULATION AND EMPLOYMENT: GERMANY
- percentage change -

	1973	1974	1975	1976	1977	1978	1979	1980	1981	1982	1983
POPULATION AND EMPLOYMENT											
TOTAL POPULATION	0.49	0.13	-0.36	-0.48	-0.21	-0.12	0.05	0.34	0.19	-0.07	-0.35
POPULATION, FROM 15 TO 64 YEARS	0.73	0.37	-0.12	-0.03	0.35	0.54	0.86	1.34	1.47	1.32	0.99
MALES, FROM 15 TO 64 YEARS	1.13	0.56	-0.13	0.06	0.59	0.84	1.26	1.85	1.74	1.40	1.01
FEMALES, FROM 15 TO 64 YEARS	0.35	0.18	-0.11	-0.13	0.12	0.24	0.46	0.85	1.20	1.23	0.97
TOTAL LABOUR FORCE	0.76	-0.18	-0.97	-0.87	-0.28	0.43	0.84	1.03	0.67	0.34	-0.07
CIVILIAN LABOUR FORCE	0.85	-0.24	-0.98	-0.91	-0.29	0.45	0.84	1.05	0.67	0.35	-0.10
MALES	0.34	-0.84	-1.28	-1.24	-0.26	0.47	0.83	0.59	0.29	0.12	-0.40
FEMALES	1.70	0.76	-0.49	-0.38	-0.34	0.42	0.87	1.79	1.27	0.72	0.38
UNEMPLOYED	10.98	113.19	84.54	-1.30	-2.83	-3.59	-11.78	1.48	43.08	44.10	23.19
CIVILIAN EMPLOYMENT	0.75	-1.41	-2.89	-0.89	-0.18	-0.62	-1.34	1.04	-0.80	-1.82	-1.80
AGRICULTURE	-4.66	-4.26	-3.75	-5.13	-5.53	-3.34	-3.71	-2.91	-2.16	-1.71	-0.72
INDUSTRY	0.28	-3.15	-5.58	-1.93	-0.73	0.05	1.17	-0.62	-2.28	-3.61	-3.44
SERVICES	2.19	0.88	-0.05	0.72	1.07	1.65	2.12	1.86	0.66	-0.31	-0.55
CIVILIAN EMPLOYMENT BY SECTORS (ISIC)											
ALL ACTIVITIES	0.75	-1.41	-2.89	-0.89	-0.18	0.62	1.34	1.04	-0.80	-1.82	-1.80
AGRICULTURE	-4.66	-4.26	-3.75	-5.13	-5.53	-3.34	-3.71	-2.91	-2.16	-1.71	-0.72
MINING AND QUARRYING	-4.33	-6.03	-4.81	0.56	-7.26	-3.92	-2.03	0.59	5.59	-8.36	-1.82
MANUFACTURING	-0.47	-2.25	-4.95	-2.25	-0.42	-0.22	0.67	0.44	-2.85	-3.25	-3.80
ELECTRICITY, GAS AND WATER	0.98	5.34	9.22	8.86	7.41	-3.45	1.34	4.41	0.42	4.20	1.21
CONSTRUCTION	0.27	-7.32	-10.11	0.00	-1.86	1.09	4.08	0.98	-1.43	-5.34	-2.41
TRADE, RESTAURANTS AND HOTELS	1.06	-1.56	-1.69	-0.19	0.88	1.13	0.99	0.41	-0.72	-2.40	-1.91
TRANSPORT, COMMUNICATION	1.84	0.37	-2.29	-2.35	-1.80	-0.20	0.99	0.91	-0.19	-0.45	-1.24
FINANCING, INSURANCE AND BUSINESS SERVICES	2.12	2.47	0.45	0.82	-0.89	2.77	5.03	4.58	2.92	1.16	0.83
COMMUNITY, SOCIAL AND PERSONAL SERVICES	3.20	2.50	1.71	2.24	2.30	2.23	2.48	2.41	1.22	0.69	0.10
WAGE EARNERS AND SALARIED EMPLOYEES IN MANUFACTURING (ISIC)											
MANUFACTURING, TOTAL	0.66	-2.29	-4.94	-2.10	-0.42	0.00	0.59	0.52	-2.85	-3.41	-3.99
FOOD, BEVERAGES AND TOBACCO	-2.36	-3.62	-2.23	0.71	3.54	0.55	1.49	1.34	1.19	-2.48	-4.02
TEXTILE, WEARING APPAREL AND LEATHER IND.	-3.90	-10.19	-7.35	-3.40	-2.70	-0.84	-1.58	-1.85	-9.07	-8.73	-3.95
WOOD, WOOD PRODUCTS	1.59	-4.49	0.00	-5.11	3.02	0.42	-0.63	3.73	-3.99	-3.12	-3.86
PAPER, PAPER PROD., PRINTING, PUBLISHING	1.46	-3.78	-6.54	-6.60	-1.93	6.77	-0.61	-0.62	-0.41	-0.62	-2.93
CHEMICALS, PETROLEUM AND PLASTIC PRODUCTS	1.42	-0.40	0.80	-3.17	-4.60	-1.28	3.58	-0.84	-0.73	-4.39	-4.05
NON-METALLIC MINERAL PRODUCTS	-0.57	-7.20	-13.35	3.94	1.72	-3.05	3.85	-4.71	3.18	-4.45	-3.94
BASIC METAL INDUSTRIES	-1.13	-0.33	-4.93	-15.57	27.46	-16.24	4.03	-10.89	43.48	-18.33	-4.06
FABR. METAL PROD., MACHINERY AND EQUIPMENT	2.31	-0.02	-5.91	-0.45	-3.30	2.34	-0.40	2.30	-8.91	0.32	-4.09
OTHER MANUFACTURING INDUSTRIES	3.70	-9.52	-6.58	-5.63	-2.99	0.00	3.08	10.45	-2.70	-13.89	-4.84

Table 1e: POPULATION AND EMPLOYMENT: FRANCE

- thousands -

	1973	1974	1975	1976	1977	1978	1979	1980	1981	1982	1983
POPULATION AND EMPLOYMENT											
TOTAL POPULATION	52119	52461	52699	52909	53145	53376	53606	53880	54182	54480	54729
POPULATION, FROM 15 TO 64 YEARS	32503	32769	32987	33214	33464	33702	33963	34320	34796	35278	35703
MALES, FROM 15 TO 64 YEARS	16349	16493	16597	16697	16810	16920	17043	17215	17444	17672	17868
FEMALES, FROM 15 TO 64 YEARS	16154	16276	16390	16517	16654	16782	16920	17105	17352	17606	17835
TOTAL LABOUR FORCE	22022	22260	22385	22610	22912	23090	23266	23387	23532	23753	23690
CIVILIAN LABOUR FORCE	21442	21680	21796	22018	22324	22491	22689	22818	22955	23173	23115
MALES	13378	13363	13419	13436	13509	13519	13542	13531	13532	13563	13443
FEMALES	8064	8217	8377	8582	8815	8972	9147	9287	9423	9610	9672
UNEMPLOYED	577	618	911	991	1122	1206	1371	1471	1729	1920	1961
CIVILIAN EMPLOYMENT	20865	21062	20885	21027	21202	21285	21317	21347	21226	21254	21154
AGRICULTURE	2348	2246	2158	2083	2013	1954	1907	1854	1790	1737	1697
INDUSTRY	8238	8298	8051	7979	7948	7828	7717	7656	7461	7339	7145
SERVICES	10279	10518	10676	10965	11241	11503	11693	11837	11975	12178	12312
CIVILIAN EMPLOYMENT BY SECTORS (ISIC)											
ALL ACTIVITIES	20814	20959	20714	20855	21036	21113	21118	21127	20950	20984	20867
AGRICULTURE	2348	2246	2158	2083	2013	1954	1907	1854	1790	1737	1697
MINING AND QUARRYING	-	-	-	-	-	-	-	-	-	-	-
MANUFACTURING	-	-	-	-	-	-	-	-	-	-	-
ELECTRICITY, GAS AND WATER	-	-	-	-	-	-	-	-	-	-	-
CONSTRUCTION	-	-	-	-	-	-	-	-	-	-	-
TRADE, RESTAURANTS AND HOTELS	-	-	-	-	-	-	-	-	-	-	-
TRANSPORT, COMMUNICATION	-	-	-	-	-	-	-	-	-	-	-
FINANCING, INSURANCE AND BUSINESS SERVICES	-	-	-	-	-	-	-	-	-	-	-
COMMUNITY, SOCIAL AND PERSONAL SERVICES	-	-	-	-	-	-	-	-	-	-	-
WAGE EARNERS AND SALARIED EMPLOYEES IN MANUFACTURING (ISIC)											
MANUFACTURING, TOTAL	5599	5658	5502	5449	5429	5346	5254	5188	5010	4927	4803
FOOD, BEVERAGES AND TOBACCO	-	-	513	512	516	519	515	516	510	511	504
TEXTILE, WEARING APPAREL AND LEATHER IND.	-	-	764	739	717	689	665	643	599	579	552
WOOD, WOOD PRODUCTS	-	-	233	229	229	228	225	223	215	210	206
PAPER, PAPER PROD., PRINTING, PUBLISHING	-	-	343	337	335	333	328	327	317	313	307
CHEMICALS, PETROLEUM AND PLASTIC PRODUCTS	-	-	606	603	607	615	615	613	595	585	567
NON-METALLIC MINERAL PRODUCTS	-	-	239	236	233	229	222	218	210	202	197
BASIC METAL INDUSTRIES	-	-	271	269	262	247	233	219	209	203	197
FABR. METAL PROD., MACHINERY AND EQUIPMENT	-	-	2434	2426	2429	2389	2354	2334	2266	2236	2185
OTHER MANUFACTURING INDUSTRIES	-	-	98	98	101	99	97	95	90	88	87

Table 1e:

POPULATION AND EMPLOYMENT: FRANCE

- percentage change -

	1973	1974	1975	1976	1977	1978	1979	1980	1981	1982	1983
POPULATION AND EMPLOYMENT											
TOTAL POPULATION	0.81	0.66	0.45	0.40	0.45	0.43	0.43	0.51	0.56	0.55	0.46
POPULATION, FROM 15 TO 64 YEARS	0.87	0.82	0.67	0.69	0.75	0.71	0.77	1.05	1.39	1.39	1.20
MALES, FROM 15 TO 64 YEARS	0.96	0.88	0.63	0.60	0.68	0.65	0.73	1.01	1.33	1.31	1.11
FEMALES, FROM 15 TO 64 YEARS	0.78	0.76	0.70	0.77	0.83	0.77	0.82	1.09	1.44	1.46	1.30
TOTAL LABOUR FORCE	1.31	1.08	0.56	1.01	1.34	0.78	0.76	0.52	0.62	0.94	-0.27
CIVILIAN LABOUR FORCE	1.29	1.11	0.54	1.02	1.39	0.75	0.88	0.57	0.60	0.95	-0.25
MALES	0.80	0.64	-0.33	0.13	0.54	0.07	0.17	-0.08	0.01	0.23	-0.88
FEMALES	2.13	1.90	1.95	2.45	2.71	1.78	1.95	1.53	1.46	1.98	0.65
UNEMPLOYED	-3.03	7.11	47.41	8.78	13.22	7.49	13.68	7.29	17.54	11.05	2.14
CIVILIAN EMPLOYMENT	1.42	0.94	-0.84	0.68	0.83	0.39	0.15	0.14	-0.57	-0.13	-0.47
AGRICULTURE	-5.02	-4.34	-3.92	-3.48	-3.36	-2.93	-2.41	-2.78	-3.45	-2.96	-2.30
INDUSTRY	1.83	0.73	-2.98	-0.89	-0.39	-1.51	-1.42	-0.79	-2.55	-1.64	-2.64
SERVICES	2.68	2.33	1.50	2.71	2.52	2.33	1.65	1.23	1.17	1.70	1.10
CIVILIAN EMPLOYMENT BY SECTORS (ISIC)											
ALL ACTIVITIES	1.27	0.70	-1.17	0.68	0.87	0.37	0.02	0.04	-0.84	0.16	-0.56
AGRICULTURE	-5.02	-4.34	-3.92	-3.48	-3.36	-2.93	-2.41	-2.78	-3.45	-2.96	-2.30
MINING AND QUARRYING	-	-	-	-	-	-	-	-	-	-	-
MANUFACTURING	-	-	-	-	-	-	-	-	-	-	-
ELECTRICITY, GAS AND WATER	-	-	-	-	-	-	-	-	-	-	-
CONSTRUCTION	-	-	-	-	-	-	-	-	-	-	-
TRADE, RESTAURANTS AND HOTELS	-	-	-	-	-	-	-	-	-	-	-
TRANSPORT, COMMUNICATION	-	-	-	-	-	-	-	-	-	-	-
FINANCING, INSURANCE AND BUSINESS SERVICES	-	-	-	-	-	-	-	-	-	-	-
COMMUNITY, SOCIAL AND PERSONAL SERVICES	-	-	-	-	-	-	-	-	-	-	-
WAGE EARNERS AND SALARIED EMPLOYEES IN MANUFACTURING (ISIC)											
MANUFACTURING, TOTAL	2.26	1.05	-2.76	-0.96	-0.37	-1.53	-1.72	-1.26	-3.43	-1.66	-2.52
FOOD, BEVERAGES AND TOBACCO	-	-	-	-0.19	-0.78	0.58	-0.77	0.19	-1.16	0.20	-1.37
TEXTILE, WEARING APPAREL AND LEATHER IND.	-	-	-	-3.27	-2.98	-3.91	-3.48	-3.31	-6.84	-3.34	-4.66
WOOD, WOOD PRODUCTS	-	-	-	-1.72	0.00	-0.44	-1.32	-0.89	-3.59	-2.33	-1.90
PAPER, PAPER PROD., PRINTING, PUBLISHING	-	-	-	-1.75	-0.59	-0.60	-1.50	-0.30	-3.06	-1.26	-1.92
CHEMICALS, PETROLEUM AND PLASTIC PRODUCTS	-	-	-	-0.50	0.66	1.32	0.00	-0.33	-2.94	-1.68	-3.08
NON-METALLIC MINERAL PRODUCTS	-	-	-	-1.26	-1.27	-1.72	-3.06	-1.80	-3.67	-3.81	-2.48
BASIC METAL INDUSTRIES	-	-	-	-0.74	-2.60	-5.73	-5.67	-6.01	-4.57	-2.87	-2.96
FABR. METAL PROD., MACHINERY AND EQUIPMENT	-	-	-	-0.33	0.12	-1.65	-1.47	-0.85	-2.91	-1.32	-2.28
OTHER MANUFACTURING INDUSTRIES	-	-	-	0.00	3.06	-1.98	-2.02	-2.06	-5.26	-2.22	-1.14

Employment Trends

Table 1f: POPULATION AND EMPLOYMENT: UNITED KINGDOM

- thousands -

	1973	1974	1975	1976	1977	1978	1979	1980	1981	1982	1983
POPULATION AND EMPLOYMENT											
TOTAL POPULATION	56210	56224	56215	56206	56179	56167	56227	56314	56379	56335	56377
POPULATION, FROM 15 TO 64 YEARS	35109	35132	35192	35329	35488	35648	35858	36078	36302	36498	36763
MALES, FROM 15 TO 64 YEARS	17474	17504	17554	17630	17713	17797	17934	18038	18138	18258	18367
FEMALES, FROM 15 TO 64 YEARS	17635	17629	17638	17699	17775	17851	17924	18040	18164	18240	18396
TOTAL LABOUR FORCE	25612	25659	25878	26092	26209	26343	26609	26819	26718	26757	26776
CIVILIAN LABOUR FORCE	25251	25314	25541	25756	25882	26023	26295	26496	26384	26433	26454
MALES	15897	15737	15842	15942	15904	15913	15919	16003	16020	15973	15859
FEMALES	9355	9577	9700	9816	9980	10112	10377	10493	10363	10459	10595
UNEMPLOYED	557	528	838	1265	1359	1343	1234	1513	2395	2770	2984
CIVILIAN EMPLOYMENT	24694	24786	24703	24491	24522	24680	25061	24983	23989	23663	23470
AGRICULTURE	724	689	677	677	675	671	658	647	635	635	628
INDUSTRY	10482	10452	10007	9720	9690	9670	9713	9424	8598	8204	7882
SERVICES	13488	13635	14019	14094	14157	14340	14691	14914	14757	14824	14961
CIVILIAN EMPLOYMENT BY SECTORS (ISIC)											
ALL ACTIVITIES	24694	24786	24703	24491	24522	24680	25061	24983	23989	23663	23470
AGRICULTURE	724	689	677	677	675	671	658	647	635	635	628
MINING AND QUARRYING	371	357	360	356	358	361	358	361	351	340	327
MANUFACTURING	8000	8046	7668	7424	7471	7436	7402	7085	6364	6056	5785
ELECTRICITY, GAS AND WATER	344	347	353	353	347	340	348	352	349	340	336
CONSTRUCTION	1767	1702	1626	1587	1514	1533	1605	1626	1534	1468	1433
TRADE, RESTAURANTS AND HOTELS	4469	4464	4506	4495	4547	4583	4722	4810	4697	4718	4753
TRANSPORT, COMMUNICATION	1592	1580	1592	1550	1544	1562	1575	1592	1536	1471	1426
FINANCING, INSURANCE AND BUSINESS SERVICES	1547	1605	1609	1610	1630	1681	1770	1842	1891	1965	2033
COMMUNITY, SOCIAL AND PERSONAL SERVICES	5878	5995	6306	6434	6434	6514	6624	6670	6633	6670	6749
WAGE EARNERS AND SALARIED EMPLOYEES IN MANUFACTURING (ISIC)											
MANUFACTURING, TOTAL	7865	7908	7526	7281	7327	7293	7260	6939	6216	5904	5629
FOOD, BEVERAGES AND TOBACCO	785	798	758	745	744	737	739	730	688	669	642
TEXTILE, WEARING APPAREL AND LEATHER IND.	1035	1005	928	889	897	865	851	760	649	603	566
WOOD, WOOD PRODUCTS	276	268	249	249	244	242	244	231	213	204	207
PAPER, PAPER PROD., PRINTING, PUBLISHING	578	592	569	545	540	544	553	547	517	505	494
CHEMICALS, PETROLEUM AND PLASTIC PRODUCTS	764	781	750	738	745	749	741	708	641	610	576
NON-METALLIC MINERAL PRODUCTS	319	316	292	279	280	281	279	265	233	220	202
BASIC METAL INDUSTRIES	568	558	549	515	530	506	490	446	365	361	325
FABR. METAL PROD., MACHINERY AND EQUIPMENT	3435	3483	3331	3217	3241	3262	3259	3157	2828	2663	2550
OTHER MANUFACTURING INDUSTRIES	106	107	101	103	106	106	103	94	81	69	65

Table 1f:

POPULATION AND EMPLOYMENT: UNITED KINGDOM
- percentage change -

	1973	1974	1975	1976	1977	1978	1979	1980	1981	1982	1983
POPULATION AND EMPLOYMENT											
TOTAL POPULATION	0.23	0.02	-0.02	-0.02	-0.05	-0.02	0.11	0.15	0.12	-0.08	0.07
POPULATION, FROM 15 TO 64 YEARS	0.14	0.07	0.17	0.39	0.45	0.45	0.59	0.61	0.62	0.54	0.73
MALES, FROM 15 TO 64 YEARS	0.22	0.17	0.29	0.43	0.47	0.47	0.71	0.64	0.55	0.56	0.86
FEMALES, FROM 15 TO 64 YEARS	0.06	-0.03	0.05	0.35	0.43	0.43	0.46	0.59	0.69	0.52	0.60
TOTAL LABOUR FORCE	1.38	0.18	0.85	0.83	0.45	0.51	1.01	0.79	-0.38	0.15	-0.07
CIVILIAN LABOUR FORCE	1.44	0.25	0.90	0.84	0.49	0.54	1.05	0.76	-0.11	0.19	-0.08
MALES	0.13	-1.01	0.67	0.63	-0.24	0.06	0.04	0.53	0.11	-0.29	-0.71
FEMALES	3.76	2.37	1.28	1.20	1.67	1.32	2.62	1.12	-1.24	0.93	1.30
UNEMPLOYED	-28.41	-5.21	58.71	50.95	7.43	-1.18	-8.29	22.61	58.29	15.66	7.73
CIVILIAN EMPLOYMENT	2.40	0.37	-0.33	-0.86	0.13	0.64	1.54	-0.31	-3.98	-1.36	-0.82
AGRICULTURE	0.42	-4.83	-1.74	0.00	-0.30	-0.59	-1.94	-1.67	-1.85	0.00	-1.10
INDUSTRY	1.53	-0.29	-4.26	-2.87	-0.30	-0.21	0.44	-2.98	-8.76	-4.58	-3.92
SERVICES	3.20	1.09	2.82	0.53	0.45	1.29	2.45	1.52	-1.05	0.45	-0.92
CIVILIAN EMPLOYMENT BY SECTORS (ISIC)											
ALL ACTIVITIES	2.40	0.37	-0.33	-0.86	0.13	0.64	1.54	-0.31	-3.98	-1.36	-0.82
AGRICULTURE	0.42	-4.83	-1.74	0.00	-0.30	-0.59	-1.94	-1.67	-1.85	0.00	-1.10
MINING AND QUARRYING	-4.13	-3.77	0.84	-1.11	0.56	0.84	-0.83	-0.84	-2.77	-3.13	-3.82
MANUFACTURING	0.57	0.57	-4.70	-3.18	0.63	-0.47	-0.46	-4.28	-10.18	-4.84	-4.47
ELECTRICITY, GAS AND WATER	-3.37	0.87	1.73	0.00	-1.70	-2.02	2.35	1.15	-0.85	-2.58	-2.06
CONSTRUCTION	8.67	-3.68	-4.47	-2.40	-4.60	1.25	4.70	1.31	-5.66	-4.30	-2.11
TRADE, RESTAURANTS AND HOTELS	3.69	-0.11	0.94	-0.24	1.16	0.79	3.03	1.86	-2.35	0.45	0.74
TRANSPORT, COMMUNICATION	-1.06	-0.75	0.76	-2.64	-0.39	1.17	0.83	1.08	-3.52	-4.23	-3.06
FINANCING, INSURANCE AND BUSINESS SERVICES	5.38	3.75	0.25	2.06	1.24	3.13	5.29	4.07	2.66	3.91	3.46
COMMUNITY, SOCIAL AND PERSONAL SERVICES	3.49	1.99	5.19	2.03	0.00	1.24	1.69	0.69	-0.55	0.56	1.18
WAGE EARNERS AND SALARIED EMPLOYEES IN MANUFACTURING (ISIC)											
MANUFACTURING, TOTAL	0.65	0.55	-4.83	-3.26	0.63	-0.46	-0.45	-4.42	-10.42	-5.02	-4.66
FOOD, BEVERAGES AND TOBACCO	-0.25	1.66	-5.01	-1.72	-0.13	-0.94	0.27	-1.22	-5.75	-2.76	-4.04
TEXTILE, WEARING APPAREL AND LEATHER IND.	-1.24	-2.90	-7.66	-4.20	-2.01	-3.57	-1.62	-10.69	-14.61	-7.09	-6.14
WOOD, WOOD PRODUCTS	6.15	2.42	-7.09	-4.22	-2.01	-0.82	0.83	-5.33	-7.79	-4.23	-1.47
PAPER, PAPER PROD., PRINTING, PUBLISHING	-0.86	2.23	-3.89	-1.60	0.95	0.74	1.65	-1.08	-5.48	-2.32	-2.18
CHEMICALS, PETROLEUM AND PLASTIC PRODUCTS	1.33	-0.34	-2.33	-4.45	0.36	0.54	-1.07	-4.45	-9.46	-4.84	-5.57
NON-METALLIC MINERAL PRODUCTS	1.27	-1.76	-1.61	-6.19	2.91	0.36	-0.71	-5.02	-12.08	-5.58	-8.18
BASIC METAL INDUSTRIES	0.71	1.40	-4.36	-3.42	0.75	-4.53	-3.16	-8.98	-18.16	-1.10	-9.97
FABR. METAL PROD., MACHINERY AND EQUIPMENT	0.77	1.03	-1.76	-3.42	2.91	0.65	-0.09	-3.13	-10.42	-5.83	-4.24
OTHER MANUFACTURING INDUSTRIES	1.92	0.94	-5.61	1.98	1.98	0.00	-2.83	-8.74	-13.83	-14.81	-5.80

Employment Trends

Table 1g:

POPULATION AND EMPLOYMENT: ITALY

- thousands -

	1973	1974	1975	1976	1977	1978	1979	1980	1981	1982	1983
POPULATION AND EMPLOYMENT											
TOTAL POPULATION	53981	54541	54967	55325	55576	55806	56016	56121	56292	56448	56577
POPULATION, FROM 15 TO 64 YEARS	35555	35980	36253	36448	36647	36993	37297	37432	37698	38185	38613
MALES, FROM 15 TO 64 YEARS	17387	17592	17724	17773	17920	18127	18276	18355	18523	18778	18985
FEMALES, FROM 15 TO 64 YEARS	18168	18388	18529	18675	18727	18866	19021	19079	19176	19406	19629
TOTAL LABOUR FORCE	20932	21126	21340	21689	22035	22143	22497	22553	22820	22727	23185
CIVILIAN LABOUR FORCE	20362	20583	20824	21168	21494	21615	21964	21964	21997	22349	22614
MALES	14197	14315	14406	14464	14433	14502	14584	14482	14574	14597	14663
FEMALES	6165	6268	6418	6704	7061	7113	7380	7515	7682	7752	7951
UNEMPLOYED	1305	1113	1230	1426	1545	1571	1698	1684	1895	2052	2264
CIVILIAN EMPLOYMENT	19057	19470	19594	19742	19948	20044	20266	20313	20361	20297	20350
AGRICULTURE	3489	3412	3274	3244	3149	3090	3012	2899	2732	2522	2526
INDUSTRY	7470	7639	7669	7566	7666	7633	7646	7699	7647	7527	7352
SERVICES	8098	8419	8651	8932	9133	9321	9610	9715	9982	10248	10472
CIVILIAN EMPLOYMENT BY SECTORS (ISIC)											
ALL ACTIVITIES	19057	19470	19594	19742	19948	20044	20266	20313	20361	20297	20350
AGRICULTURE	3489	3412	3274	3244	3149	3090	3012	2899	2732	2522	2526
MINING AND QUARRYING	-	-	-	-	208	197	212	-	-	-	-
MANUFACTURING	-	-	-	-	5476	5425	5413	-	-	-	-
CONSTRUCTION	-	-	-	-	1982	2011	2021	-	-	-	-
TRADE, RESTAURANTS AND HOTELS	-	-	-	-	3605	3640	3767	-	-	-	-
TRANSPORT, COMMUNICATION	-	-	-	-	1127	1129	1128	-	-	-	-
FINANCING, INSURANCE AND BUSINESS SERVICES	-	-	-	-	427	467	493	-	-	-	-
COMMUNITY, SOCIAL AND PERSONAL SERVICES	-	-	-	-	3974	4085	4222	-	-	-	-
WAGE EARNERS AND SALARIED EMPLOYEES IN MANUFACTURING (ISIC)											
MANUFACTURING, TOTAL	4790	4912	4893	4906	4910	4860	4883	4894	4802	4695	4546
FOOD, BEVERAGES AND TOBACCO	381	386	385	385	383	382	387	386	386	390	383
TEXTILE, WEARING APPAREL AND LEATHER IND.	1144	1133	1119	1117	1113	1099	1094	1086	1068	1060	1035
WOOD, WOOD PRODUCTS	334	337	333	338	343	339	338	339	337	335	328
PAPER, PAPER PROD., PRINTING, PUBLISHING	234	239	239	238	238	234	236	237	234	232	225
CHEMICALS, PETROLEUM AND PLASTIC PRODUCTS	475	498	499	497	498	491	488	483	469	453	426
NON-METALLIC MINERAL PRODUCTS	369	376	376	375	374	366	364	363	358	355	347
FABR. METAL PROD., MACHINERY AND EQUIPMENT	1792	1881	1879	1892	1896	1884	1912	1934	1885	1806	1740
OTHER MANUFACTURING INDUSTRIES	61	63	63	64	66	65	65	66	65	64	62

Table 1g:

POPULATION AND EMPLOYMENT: ITALY
- percentage change -

POPULATION AND EMPLOYMENT

	1973	1974	1975	1976	1977	1978	1979	1980	1981	1982	1983
TOTAL POPULATION	0.81	1.04	0.78	0.65	0.45	0.41	0.38	0.19	0.30	0.28	0.23
POPULATION, FROM 15 TO 64 YEARS	0.91	1.20	0.76	0.54	0.55	0.94	0.82	0.36	0.71	1.29	1.12
MALES, FROM 15 TO 64 YEARS	0.85	1.18	0.28	0.28	0.83	1.16	0.82	0.41	0.94	1.38	1.10
FEMALES, FROM 15 TO 64 YEARS	0.96	1.21	0.77	0.79	0.28	0.74	0.82	0.30	0.51	1.20	1.15
TOTAL LABOUR FORCE	0.93	0.93	1.01	1.64	1.60	0.49	1.60	0.25	1.18	0.47	1.13
CIVILIAN LABOUR FORCE	0.94	0.83	1.17	1.65	1.54	0.56	1.61	-0.00	0.15	1.60	1.19
MALES	-0.16	0.83	0.64	0.40	-0.21	0.48	0.57	-0.70	0.64	0.16	0.45
FEMALES	3.58	1.67	2.39	4.46	5.33	0.74	3.75	1.83	2.22	0.91	2.57
UNEMPLOYED	0.62	-14.71	10.51	15.93	8.35	1.68	8.08	-0.82	12.53	8.28	10.33
CIVILIAN EMPLOYMENT	0.96	2.17	0.64	0.76	1.04	0.48	1.11	-0.23	0.24	-0.31	0.26
AGRICULTURE	-2.89	-2.21	-4.04	-0.92	-2.93	-1.87	-2.52	-3.75	-5.76	-7.69	0.16
INDUSTRY	-0.09	2.26	-0.39	-1.34	1.32	-0.43	0.17	-0.69	-0.68	-1.57	-2.32
SERVICES	3.75	3.96	2.76	3.25	2.25	2.06	3.10	1.09	2.75	2.66	2.19

CIVILIAN EMPLOYMENT BY SECTORS (ISIC)

	1973	1974	1975	1976	1977	1978	1979	1980	1981	1982	1983
ALL ACTIVITIES	0.96	2.17	0.64	0.76	1.04	0.48	1.11	-0.23	0.24	-0.31	0.26
AGRICULTURE	-2.89	-2.21	-4.04	-0.92	-2.93	-1.87	-2.52	-3.75	-5.76	-7.69	0.16
MINING AND QUARRYING	-	-	-	-	-	-	-	-	-	-	-
MANUFACTURING	-	-	-	-	-	-	-	-	-	-	-
CONSTRUCTION	-	-	-	-	-	-	-	-	-	-	-
TRADE, RESTAURANTS AND HOTELS	-	-	-	-	-	-	-	-	-	-	-
TRANSPORT, COMMUNICATION	-	-	-	-	-	-	-	-	-	-	-
FINANCING, INSURANCE AND BUSINESS SERVICES	-	-	-	-	-	-	-	-	-	-	-
COMMUNITY, SOCIAL AND PERSONAL SERVICES	-	-	-	-	-	-	-	-	-	-	-

WAGE EARNERS AND SALARIED EMPLOYEES IN MANUFACTURING (ISIC)

	1973	1974	1975	1976	1977	1978	1979	1980	1981	1982	1983
MANUFACTURING, TOTAL	2.15	2.55	-0.39	0.27	0.08	-1.02	0.47	0.23	-1.88	-2.23	-3.17
FOOD, BEVERAGES AND TOBACCO	1.06	1.31	-0.26	0.00	-0.52	-0.26	1.31	-0.26	0.00	1.04	-1.79
TEXTILE, WEARING APPAREL AND LEATHER IND.	0.35	-0.96	-1.24	-0.18	-0.36	-1.26	-0.45	-0.73	-1.66	-0.75	-2.36
WOOD, WOOD PRODUCTS	0.91	0.90	-1.19	1.50	1.48	-1.17	-0.29	0.30	-0.59	-0.59	-2.09
PAPER, PAPER PROD., PRINTING, PUBLISHING	2.18	2.14	0.00	-0.42	0.00	-1.68	0.85	0.42	-1.27	-0.85	-3.02
CHEMICALS, PETROLEUM AND PLASTIC PRODUCTS	1.71	4.84	0.20	-0.40	0.20	-1.41	-0.61	-1.02	-2.90	-3.41	-5.96
NON-METALLIC MINERAL PRODUCTS	1.10	1.90	0.00	-0.27	-0.27	-2.14	-0.55	-0.27	-1.38	-0.84	-2.25
FABR. METAL PROD., MACHINERY AND EQUIPMENT	4.07	4.97	-0.11	0.69	0.21	-0.63	1.49	1.15	-2.53	-4.19	-3.65
OTHER MANUFACTURING INDUSTRIES	5.17	3.28	0.00	1.59	3.13	-1.52	0.00	1.54	-1.52	1.54	-3.13

Table 2: NOMINAL AND REAL WAGES PER MAN AND PER MAN-HOUR, WHOLE ECONOMY

a) Index 1970 = 100

REAL WAGES PER MAN

	1970	1971	1972	1973	1974	1975	1976	1977	1978	1979	1980	1981	1982	1983
UNITED STATES	100.0	101.5	104.6	106.3	105.2	104.4	106.9	108.7	109.1	109.3	109.1	109.8	110.0	111.5
JAPAN	100.0	109.4	117.0	128.4	134.1	144.6	150.0	156.3	159.8	165.5	171.1	177.6	181.9	185.8
GERMANY	100.0	103.5	108.0	113.7	118.8	120.0	125.3	128.8	130.5	132.8	135.8	137.2	136.7	137.3
FRANCE	100.0	105.4	109.5	114.6	121.2	126.8	132.4	136.8	140.6	142.3	146.6	149.9	151.4	153.0
UNITED KINGDOM	100.0	101.8	106.3	112.4	116.3	120.0	119.9	116.4	118.8	119.2	118.6	120.5	122.7	127.5
ITALY	100.0	105.5	110.3	118.2	121.8	125.3	128.4	130.9	133.6	135.8	138.1	142.3	141.4	142.5

NOMINAL WAGES PER MAN

	1970	1971	1972	1973	1974	1975	1976	1977	1978	1979	1980	1981	1982	1983
UNITED STATES	100.0	106.9	114.9	123.3	133.0	144.1	156.2	167.9	181.2	196.9	215.5	236.0	252.8	267.8
JAPAN	100.0	115.0	131.7	159.0	200.3	232.8	257.0	283.0	302.7	321.5	341.8	364.5	379.8	390.0
GERMANY	100.0	111.6	122.7	137.6	153.4	164.5	177.4	189.1	199.7	211.4	225.9	237.7	247.9	257.0
FRANCE	100.0	111.5	123.0	138.7	163.1	193.5	222.0	249.9	281.2	318.6	363.3	415.3	472.4	523.0
UNITED KINGDOM	100.0	111.4	126.0	142.6	169.6	222.7	255.6	282.7	320.8	368.5	439.1	498.3	543.4	593.6
ITALY	100.0	113.1	125.6	150.2	183.3	221.8	268.2	325.5	378.3	445.8	546.9	666.9	781.0	905.5

REAL WAGES PER MAN-HOUR

	1970	1971	1972	1973	1974	1975	1976	1977	1978	1979	1980	1981	1982	1983
UNITED STATES	100.0	101.3	104.2	105.7	106.7	107.1	108.6	110.1	110.5	110.9	112.0	112.7	114.8	113.9
JAPAN	100.0	111.2	121.8	132.4	145.2	161.4	161.6	167.9	170.7	174.8	180.1	188.9	193.9	197.1
GERMANY	100.0	105.4	110.9	116.2	126.1	130.7	132.6	138.3	142.1	145.5	150.1	153.5	153.6	154.7
FRANCE	100.0	106.1	105.1	111.2	126.8	136.8	142.3	148.2	153.4	157.2	159.5	164.1	170.9	177.6
UNITED KINGDOM	100.0	104.8	113.5	117.6	123.4	129.1	128.6	123.9	126.8	127.4	131.0	134.8	135.0	139.3
ITALY	100.0	106.3	111.2	123.0	136.5	148.3	146.7	148.2	151.6	155.6	158.0	166.8	168.8	172.0

NOMINAL WAGES PER MAN-HOUR

	1970	1971	1972	1973	1974	1975	1976	1977	1978	1979	1980	1981	1982	1983
UNITED STATES	100.0	106.6	114.5	122.6	134.9	147.8	158.7	170.2	183.4	199.8	221.0	242.2	263.9	273.5
JAPAN	100.0	116.9	134.8	164.0	216.9	259.8	276.9	304.1	323.2	339.6	361.4	387.7	404.7	413.7
GERMANY	100.0	113.7	126.0	143.0	162.9	179.1	187.8	203.1	217.4	231.6	249.6	265.9	278.5	289.6
FRANCE	100.0	112.3	118.1	134.6	170.5	208.7	238.5	270.7	306.6	347.8	395.3	454.6	531.1	607.0
UNITED KINGDOM	100.0	114.7	134.4	147.2	180.1	239.6	274.2	300.9	342.4	393.8	485.0	557.5	597.7	648.5
ITALY	100.0	113.9	126.7	156.4	205.6	262.4	306.3	368.6	429.3	510.7	625.4	781.7	937.2	1093.3

Table 2:   NOMINAL AND REAL WAGES PER MAN AND PER MAN-HOUR, WHOLE ECONOMY

b) percentage change

REAL WAGES PER MAN

	1971	1972	1973	1974	1975	1976	1977	1978	1979	1980	1981	1982	1983
UNITED STATES	1.5	3.0	1.6	-1.0	-0.8	2.4	1.7	0.4	0.2	-0.2	0.6	0.2	1.4
JAPAN	9.4	8.8	7.9	4.4	7.8	3.7	4.2	3.4	3.5	3.1	3.8	2.5	2.1
GERMANY	3.5	4.3	5.3	4.4	1.1	4.3	3.3	1.3	1.8	2.3	1.0	-0.4	0.5
FRANCE	5.4	3.9	4.7	5.8	4.6	4.2	3.3	2.8	0.3	1.0	1.6	1.0	1.1
UNITED KINGDOM	1.8	4.5	5.7	3.5	3.2	-0.1	-2.9	2.1	-0.3	-0.5	1.6	1.9	3.9
ITALY	5.5	4.5	7.1	3.0	2.9	2.4	1.9	2.1	1.7	1.7	3.0	-0.7	0.8

NOMINAL WAGES PER MAN

	1971	1972	1973	1974	1975	1976	1977	1978	1979	1980	1981	1982	1983
UNITED STATES	6.9	7.5	7.3	7.9	8.3	8.4	7.5	7.9	8.7	9.4	9.5	7.1	6.0
JAPAN	15.0	14.4	20.8	26.0	16.2	10.4	10.1	7.0	6.2	6.3	6.6	4.2	2.7
GERMANY	11.6	9.9	12.1	11.5	7.2	7.9	6.6	5.6	5.9	6.8	5.2	4.3	3.7
FRANCE	11.5	10.3	12.8	17.6	18.6	14.7	12.6	12.5	13.3	14.0	14.3	13.7	10.7
UNITED KINGDOM	11.4	13.1	13.2	18.9	31.3	14.8	10.6	13.5	14.9	19.2	13.5	9.1	9.2
ITALY	13.1	11.1	19.6	22.1	21.0	20.9	21.4	16.2	17.9	22.7	21.9	17.1	15.9

REAL WAGES PER MAN-HOUR

	1971	1972	1973	1974	1975	1976	1977	1978	1979	1980	1981	1982	1983
UNITED STATES	1.3	2.9	1.5	0.9	0.3	1.4	1.5	0.3	0.4	1.0	0.6	1.9	-0.8
JAPAN	11.2	9.6	8.7	9.7	11.1	0.2	3.9	1.6	2.4	3.5	4.5	2.6	1.7
GERMANY	5.4	5.2	6.5	6.7	3.6	4.0	4.4	2.7	2.4	3.2	2.3	0.1	0.8
FRANCE	6.1	-0.9	5.8	14.0	7.9	4.0	4.1	3.5	2.7	2.8	2.9	4.1	4.0
UNITED KINGDOM	4.8	8.2	3.6	5.0	4.6	-0.4	-3.6	2.4	0.4	2.8	2.9	1.1	3.2
ITALY	6.3	4.7	10.6	11.0	8.6	-1.1	1.0	2.3	2.6	1.5	5.6	1.1	1.9

NOMINAL WAGES PER MAN-HOUR

	1971	1972	1973	1974	1975	1976	1977	1978	1979	1980	1981	1982	1983
UNITED STATES	6.6	7.4	7.1	10.0	9.5	7.4	7.3	7.7	9.0	10.7	9.5	9.0	3.7
JAPAN	16.6	15.3	21.7	32.3	19.8	6.6	9.8	7.0	5.1	6.4	7.3	4.4	2.2
GERMANY	13.7	10.8	13.5	14.0	9.9	4.9	8.2	7.0	6.5	7.8	6.6	4.7	4.0
FRANCE	12.3	5.2	14.0	20.7	22.4	14.3	13.5	13.3	13.4	13.6	15.0	17.3	13.8
UNITED KINGDOM	14.7	17.2	11.0	20.7	33.1	14.4	9.8	13.8	15.0	23.2	14.9	7.2	8.5
ITALY	13.9	11.2	23.5	31.5	27.6	16.8	20.3	16.5	19.0	22.5	25.0	19.3	17.3

Employment Trends

Table 3:

PRODUCTIVITY TRENDS[1], WHOLE ECONOMY

a) Index 1970 = 100

PRODUCTIVITY PER PERSON EMPLOYED

	1970	1971	1972	1973	1974	1975	1976	1977	1978	1979	1980	1981	1982	1983
UNITED STATES	100.0	103.1	106.3	108.0	105.5	106.6	108.9	110.9	111.0	110.2	109.1	111.9	109.7	112.2
JAPAN	100.0	104.0	112.9	119.7	118.8	121.9	126.0	130.9	135.7	141.0	146.8	152.0	155.3	158.0
GERMANY	100.0	102.5	107.0	111.1	113.1	114.5	121.8	125.7	128.8	132.4	133.5	134.6	135.7	139.5
FRANCE	100.0	105.0	110.7	115.1	118.0	119.5	124.7	127.5	131.8	136.3	136.3	137.7	140.1	141.8
UNITED KINGDOM	100.0	103.6	106.1	111.9	110.4	110.0	115.2	116.2	119.7	120.4	118.1	121.5	125.7	131.1
ITALY	100.0	101.7	106.2	112.8	115.7	111.3	116.9	118.4	120.8	125.4	129.4	129.0	128.7	127.0

PRODUCTIVITY PER MAN-HOUR

	1970	1971	1972	1973	1974	1975	1976	1977	1978	1979	1980	1981	1982	1983
UNITED STATES	100.0	102.9	105.9	107.4	107.0	109.3	110.6	112.4	112.3	111.9	112.0	114.8	114.6	114.6
JAPAN	100.0	105.7	115.5	123.4	128.6	136.0	135.8	140.7	144.9	148.9	155.2	161.7	165.5	167.6
GERMANY	100.0	104.4	109.8	115.4	120.1	124.7	128.9	135.0	140.2	145.0	147.5	150.5	152.5	157.2
FRANCE	100.0	105.7	106.3	111.7	123.4	128.9	134.0	138.1	143.7	148.8	148.3	150.8	158.1	164.5
UNITED KINGDOM	100.0	106.7	113.2	117.1	117.2	118.3	123.5	123.7	127.8	128.7	130.5	135.9	138.2	143.3
ITALY	100.0	102.5	107.0	117.4	129.8	131.7	133.6	134.1	137.1	143.7	148.0	151.2	153.6	153.3

1 Gross Domestic Product at constant prices per person employed or per man-hour.

Employment Trends

Table 3:

PRODUCTIVITY TRENDS, WHOLE ECONOMY

b) percentage change

PRODUCTIVITY PER PERSON EMPLOYED

	1971	1972	1973	1974	1975	1976	1977	1978	1979	1980	1981	1982	1983
UNITED STATES	3.1	3.1	1.6	-2.3	1.0	2.2	1.8	0.1	-0.7	-1.0	2.6	-2.0	2.2
JAPAN	4.0	8.5	6.1	-0.8	2.6	3.4	3.9	3.7	3.9	4.1	3.6	2.2	1.7
GERMANY	2.5	4.4	3.8	1.9	1.2	6.4	3.2	2.5	2.8	0.8	0.8	0.9	2.8
FRANCE	5.0	5.4	4.1	2.5	1.2	4.4	2.2	3.0	3.4	0.0	1.0	1.7	1.2
UNITED KINGDOM	3.6	2.4	5.5	-1.3	-0.4	4.7	0.9	3.0	0.6	-1.9	2.9	3.4	4.4
ITALY	1.7	4.4	6.2	2.6	-3.8	5.0	1.2	2.0	3.8	3.2	-0.3	-0.3	-1.3

PRODUCTIVITY PER MAN-HOUR

	1971	1972	1973	1974	1975	1976	1977	1978	1979	1980	1981	1982	1983
UNITED STATES	2.9	3.0	1.4	-0.4	2.2	1.2	1.6	-0.1	-0.4	0.1	2.6	-0.3	-0.0
JAPAN	5.7	9.3	6.9	4.2	5.8	-0.2	3.6	3.0	2.8	4.2	4.2	2.4	1.2
GERMANY	4.4	5.2	5.1	4.1	3.7	3.4	4.8	3.9	3.4	1.7	2.1	1.3	3.1
FRANCE	5.7	0.5	5.2	10.4	4.5	4.0	3.0	4.1	3.5	-0.3	1.7	4.8	4.1
UNITED KINGDOM	6.7	6.1	3.4	0.1	1.0	4.4	0.1	3.3	0.7	1.4	4.2	1.7	3.7
ITALY	2.5	4.5	9.7	10.5	1.5	1.4	0.4	2.3	4.8	3.0	2.2	1.5	-0.2

Table 4:

REAL WAGE GAP[1]

a) Index 1970 = 100

REAL WAGE GAP, BASED ON PERSONS EMPLOYED

	1970	1971	1972	1973	1974	1975	1976	1977	1978	1979	1980	1981	1982	1983
UNITED STATES	100.0	99.3	99.7	99.9	102.0	101.4	101.8	101.7	101.9	103.1	104.9	103.7	107.3	107.4
JAPAN	100.0	107.6	110.5	114.6	123.1	131.8	133.7	135.8	135.6	137.1	138.6	141.4	144.2	146.9
GERMANY	100.0	102.3	103.6	106.2	110.4	111.3	111.3	112.1	111.8	111.5	114.1	115.9	116.2	115.4
FRANCE	100.0	101.8	101.8	103.9	108.7	114.3	115.9	118.6	119.5	120.3	123.6	127.2	128.1	130.0
UNITED KINGDOM	100.0	99.3	102.4	103.0	108.9	113.8	109.5	106.3	106.0	106.1	108.5	109.4	109.1	109.9

REAL WAGE GAP, BASED ON MAN-HOURS

	1970	1971	1972	1973	1974	1975	1976	1977	1978	1979	1980	1981	1982	1983
UNITED STATES	100.0	99.2	99.6	99.8	102.3	102.0	102.1	101.9	102.2	103.4	105.5	104.3	108.5	107.9
JAPAN	100.0	107.9	111.0	115.3	125.5	135.7	136.4	138.5	138.1	139.3	140.8	146.0	147.0	149.5
GERMANY	100.0	102.7	104.2	107.2	112.1	114.8	113.0	114.3	114.5	114.5	117.5	119.8	120.5	119.9
FRANCE	100.0	102.1	100.8	103.1	110.5	117.6	119.2	122.4	123.8	124.8	128.2	132.4	135.0	138.8
UNITED KINGDOM	100.0	99.9	104.0	104.1	110.5	116.0	111.5	108.0	107.8	108.0	111.6	113.0	112.2	112.8

1 Increase of real wages reduced by "employment-neutral" increase of productivity. For Italy not available.

Appendix

Table 4:

REAL WAGE GAP

b) percentage change

REAL WAGE GAP, BASED ON PERSONS EMPLOYED

	1971	1972	1973	1974	1975	1976	1977	1978	1979	1980	1981	1982	1983
UNITED STATES	-0.7	0.4	0.2	2.1	-0.5	0.4	-0.2	-0.3	1.1	1.8	-1.1	3.4	0.1
JAPAN	7.6	2.7	3.8	7.4	7.1	1.4	1.6	-0.1	-1.2	1.0	2.1	1.9	1.9
GERMANY	2.3	1.3	2.5	4.0	1.6	-0.8	0.7	-0.3	-0.2	2.3	1.5	0.3	-0.7
FRANCE	1.8	-0.0	2.0	4.7	5.1	1.4	2.3	0.8	0.7	2.7	2.9	0.7	1.5
UNITED KINGDOM	-0.7	3.1	0.6	5.7	4.6	-3.8	-3.0	-0.3	0.1	2.3	0.8	-0.3	0.7

REAL WAGE GAP, BASED ON MAN-HOURS

	1971	1972	1973	1974	1975	1976	1977	1978	1979	1980	1981	1982	1983
UNITED STATES	-0.8	0.3	0.2	2.6	-0.3	0.1	-0.2	0.2	1.2	2.1	-1.1	4.0	-0.6
JAPAN	7.9	2.8	3.9	8.9	8.1	0.5	1.5	-0.3	0.9	1.1	2.3	2.0	1.7
GERMANY	2.7	1.5	2.8	4.6	2.4	-1.5	1.1	0.2	-0.0	2.7	2.0	0.6	-0.5
FRANCE	2.1	-1.3	2.3	7.2	6.4	1.3	2.7	1.1	0.9	2.7	3.3	2.0	2.8
UNITED KINGDOM	-0.1	4.0	0.1	6.1	5.0	-3.8	-3.1	-0.2	0.1	3.4	1.2	-0.7	0.5

Employment Trends

Table 5:

FACTOR PRICE RATIO[1]

a) Index 1970 = 100

FACTOR PRICE RATIO, VAR.1

	1970	1971	1972	1973	1974	1975	1976	1977	1978	1979	1980	1981	1982	1983
UNITED STATES	100.0	100.4	103.2	105.4	103.1	99.4	102.0	103.0	102.5	102.5	103.9	105.5	111.2	115.9
JAPAN	100.0	114.9	129.1	140.9	147.5	169.2	173.0	184.4	193.2	193.7	195.8	206.6	220.8	230.1
GERMANY	100.0	106.7	114.9	125.2	132.4	139.6	141.9	149.1	153.3	154.7	156.6	160.4	163.7	167.9
FRANCE	100.0	106.7	107.2	114.9	125.8	136.2	140.6	147.8	156.5	162.5	165.7	171.7	182.5	193.9
UNITED KINGDOM	100.0	104.0	111.3	109.4	109.8	118.4	118.0	114.7	117.3	116.9	122.0	128.6	133.9	141.1
ITALY	100.0	105.4	111.1	118.3	122.4	130.7	128.0	130.2	136.8	141.6	145.7	152.3	156.6	162.2

FACTOR PRICE RATIO, VAR.2

	1970	1971	1972	1973	1974	1975	1976	1977	1978	1979	1980	1981	1982	1983
UNITED STATES	100.0	101.3	102.7	102.7	101.8	101.2	100.9	99.3	97.3	97.6	98.3	95.7	100.2	99.7
JAPAN	100.0	116.4	124.0	143.1	184.1	205.5	145.4	139.1	149.8	135.3	132.1	146.9	153.5	151.9
GERMANY	100.0	110.3	106.9	112.4	121.1	126.8	115.5	123.3	131.9	125.0	124.4	122.0	123.4	125.6
FRANCE	100.0	108.8	100.6	108.1	153.3	192.6	166.5	152.1	161.2	165.2	156.4	156.9	176.1	191.6
UNITED KINGDOM	100.0	116.4	128.6	114.8	111.0	167.6	151.9	108.7	110.8	117.7	138.5	143.0	122.9	124.0
ITALY	100.0	101.5	100.1	122.7	162.2	177.4	134.6	118.9	126.8	127.7	137.6	144.4	140.7	137.2

1 Ratio of the price of labour to the price of capital.
  Var. 1: Ratio of real wages to real prices of capital goods.
  Var. 2: Ratio of real wages to real prices of capital goods, including expected wage increases and interest on capital.

Table 5:

FACTOR PRICE RATIO

b) percentage change

FACTOR PRICE RATIO, VAR.1

	1971	1972	1973	1974	1975	1976	1977	1978	1979	1980	1981	1982	1983
UNITED STATES	0.4	2.8	2.1	-2.2	-3.6	2.7	0.9	-0.5	0.0	1.4	1.6	5.4	4.1
JAPAN	14.9	12.4	9.1	4.7	14.7	2.3	6.6	4.8	0.3	1.1	0.5	5.9	4.2
GERMANY	6.9	7.6	8.9	5.8	5.4	1.7	5.1	2.8	0.9	1.2	2.4	2.0	2.6
FRANCE	6.7	0.5	7.2	9.4	8.3	3.2	5.2	5.9	3.9	1.9	3.7	6.3	6.3
UNITED KINGDOM	4.0	7.0	-1.7	0.4	7.8	-0.3	-2.8	2.3	-0.4	4.4	5.5	4.1	5.4
ITALY	5.4	5.3	6.5	3.5	6.8	-2.0	1.7	5.1	3.5	2.9	4.5	2.8	3.5

FACTOR PRICE RATIO, VAR.2

	1971	1972	1973	1974	1975	1976	1977	1978	1979	1980	1981	1982	1983
UNITED STATES	1.3	1.4	-0.0	-0.9	-0.6	-0.3	-1.7	-2.0	0.3	0.7	-2.7	4.7	-0.5
JAPAN	16.4	6.5	15.4	28.7	11.6	-29.3	-4.3	7.7	-9.7	-2.4	11.2	4.5	-1.1
GERMANY	10.3	-3.0	5.1	7.8	4.7	-8.9	6.8	7.0	-5.2	-0.5	-1.9	1.1	1.8
FRANCE	8.8	-7.6	7.5	41.7	25.7	-13.5	-8.6	6.0	2.5	-5.3	0.3	12.3	8.8
UNITED KINGDOM	16.4	10.5	-10.7	-3.3	51.0	-9.4	-28.5	2.0	6.2	17.7	3.3	-14.0	0.8
ITALY	1.5	-1.4	22.6	32.2	9.4	-24.1	-11.7	6.7	0.7	7.8	4.9	-2.6	-2.5

Employment Trends

Table 6:

CAPITAL INTENSITY[1]

a) Index 1970 = 100

CAPITAL PER PERSON EMPLOYED

	1970	1971	1972	1973	1974	1975	1976	1977	1978	1979	1980	1981	1982	1983
UNITED STATES	100.0	103.7	105.5	106.4	109.4	114.8	115.5	115.5	115.2	116.5	120.4	124.1	129.8	133.7
JAPAN	100.0	112.4	126.2	137.3	150.1	161.6	168.3	176.0	183.9	193.7	205.1	217.0	228.3	238.2
GERMANY	100.0	105.2	111.1	115.7	121.9	129.8	135.5	140.5	144.7	148.3	152.4	158.8	166.4	174.3
FRANCE	100.0	105.5	111.3	116.5	122.0	129.1	134.7	139.8	145.5	151.9	156.8	164.2	170.4	177.5
UNITED KINGDOM	100.0	105.0	109.1	110.8	114.5	118.7	123.4	127.1	129.9	131.7	135.8	145.0	151.0	156.5

CAPITAL PER MAN-HOUR

	1970	1971	1972	1973	1974	1975	1976	1977	1978	1979	1980	1981	1982	1983
UNITED STATES	100.0	103.6	107.7	110.3	112.9	115.9	120.5	121.6	122.3	122.3	124.5	128.7	134.4	137.8
JAPAN	100.0	114.2	129.1	141.6	162.5	180.3	181.4	189.1	196.4	204.6	216.9	230.9	243.4	252.7
GERMANY	100.0	107.2	114.1	120.3	129.4	141.3	143.4	150.9	157.6	162.4	168.4	177.6	186.9	196.4
FRANCE	100.0	106.2	110.9	113.1	127.5	139.3	144.7	151.5	158.6	165.8	170.6	179.7	192.3	206.0
UNITED KINGDOM	100.0	108.1	116.4	115.9	121.6	127.7	132.4	135.2	138.7	140.7	150.1	162.2	166.1	171.0

1 Stock of fixed capital in constant prices (excluding dwellings) per person employed respectively per man-hour.

Appendix

271

Table 6:

CAPITAL INTENSITY

b) percentage change

CAPITAL PER PERSON EMPLOYED

	1971	1972	1973	1974	1975	1976	1977	1978	1979	1980	1981	1982	1983
UNITED STATES	3.7	1.8	0.8	2.8	4.9	0.6	0.0	-0.3	1.1	3.3	3.1	4.6	3.0
JAPAN	12.4	12.2	8.8	9.3	7.7	4.2	4.6	4.5	5.3	5.9	5.8	5.2	4.3
GERMANY	5.2	5.5	4.2	4.7	6.5	4.4	3.7	3.0	2.5	2.8	4.2	4.8	4.7
FRANCE	5.5	5.5	4.7	4.7	5.9	4.3	3.8	4.0	4.4	3.2	4.7	3.8	4.2
UNITED KINGDOM	5.0	3.8	1.6	3.4	3.7	3.9	2.9	2.2	1.4	3.1	6.7	4.1	3.7

CAPITAL PER MAN-HOUR

	1971	1972	1973	1974	1975	1976	1977	1978	1979	1980	1981	1982	1983
UNITED STATES	3.6	4.0	2.4	2.3	2.7	4.0	0.9	0.5	0.1	1.3	3.3	4.4	2.6
JAPAN	14.2	13.1	9.6	14.7	11.0	0.6	4.3	3.8	4.2	6.0	6.4	5.4	3.8
GERMANY	7.2	6.5	5.4	7.6	9.2	1.4	5.2	4.4	3.1	3.7	5.5	5.2	5.0
FRANCE	6.2	0.6	5.8	12.8	9.2	3.6	4.6	4.7	4.5	2.9	5.3	7.0	7.1
UNITED KINGDOM	8.1	7.6	-0.4	4.9	5.0	3.6	2.2	2.6	1.5	6.6	8.1	2.4	3.0

Employment Trends

Table 7a: TOTAL FACTOR PRODUCTIVITY, LABOUR PRODUCTIVITY,
             FACTOR SUBSTITUTION COMPONENT AND CAPITAL INTENSITY
             - annual changes -

U n i t e d   S t a t e s

YEAR	TOTAL FACTOR PRODUCTIVITY	LABOUR PROD.	FACTOR SUBST. COMPONENT	CAPITAL INTENSITY
1963	2.1	2.4	0.3	1.5
1964	2.4	2.7	0.3	1.3
1965	3.1	3.6	0.4	2.0
1966	2.6	3.2	0.6	2.5
1967	0.2	0.8	0.6	2.4
1968	1.3	1.9	0.6	2.4
1969	-0.4	0.1	0.5	2.0
1970	-1.0	0.0	1.1	4.3
1971	2.2	3.1	0.9	3.6
1972	2.6	3.1	0.5	1.8
1973	1.4	1.6	0.2	0.8
1974	-3.1	-2.3	0.7	2.8
1975	-0.2	1.0	1.3	4.7
1976	2.0	2.2	0.2	0.6
1977	1.8	1.8	0.0	0.0
1978	0.2	0.1	-0.1	-0.3
1979	-1.0	-0.7	0.3	1.1
1980	-1.9	-1.0	0.9	3.2
1981	1.7	2.6	0.9	3.0
1982	-3.3	-2.0	1.3	4.4
1983	1.3	2.2	0.9	2.9
62/73	1.5	2.0	0.6	2.2
73/83	-0.3	0.4	0.7	2.3
62/83	0.6	1.2	0.7	2.2

Source: Authors' calculations based on OECD data and national data.

Table 7b: TOTAL FACTOR PRODUCTIVITY, LABOUR PRODUCTIVITY,
            FACTOR SUBSTITUTION COMPONENT AND CAPITAL INTENSITY
            - annual changes -

J a p a n

YEAR	TOTAL FACTOR PRODUCTIVITY	LABOUR PROD.	FACTOR SUBST. COMPONENT	CAPITAL INTENSITY
1965	2.6	3.5	0.8	6.9
1966	7.6	8.4	0.8	6.3
1967	7.6	8.7	1.1	8.2
1968	9.4	10.9	1.5	9.9
1969	9.5	11.4	1.9	11.4
1970	6.5	8.6	2.1	11.7
1971	1.8	4.0	2.2	11.0
1972	6.1	8.5	2.4	10.9
1973	4.2	6.1	1.9	8.1
1974	-2.9	-0.8	2.1	8.5
1975	0.7	2.6	1.9	7.1
1976	2.3	3.4	1.1	4.0
1977	2.6	3.9	1.2	4.4
1978	2.4	3.7	1.3	4.3
1979	2.4	3.9	1.5	5.0
1980	2.3	4.1	1.8	5.6
1981	1.8	3.6	1.8	5.5
1982	0.5	2.2	1.7	5.0
1983	0.3	1.7	1.4	4.1
64/73	5.5	7.8	2.2	9.4
73/83	0.9	2.8	1.9	5.4
64/83	2.6	5.1	2.5	7.3

Source: Authors' calculations based on OECD data and national data.

Table 7c: TOTAL FACTOR PRODUCTIVITY, LABOUR PRODUCTIVITY,
            FACTOR SUBSTITUTION COMPONENT AND CAPITAL INTENSITY
                        - annual changes -

G e r m a n y

YEAR	TOTAL FACTOR PRODUCTIVITY	LABOUR PROD.	FACTOR SUBST. COMPONENT	CAPITAL INTENSITY
1963	2.0	3.0	1.0	5.9
1964	5.7	6.8	1.2	6.3
1965	4.0	5.1	1.1	5.7
1966	1.8	3.0	1.2	6.0
1967	1.6	3.3	1.6	7.6
1968	4.8	5.8	1.0	4.3
1969	5.1	5.9	0.8	3.6
1970	2.9	3.9	1.1	4.5
1971	1.2	2.5	1.2	5.0
1972	3.0	4.4	1.4	5.3
1973	2.8	3.8	1.1	4.0
1974	0.5	1.9	1.4	5.0
1975	-0.6	1.2	1.7	6.1
1976	5.1	6.4	1.2	4.2
1977	2.1	3.2	1.1	3.6
1978	1.6	2.5	0.9	2.9
1979	2.0	2.8	0.8	2.4
1980	-0.1	0.8	0.9	2.7
1981	-0.5	0.8	1.3	4.0
1982	-0.7	0.9	1.6	4.6
1983	1.2	2.8	1.6	4.5
62/73	2.9	4.3	1.4	5.3
73/83	0.9	2.3	1.4	4.0
62/83	1.7	3.3	1.6	4.7

Source: Authors' calculations based on OECD data and national data.

Table 7d: TOTAL FACTOR PRODUCTIVITY, LABOUR PRODUCTIVITY,
            FACTOR SUBSTITUTION COMPONENT AND CAPITAL INTENSITY
                        - annual changes -

F r a n c e

YEAR	TOTAL FACTOR PRODUCTIVITY	LABOUR PROD.	FACTOR SUBST. COMPONENT	CAPITAL INTENSITY
1963	3.0	3.5	0.6	2.6
1964	4.1	4.7	0.7	3.0
1965	3.1	4.0	0.9	4.0
1966	3.4	4.4	1.0	4.2
1967	3.2	4.3	1.1	4.5
1968	3.2	4.4	1.3	5.0
1969	4.3	5.4	1.0	4.0
1970	3.2	4.3	1.1	4.3
1971	3.6	5.0	1.4	5.2
1972	3.9	5.4	1.5	5.2
1973	2.7	4.1	1.4	4.5
1974	1.1	2.5	1.4	4.5
1975	-0.5	1.2	1.8	5.5
1976	3.1	4.4	1.4	4.1
1977	1.0	2.2	1.2	3.7
1978	2.0	3.4	1.3	3.9
1979	1.9	3.4	1.5	4.2
1980	-1.1	0.0	1.1	3.1
1981	-0.7	1.0	1.7	4.5
1982	0.3	1.7	1.4	3.6
1983	-0.4	1.2	1.6	4.0
62/73	3.2	4.5	1.3	4.2
73/83	0.5	2.1	1.6	4.1
62/83	1.7	3.4	1.6	4.2

Source: Authors' calculations based on OECD data and national data.

Table 7e: TOTAL FACTOR PRODUCTIVITY, LABOUR PRODUCTIVITY,
            FACTOR SUBSTITUTION COMPONENT AND CAPITAL INTENSITY
            - annual changes -

U n i t e d   K i n g d o m

YEAR	TOTAL FACTOR PRODUCTIVITY	LABOUR PROD.	FACTOR SUBST. COMPONENT	CAPITAL INTENSITY
1963	3.4	4.0	0.6	3.3
1964	3.4	4.0	0.6	2.9
1965	0.6	1.2	0.6	3.1
1966	0.5	1.3	0.7	3.5
1967	3.1	4.3	1.2	5.6
1968	3.7	4.8	1.1	4.8
1969	0.2	1.2	0.9	3.9
1970	1.5	2.6	1.1	4.5
1971	2.4	3.6	1.2	4.8
1972	1.4	2.4	1.0	3.7
1973	5.0	5.5	0.4	1.6
1974	-2.2	-1.3	0.9	3.3
1975	-1.3	-0.4	1.0	3.5
1976	3.7	4.7	1.1	3.8
1977	0.1	0.9	0.8	2.9
1978	2.4	3.0	0.6	2.2
1979	0.2	0.6	0.4	1.4
1980	-2.8	-1.9	0.9	3.0
1981	0.9	2.9	2.0	6.3
1982	2.1	3.4	1.3	4.0
1983	3.2	4.4	1.2	3.5
62/73	2.2	3.1	1.0	3.8
73/83	0.5	1.6	1.1	3.4
62/83	1.2	2.4	1.2	3.6

Source: Authors' calculations based on OECD data and national data.

REAL WAGES, PRODUCTIVITY AND EMPLOYMENT

- whole economy, 1970 = 100 -

USA

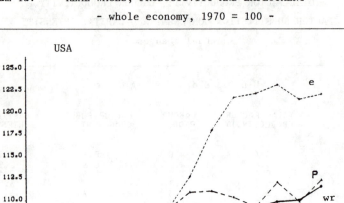

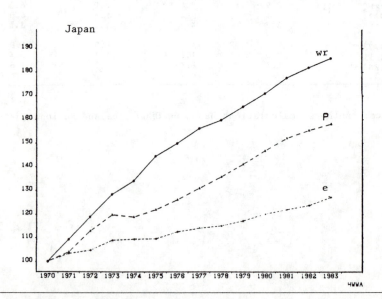

e = wage and salary earners, p = productivity, wr = real wages

Source: Authors' calculations based on OECD data.

Employment Trends

Diagram 1b: REAL WAGES, PRODUCTIVITY AND EMPLOYMENT

- whole economy, 1970 = 100 -

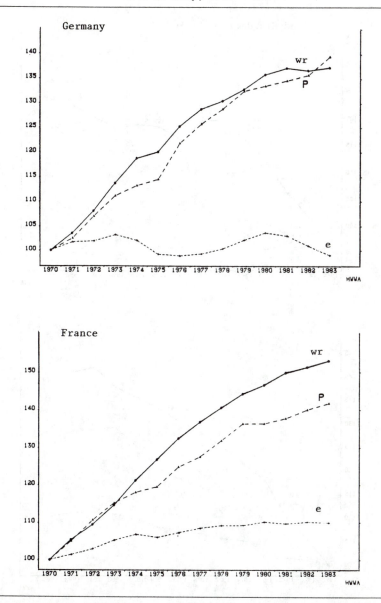

e = wage and salary earners, p = productivity, wr = real wages

Source: Authors' calculations based on OECD data.

Diagram 1c: REAL WAGES, PRODUCTIVITY AND EMPLOYMENT
- whole economy, 1970 = 100 -

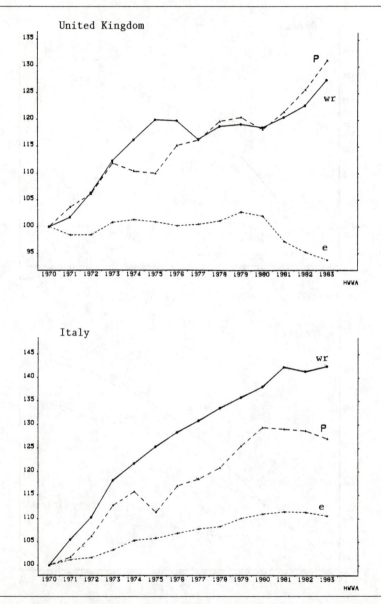

e = wage and salary earners, p = productivity, wr = real wages
Source: Authors' calculations based on OECD data.

Employment Trends

Diagram 2a: COMPONENTS OF PRODUCTIVITY

- percentage annual changes -

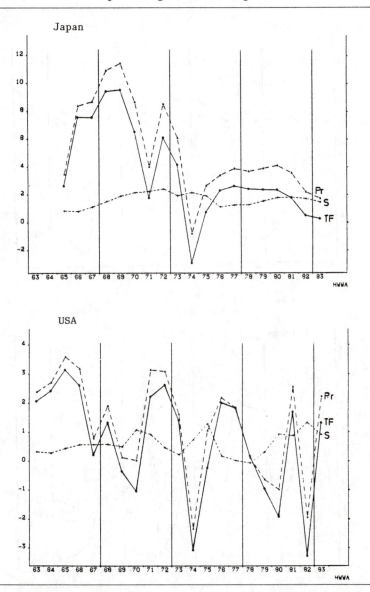

Pr = labour productivity, TF = total factor productivity, S = substitution component

Source: Authors' calculations based on OECD data and national data.

Appendix   281

Diagram 2b:　　　　　　COMPONENTS OF PRODUCTIVITY

- percentage annual changes -

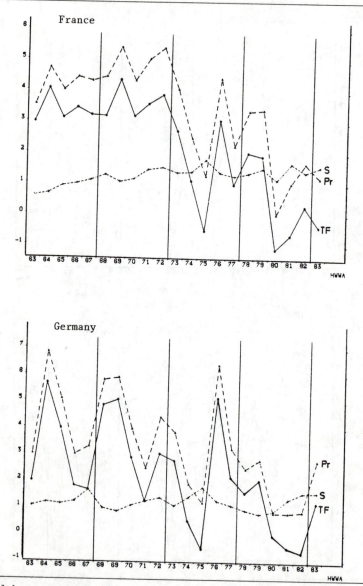

Pr = labour productivity, TF = total factor productivity, S = substitution component

Source: Authors' calculations based on OECD data and national data.

　　　　　　Employment Trends

Diagram 2c: COMPONENTS OF PRODUCTIVITY

- percentage annual changes -

United Kingdom

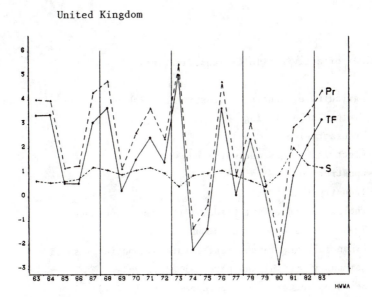

Pr = labour productivity, TF = total factor productivity, S = substitution component

Source: Authors' calculations based on OECD data and national data.

Diagram 3a-e: SECTORAL WAGE STRUCTURES, UNITED STATES AND EC-
COUNTRIES, 10 BRANCHES OF ACTIVITY[1]

Branches of activity (ISIC-classification)

1   Agriculture, hunting, forestry and fishing

2   Mining and quarrying

3   Manufacturing

4   Electricity, gas and water

5   Construction

6   Industry (ISIC 2-5)

7   Wholesale and retail trade, restaurants and hotels

8   Transport, storage and communication

9   Financial, insurance, real estate and business services

10 Community, social and personal services

11 Services sector, excl. government (ISIC 7-10)

12 Total industries

13 Government services

14 Services sector, incl. government

1 Compensation of employees per worker, percentage deviation from average.

Source: Authors' calculations based on OECD data and national data.

Employment Trends

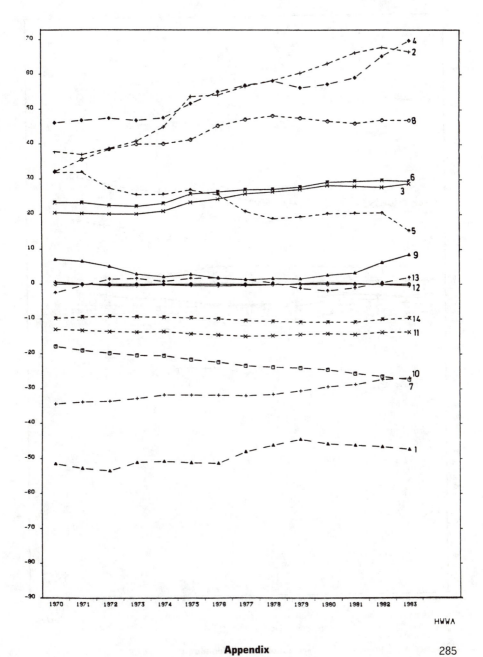

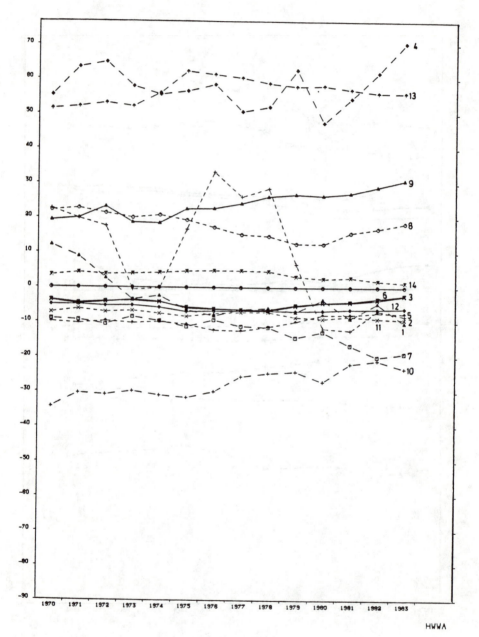

HWWA

Employment Trends

Germany

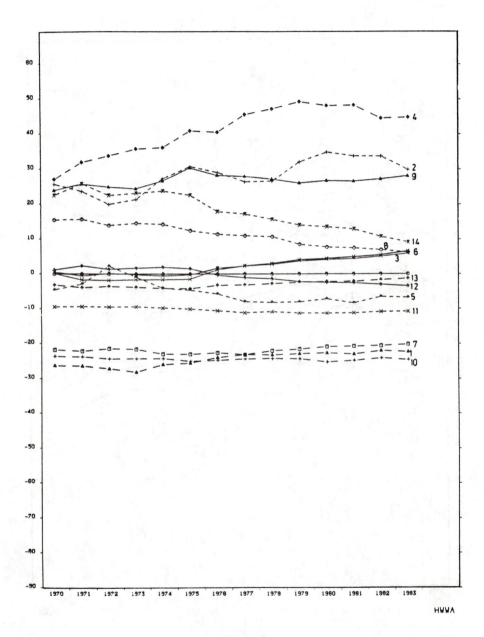

HWWA

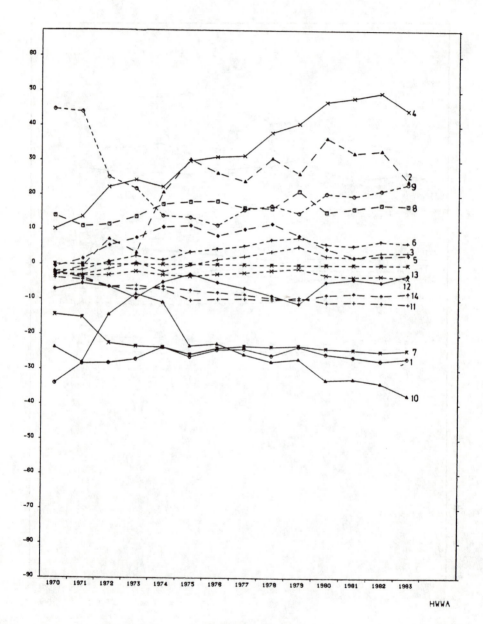

HWWA

Employment Trends

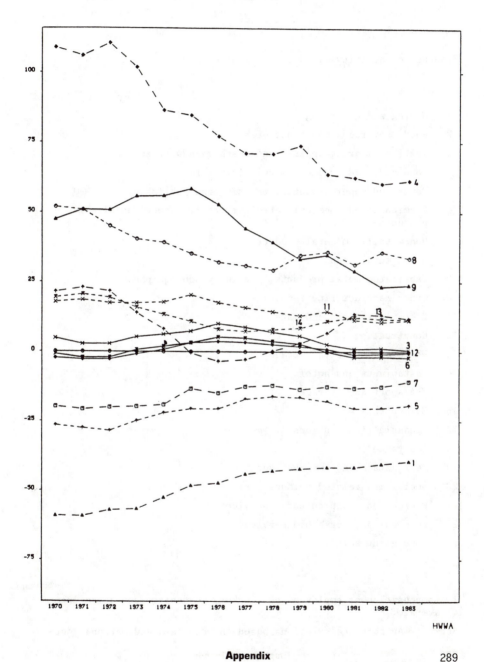

Diagrams 4a,b: SECTORAL WAGE STRUCTURES, UNITED STATES AND GERMANY,
                   23 RESPECTIVELY 19 BRANCHES OF ACTIVITY[1]

Branches of activity (ISIC classification)

United States:

1   Mining and quarrying

2   Food, beverages and tobacco

3   Textile, wearing apparel and leather industries

4   Wood and wood products, incl. furniture

5   Paper and paper products, printing and publishing

6   Chemicals and chemical petroleum, coal, rubber and plastic
     products

7   Non-metallic mineral products

8   Basic metal industry

9   Fabricated metal products, machinery and equipment

10   Other manufacturing industries

11   Electricity, gas and water

12   Construction

13   Wholesale and retail trade

14   Restaurants and hotels

15   Transport and storage

16   Communication

17   Financial institutions

18   Insurance

19   Real estate and business services

20   Social and related community services

21   Recreational and cultural services

22   Personal and household services

23   Government services

1   Compensation of employees per worker, percentage deviation from
    average.

Source: Authors' calculations based on OECD data and national data.

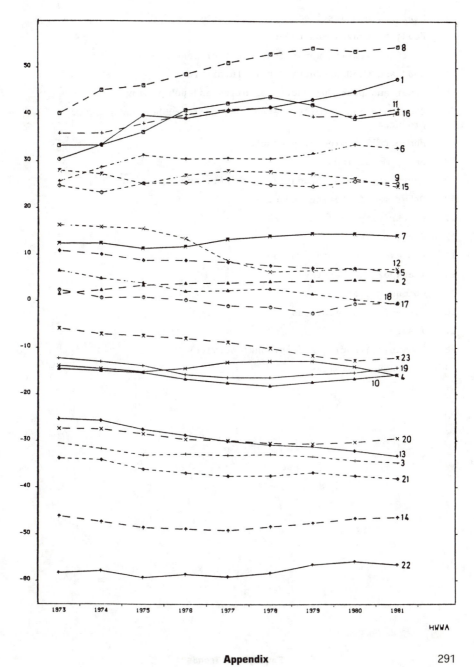

HWWA

Germany:

1   Mining and quarrying

2   Food, beverages and tobacco

3   Textile, wearing apparel and leather industries

4   Wood and wood products, incl. furniture

5   Paper and paper products, printing and publishing

6   Chemicals and chemical petroleum, coal, rubber and plastic products

7   Non-metallic mineral products

8   Basic metal industry

9   Fabricated metal products, machinery and equipment

10   Other manufacturing industries

11   Electricity, gas and water

12   Construction

13   Wholesale and retail trade

14   Transport and storage

15   Communication

16   Financial institutions

17   Insurance

18   Community, social and personal services

19   Government services

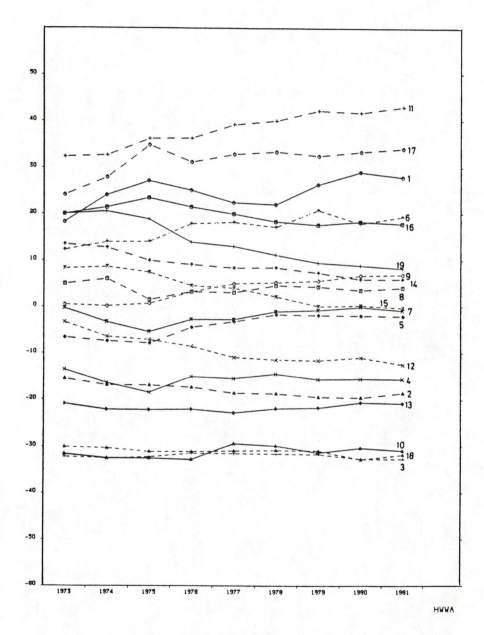

HWWA